The
GOURMAN REPORT

LATEST EDITION
IS 10th, 1997.
IT IS NO LONGER
BEING PUBLISHED.
KAREN McQ
7/18/00

A Rating of Undergraduate Programs in American and International Universities

NINTH EDITION
Revised

Dr. Jack Gourman

National Education Standards

Editorial inquiries concerning this book should be addressed to:
Editor
National Education Standards
One Wilshire Building
Suite 1210
624 South Grand Avenue
Los Angeles, California 90017

International Standard Serial Number (ISSN) 1049-7188

Library of Congress Catalog Card Number 95-072302

ISBN: 0-918192-16-1

Printed in the United States of America

This book is dedicated to the memory of
BLANKA GOURMAN
a kind and generous spirit.

PREFACE to the ninth edition

THE GOURMAN REPORT: A Rating of Undergraduate Programs in America and International Universities Ninth Edition is designed to provide easily acceptable, comparative information on selective undergraduate programs.

The content and format of this edition have remained the same as previous editions.

Since 1967, the author has made an intensive effort to determine what constitutes academic excellence or quality in American colleges and universities. I admit that the choice of means to display colleges accurately and comprehensively is a large problem requiring full exploration. Fact and fiction with regard to the quality of the work done by the institutions is a delicate subject.

My work is concerned with disseminating specific and critical information on the quality of the undergraduate colleges and universities. Institutions do differ by quality and The Gourman Report can be used as a basis for distinguishing them.

Quality is vital because reputation or image and quality do not always coincide. For instance the regional and national accrediting associations are concerned about quality but not in any precise or useful way to the public. Accreditation is mainly a finding that an institution is not conspicuously defective in physical and faculty resources. I find that the assets and liabilities are not known. There are clusters of accredited institutions lacking in essential elements. Institutions which are far apart in quality receive the same approval in terms of certification to the public. The public is not informed about the facts. I uphold that public trust is the greatest public relations asset and investment an institution can have. Furthermore, public relations should rest solidly and squarely on facts. The majority of institutions are reluctant to relate to the public a truthful image.

Even among established schools, many institutions again scored poorly based on one or more of the following shortcomings:

1. Objectives of the program are ill-defined and misunderstood.

2. The present program is not constituted to meet the needs and problems of students and faculty.

3. Institutional reports are not evaluated and beneficial changes are not recommended.

4. Administrators are reluctant to reveal the weakness of programs.

5. Administration – poor communication (this affects the faculty).

6. Administration – weak or unstable leadership (this affects the faculty).

7. Special interest pressure is exerted by administrators, to the detriment of the educators and teaching experience.

8. Faculty salaries are inadequate.

9. Funds for faculty research are inadequate.

10. Faculty – potential instability including poor morale.

11. Faculty – inadequate opportunities for professional development.

12. Failure to integrate computer into the curriculum.

13. Requisite improvements are not made in the quality of administrators, faculty instruction, curriculum, library resources and the physical plant.

14. Funds designation for the improvement of faculty, curriculum, library resources and physical areas are misused.

15. The public relations of the institution provides a false image to cover up deficiencies in programs.

16. Inadequate laboratory space.

17. Serious lack of secretarial help.

18. Student grants and scholarships are inadequate or nonexistent.

19. Students suffer from poor counseling.

20. Inferior undergraduate programs.

21. Lack of depth in humanities and social sciences.

22. Psychology undergraduate programs need to improve. (See lower ratings of psychology disciplines – 9th Edition).

23. Education programs and training are below average.
    Credential Note:
    A student with a baccalaureate degree or higher (and approved by THE GOURMAN REPORT) with a 3.5 grade point average in the major (excluding education majors) and an overall 3.3 grade point average are eligible for a teaching credential.

    In addition, the candidate must submit two letters from faculty who can assess their professional potential.

    Prospective candidates would apply directly to the state board of education for a teaching credential.

    We strongly recommend credential programs be *discontinued* by the educational institution.

24. The Undergraduate Schools of Education are not approved by THE GOURMAN REPORT and should be *discontinued* by the educational institution.

25. Criminal Justice/Criminology Correction programs are inadequate and not approved by THE GOURMAN REPORT.

26. Athletic-Academic imbalance.

27. THE GOURMAN REPORT does not approve of underclassmen departing early for professional sports. They are to *honor* their *commitment* to their respective institution.

28. THE GOURMAN REPORT does not approve of institutions reneging on their respective conference to join other leagues.

29. Sports Administration is not on the approved list of THE GOURMAN REPORT.

30. Sports Medicine is not on the approved list of THE GOURMAN REPORT.

31. The U.S. Department of Education is not on the approved list of THE GOURMAN REPORT. We recommend it's closure.

32. The community's ability and willingness to provide financial support for educational programs.

33. Inadequate library holdings.

34. Library mismanagement.

THE GOURMAN REPORT Now examines more than 140 separate disciplines.

Excluded from the ninth edition are the Soviet universities because of internal affairs and political instability.

I am grateful to many people for their contributions to this text. Paul Gregory Gourman again gave unstintingly of his time for research and technical assistance. Finally, a deep sense of gratitude is expressed to my wife Blanka, whose assistance and encouragement served to bring a difficult and complicated job to a successful conclusion.

Finally, I must express my obligation and appreciation to those college and university faculty members, presidents, administrators and trustees/regents without whom our survey would be impossible. While I cannot recognize these individuals by name, I know all readers of my book will join me in thanking them for their anonymous, and therefore selfless, contribution to the cause of quality in higher education.

Jack Gourman
Los Angeles, California
January, 1996

Preface
Introduction
Table of Contents

The Disciplines – A Rating of Undergraduate Programs

Part I

UNDERGRADUATE PROGRAMS

Table of Contents

Table of Contents

Table of Contents

Table of Contents

Introduction to the ninth edition

THE GOURMAN REPORT is the only qualitative guide to American and International institutions of higher education which assigns a precise, numerical score in assessing the strengths and shortcomings of each school and program. This methodology vastly simplifies the reader's task in examining the effectiveness of a given educational program, or comparing one program against another; and yet the Gourman rating takes into account a wide variety of empirical data, as described below.

This text is intended for use by:

– Young people, and parents, wishing to make an informed choice about higher education.

– Educators and administrators desirous of an independent evaluation of their programs.

– Prospective employers who want to avoid retraining of inadequately prepared graduates from ineffective institutions.

– Schools wishing to improve undergraduate programs.

– Foundations involved in fund-giving to colleges and universities.

– Licensing authorities in need of objective educational assessments.

– Individuals interested in identifying, and eliminating, fraudulent and inferior institutions.

– Citizens concerned about the quality of today's higher education.

If each institution did its utmost to insure a superior educational experience, and then frankly informed the public of any unavoidable compromises caused by funding, geography or educational focus, then there might be no need for a book such as this one. However, the facts remain that:

– Institutional policy dictates decisions about faculty, curriculum and physical plant for reasons which have little to do with education.

– Faculty members and administrators are intimidated, by internal and external political pressures from making critical comments about their own institutions.

– Public relations efforts by institutions tend to exaggerate strong areas, and ignore weak ones.

– Frankly fraudulent institutions exist as profit centers, rather than as promulgators of quality education.

– Accreditation appears to be mainly a finding that an institution is not conspicuously defective in physical and staff resources.

We must remember that the quality of higher education affects the future not only of individuals, but of the nation and its economy. If the following pages can make a contribution, no matter how minor, toward raising awareness of the need for better educational standards, then the purpose of THE GOURMAN REPORT is well served.

Method of Evaluation

In an age of disinformation, the user of this text should keep in mind that THE GOURMAN REPORT is not a "popularity contest", or an "opinion poll", but an objective evaluation which synthesizes complex data into a deceptively convenient numerical rating.

Obviously, much of the material used in compiling THE GOURMAN REPORT is internal – drawn from educators and administrators at the schools themselves. These individuals are permitted to evaluate *only* their own program – as they know them from daily interface with the educational experience – and not the programs of other institutions. Unsolicited appraisals are occasionally considered (and weighed accordingly), but the bulk of our contributions are requested from persons chosen for their academic qualifications, their published works, and their interest in improving the quality of higher education. It attests to the dedication of these individuals (and also to the serious problems in higher education today) that over 90% of our requests for contributions are met with a positive response.

In addition, THE GOURMAN REPORT draws on many external resources which are a matter of record – e.g., funding for public universities as authorized by legislative bodies, required filings by schools to meet standards of nondiscrimination, and material provided by the institutions (and independently verified) about faculty makeup and experience, fields of study offered, and physical plant. Such resources, while public, are not always accessible to the individual researcher; and someone wishing to utilize this data for comparing a number of institutions and programs would face a daunting task.

Finally, THE GOURMAN REPORT is fortunate to have among its contributors a number of individuals, associations and agencies whose business it is to make correct projections of the success graduates from given institutions and disciplines will enjoy in the "real world". While the methods employed by these resources are proprietary, their findings have consistently been validated by experience, and they are an important part of our research.

To critics who might question the feasibility of an evaluation which draws from such diverse resources, we offer the comparison to the grading of a college essay examination. What may appear to be a subjective process is in fact a patient sifting of empirical data by analysts who understand both the "subject matter" (the fields of study under evaluation), and the "students" (the colleges and universities themselves). The fact that there are virtually no "tie" scores indicates the accuracy and effectiveness of this methodology, as does the consistent affirmation of the ratings in THE GOURMAN REPORT from readers in a position to independently evaluate the attributes of specific educational programs.

Criteria

The following criteria are taken into consideration in the evaluation of each educational program and institution. It should be noted that, because different disciplines vary in their educational methodology, the significance given each criterion will vary from the rating of one discipline to the next; however, our evaluation is consistent for all schools listed within each field of study.

1. Auspices, control and organization of the institution;

2. Total educational programs offered and degrees conferred (with additional attention to "subfields" available to students within a particular discipline);

3. Age (experience level) of the institution and of the individual discipline or program and division;

4. Faculty, including qualifications, experience, intellectual interests, attainments, and professional productivity (including research);

5. Students, including quality of scholastic work and records of graduates both in graduate study and in practice;

6. Basis of and requirements for admission of students (overall and by individual discipline);

7. Number of students enrolled (overall and for each discipline);

8. Curriculum and curricular content of the program or discipline and division;

9. Standards and quality of instruction (including teaching loads);

10. Quality of administration, including attitudes and policy toward teaching, research and scholarly production in each discipline, and administration research;

11. Quality and availability of non-departmental areas such as counseling and career placement services;

12. Quality of physical plant devoted to undergraduate, graduate and professional levels;

13. Finances, including budgets, investments, expenditures and sources of income for both public and private institutions;

14. Library, including number of volumes, appropriateness of materials to individual disciplines, and accessibility of materials;

15. Computer facility sufficient to support current research activities for both faculty and students;

16. Sufficient funding for research equipment and infrastructure;

17. Number of teaching and research assistantships;

18. Academic-athletic balance.

A guide to using THE GOURMAN REPORT

Because the actual ratings within this text are presented without extraneous commentary, the following observations should be helpful in guiding both the first-time reader and the experienced user of THE GOURMAN REPORT.

PART I contains ratings of leading institutions in over 141 individual fields, from Accounting to Zoology. Out intent is not to create a visually attractive and consistent format, but simply to identify the most effective schools in each field; therefore, the number of institutions listed, and the numerical rating range employed, will vary from one field to another. Scores for institutions evaluated by THE GOURMAN REPORT, but not listed here, may be found in Part IX.

PART II includes ratings of Canadian programs in engineering, listed for the nation in total and also grouped by Province.

PART III, new for the ninth edition includes the section on Canadian colleges and universities.

PART IV includes ratings of 50 top schools in prelegal education and 58 leading institutions offering premedical education.

PART V evaluates institutions in eleven administrative areas: administration, alumni associations, athletic-academic balance, comparative competition for fellowships/scholarships, counseling centers, curriculum, intercollegiate athletic departments, libraries, public relations, trustees/regents (public/federal) not on the approved list and trustees/regents of the following private colleges and universities on the approved list of THE GOURMAN REPORT.

PART VI offers a comparative rating of selective university administrations, regents and trustees.

PART VII list the top fifty undergraduate schools in the United States, in rank order. These institutions have distinguished themselves by their commitment to a leadership position in quality education; it is only appropriate that their achievement be recognized in a separate section.

PART VIII provides a rating of leading international universities, ranked by curriculum, faculty, and overall.

PART IX is an overall ranking of American undergraduate institutions, listed alphabetically by state. This section is included primarily for use by readers who desire information about a particular institution. By no means should a school's listing be taken as an endorsement or an indication of quality, as ratings vary from "strong" (4.41 to 4.99) to "marginal" (2.01 to 2.99).

PART X is a rating of undergraduate schools of business administration on the approved list of THE GOURMAN REPORT. This section recognizes institutions which have attained and maintain rigorous standards of quality.

PART XI ranks undergraduate schools of engineering on the approved list of THE GOURMAN REPORT. As with Part X, this section recognizes institutions of quality whose engineering programs are ranked from "adequate" to "very strong".

PART XII includes the section of colleges and universities offering work in criminal justice and forensic science not on the approved list of THE GOURMAN REPORT. Furthermore we do not approve of junior/community college associated degrees (AA) in criminal justice. Criminal justice/criminology including corrections (adult and juvenile), law enforcement (police science) and juvenile justice do not emphasize those areas of study that are consistent with the advancement of our nation's social system. THE GOURMAN REPORT does not approve criminal justice as a social science discipline. Criminal justice is a technical field. Such programs should not be taken as equivalent to baccalaureate degrees in disciplines such as chemistry, biology, geo-science, engineering, mathematics, physics, English, economics, romance languages, history, political science, etc. *Postscript* — The criminal justice process in the United States is a failure. The various states (50) have no formulation of responsible policies and practices. In our studies we have made a thorough and solid review of practices and controversies in law enforcement, the criminal courts, corrections, etc. Not on the approved list of THE GOURMAN REPORT are the following: Administration of Parole, Administration of Probation, The Parole Board and the State Departments of Correction.

PART XIII includes the section entitled Education not on the approved list of THE GOURMAN REPORT. Unacceptable to the Report: Education degrees/majors (at any level), elementary education, secondary education, teacher education, undergraduate department of education including faculty members, Postsecondary Education Commission (all state and The State Department of Education (all-state). Education majors do not meet the standard of *quality* undergraduate training with regard to the effectiveness of curriculum, faculty research or scholarship. Degrees in education granted by these institutions should not be taken as equivalent in disciplines such as economics, English, engineering, mathematics, physics, history, political science, etc.

PART XIV – APPENDIXES lists, in table form, the total number of areas which were evaluated in preparing each part of THE GOURMAN REPORT. Also in the appendixes, the reader will find a listing of all International universities considered by this Ninth Edition.

The GOURMAN REPORT

PART I

Accounting
Aerospace Engineering
Agricultural Business
Agricultural Economics
Agricultural Engineering
Agriculture
Agronomy
American Studies
Animal Science
Anthropology
Applied Mathematics
Arabic
Architectural Engineering
Architecture
Art
Art History
Asian/Oriental Studies
Astronomy
Astrophysics
Atmospheric Sciences

Bacteriology/Microbiology
Behavioral Sciences
Biochemistry
Bioengineering/Biomedical Engineering
Biology
Biophysics
Botany
Business Administration

Cell Biology
Ceramic Art/Design
Ceramic Engineering
Chemical Engineering
Chemistry
Child Psychology
Chinese
Civil Engineering
Classics
Communication
Comparative Literature
Computer Engineering
Computer Science

Dairy Sciences
Dietetics
Drama/Theatre

Earth Science
East Asian Studies
Ecology/Environmental Studies
Economics
Electrical Engineering
Engineering/General
Engineering Mechanics
Engineering Physics
Engineering Science
English
Entomology
Environmental Design
Environmental Engineering
Environmental Sciences

Farm/Ranch Management
Film
Finance
Fish/Game Management
Food Sciences
Food Services Management
Forestry
French

Genetics
Geography
Geological Engineering
Geology/Geoscience
Geophysics/Geoscience
German
Greek

Hebrew
History
Home Economics
Horticulture
Hotel, Restaurant, Institutional Management

Industrial Engineering
Information Science
International Relations
Italian

Japanese
Journalism and Mass Communications

(Continued)

The GOURMAN REPORT

PART I

Labor and Industrial Relations
Landscape Architecture
Latin
Latin American Studies
Linguistics

Management
Manufacturing Engineering
Marine Biology
Marine Sciences
Marketing
Materials Engineering/Materials Science
  and Engineering
Mathematics
Mechanical Engineering
Medieval Studies
Metallurgical Engineering
Meteorology
Mining and Mineral Engineering
Molecular Biology
Music

Natural Resource Management
Naval Architecture & Marine Engineering
Near/Middle Eastern Studies
Nuclear Engineering
Nursing
Nutrition

Occupational Therapy
Ocean Engineering
Operations Research
Ornamental Horticulture

Parks Management
Petroleum Engineering
Philosophy
Physical Therapy
Physics
Political Science
Portuguese
Poultry Sciences
Psychology

Radio/Television Studies
Religious Studies
Russian
Russian/Slavic Studies

Scandinavian Languages
Slavic Languages
Social Work/Social Welfare
Sociology
South Asian Studies
Southeast Asian Studies
Spanish
Speech/Rhetoric
Speech Pathology/Audiology
Statistics
Systems Engineering

Urban Studies

Wildlife Biology

Zoology

ACCOUNTING
Leading Institutions – Rating of Undergraduate Program

Forty-one institutions with scores in the 4.0-5.0 range, in rank order

INSTITUTION	Rank	Score	INSTITUTION	Rank	Score
PENNSYLVANIA	1	4.92	TEXAS A&M (College Station)	22	4.49
INDIANA (Bloomington)	2	4.90	UTAH (Salt Lake City)	23	4.47
MICHIGAN (Ann Arbor)	3	4.87	LEHIGH	24	4.46
CALIFORNIA, BERKELEY	4	4.86	FLORIDA (Gainesville)	25	4.40
TEXAS (Austin)	5	4.84	SOUTHERN METHODIST	26	4.39
N.Y.U.	6	4.82	MASSACHUSETTS (Amherst)	27	4.37
NOTRE DAME	7	4.81	ARIZONA (Tucson)	28	4.34
ILLINOIS (Urbana)	8	4.79	LSU (Baton Rouge)	29	4.32
PURDUE (Lafayette)	9	4.76	TEMPLE (Philadelphia)	30	4.28
WISCONSIN (Madison)	10	4.73	MARYLAND (College Park)	31	4.27
WASHINGTON (Seattle)	11	4.70	GEORGIA STATE	32	4.23
MICHIGAN STATE	12	4.68	SOUTH CAROLINA (Columbia)	33	4.20
VIRGINIA (Charlottesville)	13	4.67	OREGON (Eugene)	34	4.16
CUNY (Baruch College)	14	4.64	GEORGE WASHINGTON	35	4.14
MINNESOTA (Minneapolis)	15	4.62	SUNY (Buffalo)	36	4.13
WASHINGTON (St. Louis)	16	4.60	MISSOURI (Columbia)	37	4.12
CASE WESTERN RESERVE	17	4.59	COLORADO (Boulder)	38	4.08
SOUTHERN CALIFORNIA (USC)	18	4.58	ARIZONA STATE	39	4.06
HOUSTON (University Park)	19	4.55	IOWA (Iowa City)	40	4.05
PENN STATE (University Park)	20	4.52	EMORY	41	4.02
OHIO STATE (Columbus)	21	4.50			

AEROSPACE ENGINEERING
Leading Institutions – Rating of Undergraduate Program

Forty-three institutions with scores in the 4.0-5.0 range, in rank order

INSTITUTION	Rank	Score	INSTITUTION	Rank	Score
M.I.T.[4]	1	4.91	CINCINNATI[5]	23	4.42
MICHIGAN (Ann Arbor)[5]	2	4.89	OKLAHOMA[5]	24	4.40
PRINCETON[5]	3	4.84	SUNY (Buffalo)[5]	25	4.38
MINNESOTA (Minneapolis)[7]	4	4.82	FLORIDA (Gainesville)[5]	26	4.37
ILLINOIS (Urbana)[2]	5	4.80	TENNESSEE (Knoxville)[5]	27	4.33
OHIO STATE (Columbus)[2]	6	4.78	SYRACUSE[5]	28	4.32
MARYLAND (College Park)[5]	7	4.76	V.P.I. & STATE U.[5]	29	4.30
KANSAS[5]	8	4.73	NOTRE DAME[5]	30	4.28
PURDUE (Lafayette)[2]	9	4.71	UCLA[5]	31	4.26
ARIZONA (Tucson)[5]	10	4.68	NORTH CAROLINA STATE (Raleigh)[5]	32	4.24
IOWA STATE (Ames)[5]	11	4.65	U.S. NAVAL ACADEMY[5]	33	4.23
RENSSELAER (N.Y.)[1]	12	4.64	ALABAMA[5]	34	4.22
VIRGINIA [5]	13	4.62	AUBURN[5]	35	4.21
WASHINGTON (Seattle)[3]	14	4.60	WEST VIRGINIA[5]	36	4.19
TEXAS A&M (College Station)[5]	15	4.57	WICHITA STATE[1]	37	4.17
PENN STATE (University Park)[5]	16	4.52	CALIFORNIA DAVIS[3]	38	4.15
GEORGIA TECH[5]	17	4.53	BOSTON U.[5]	39	4.14
SOUTHERN CALIFORNIA[5]	18	4.52	POLYTECHNIC U. (Brooklyn, N.Y.)[5]	40	4.13
TEXAS (Austin)[5]	19	4.51	PARKS COLLEGE (St. Louis U.)[5]	41	4.12
COLORADO (Boulder)[8]	20	4.50	MISSISSIPPI STATE[5]	42	4.11
U.S. AIR FORCE ACADEMY[1,9]	21	4.46	OKLAHOMA STATE[6]	43	4.08
MISSOURI (Rolla)[5]	22	4.44			

Explanatory Note: Actual titles by the institution to identify their curricula

[1] Aeronautical Engineering

[2] Aeronautical and Astronautical Engineering

[3] Aeronautical Science and Engineering

[4] Aeronautics and Astronautics

[5] Aerospace Engineering

[6] Aerospace Option in Mechanical Engineering

[7] Aerospace Engineering and Mechanics

[8] Aerospace Engineering Sciences

[9] Astronautical Engineering

AGRICULTURAL BUSINESS
Leading Institutions – Rating of Undergraduate Program

Nine institutions with scores
in the 4.0-5.0 range, in rank order

INSTITUTION	Rank	Score
CORNELL (N.Y.)	1	4.83
MICHIGAN STATE	2	4.80
PENN STATE (University Park)	3	4.77
ILLINOIS (Urbana)	4	4.73
MINNESOTA (Minneapolis)	5	4.69
IOWA STATE (Ames)	6	4.66
COLORADO STATE	7	4.60
PURDUE (West Lafayette)	8	4.56
WISCONSIN (Madison)	9	4.50

AGRICULTURAL ECONOMICS
Leading Institutions – Rating of Undergraduate Program

Twenty-one institutions with scores
in the 4.0-5.0 range, in rank order

INSTITUTION	Rank	Score
MINNESOTA (Minneapolis)	1	4.91
WISCONSIN (Madison)	2	4.88
MARYLAND (College Park)	3	4.85
CORNELL (N.Y.)	4	4.83
MICHIGAN STATE	5	4.80
ILLINOIS (Urbana)	6	4.77
V.P.I. & STATE U.	7	4.75
CALIFORNIA, DAVIS	8	4.73
TEXAS A&M (College Station)	9	4.71
PURDUE (Lafayette)	10	4.67
MASSACHUSETTS (Amherst)	11	4.62
OHIO STATE (Columbus)	12	4.57
PENN STATE (University Park)	13	4.50
COLORADO STATE	14	4.46
MISSOURI (Columbia)	15	4.43
OKLAHOMA STATE	16	4.40
CONNECTICUT (Storrs)	17	4.35
NEBRASKA (Lincoln)	18	4.32
HAWAII (Manoa)	19	4.27
WASHINGTON STATE	20	4.20
WEST VIRGINIA (Morgantown)	21	4.19

AGRICULTURAL ENGINEERING
Leading Institutions – Rating of Undergraduate Program

Thirty-eight institutions with scores in the 4.0-5.0 range, in rank order

INSTITUTION	Rank	Score	INSTITUTION	Rank	Score
CORNELL (N.Y.)[1]	1	4.91	AUBURN (Auburn)	20	4.37
TEXAS A&M (College Station)	2	4.90	RUTGERS (New Brunswick)[3]	21	4.36
IOWA STATE (Ames)	3	4.86	CLEMSON	22	4.34
MICHIGAN STATE	4	4.84	FLORIDA (Gainesville)	23	4.32
WISCONSIN (Madison)	5	4.82	WASHINGTON STATE	24	4.30
ILLINOIS (Urbana)	6	4.80	KENTUCKY	25	4.28
OHIO STATE (Columbus)	7	4.77	V.P.I. & STATE U.[5]	26	4.27
MINNESOTA (Minneapolis)	8	4.75	ARIZONA (Tucson)[2]	27	4.25
PURDUE (Lafayette)	9	4.71	TEXAS TECH	28	4.23
MISSOURI (Columbia)	10	4.69	IDAHO (Moscow)	29	4.21
CALIFORNIA, DAVIS	11	4.65	ARKANSAS (Fayetteville)[4]	30	4.18
PENN STATE (University Park)	12	4.61	SOUTH DAKOTA STATE	31	4.16
MARYLAND (College Park)	13	4.59	NORTH CAROLINA STATE (Raleigh)[4]	32	4.15
KANSAS STATE	14	4.54	MAINE (Orono)[3]	33	4.14
OKLAHOMA STATE[6]	15	4.50	NORTH DAKOTA STATE	34	4.12
TENNESSEE (Knoxville)	16	4.44	NEBRASKA (Lincoln)	35	4.10
LOUISIANA STATE (Baton Rouge)[4]	17	4.42	GEORGIA (Athens)	36	4.08
UTAH STATE[4]	18	4.40	NEW MEXICO STATE	37	4.06
COLORADO STATE	19	4.38	CALIFORNIA POLY. STATE (SLO)	38	4.04

Explanatory Note: Actual titles used by the institution to identify their curricula

[1] Agricultural and Biological Engineering

[2] Agricultural and Biosystems Engineering

[3] Bio-Resource Engineering

[4] Biological and Agricultureal Engineering

[5] Biological Engineering

[6] Biosystems Engineering

AGRICULTURE
Leading Institutions – Rating of Undergraduate Program

Forty-six institutions with scores in the 4.0-5.0 range, in rank order

INSTITUTION	Rank	Score	INSTITUTION	Rank	Score
CORNELL (N.Y.)	1	4.93	AUBURN (Auburn)	24	4.36
TEXAS A&M (College Station)	2	4.91	UTAH STATE	25	4.35
IOWA STATE (Ames)	3	4.88	WASHINGTON STATE	26	4.34
PURDUE (Lafayette)	4	4.85	MAINE (Orono)	27	4.33
ILLINOIS (Urbana)	5	4.82	MASSACHUSETTS (Amherst)	28	4.32
MICHIGAN STATE	6	4.79	NEW HAMPSHIRE	29	4.31
CALIFORNIA, DAVIS	7	4.74	NORTH DAKOTA STATE	30	4.30
WISCONSIN (Madison)	8	4.70	MONTANA STATE	31	4.29
MINNESOTA (Minneapolis)	9	4.66	VERMONT	32	4.28
OHIO STATE (Columbus)	10	4.62	WYOMING	33	4.27
MISSOURI (Columbia)	11	4.58	FLORIDA (Gainesville)	34	4.25
KANSAS STATE	12	4.55	CLEMSON	35	4.23
PENN STATE (University Park)	13	4.52	ARKANSAS (Fayetteville)	36	4.21
RUTGERS (New Brunswick)	14	4.51	KENTUCKY	37	4.20
COLORADO STATE	15	4.50	SOUTH DAKOTA STATE	38	4.18
LOUISIANA STATE (Baton Rouge)	16	4.48	WEST VIRGINIA (Morgantown)	39	4.16
MARYLAND (College Park)	17	4.47	ARIZONA (Tucson)	40	4.15
NORTH CAROLINA STATE (Raleigh)	18	4.45	IDAHO (Moscow)	41	4.13
NEBRASKA (Lincoln)	19	4.44	MISSISSIPPI STATE	42	4.12
OKLAHOMA STATE	20	4.42	V.P.I. & STATE U.	43	4.09
OREGON STATE	21	4.41	TEXAS TECH	44	4.06
TENNESSEE (Knoxville)	22	4.39	NEW MEXICO STATE	45	4.05
GEORGIA (Athens)	23	4.37	CONNECTICUT (Storrs)	46	4.03

AGRONOMY
Leading Institutions – Rating of Undergraduate Program

Forty-five institutions with scores in the 4.0-5.0 range, in rank order

INSTITUTION	Rank	Score	INSTITUTION	Rank	Score
CORNELL (N.Y.)	1	4.90	AUBURN (Auburn)	24	4.40
TEXAS A&M (College Station)	2	4.88	GEORGIA (Athens)	25	4.39
IOWA STATE (Ames)	3	4.86	WASHINGTON STATE	26	4.38
PURDUE (Lafayette)	4	4.84	FLORIDA (Gainesville)	27	4.37
OHIO STATE (Columbus)	5	4.82	MAINE (Orono)	28	4.35
ILLINOIS (Urbana)	6	4.81	NEW HAMPSHIRE	29	4.33
MICHIGAN STATE	7	4.79	ARIZONA (Tucson)	30	4.30
WISCONSIN (Madison)	8	4.76	KENTUCKY	31	4.26
MINNESOTA (Minneapolis)	9	4.75	VERMONT	32	4.23
MISSOURI (Columbia)	10	4.72	MISSISSIPPI STATE	33	4.20
KANSAS STATE	11	4.69	NORTH DAKOTA STATE	34	4.18
CALIFORNIA, DAVIS	12	4.67	IDAHO (Moscow)	35	4.17
PENN STATE (University Park)	13	4.66	WYOMING	36	4.16
RUTGERS (New Brunswick)	14	4.62	SOUTH DAKOTA STATE	37	4.15
LOUISIANA STATE (Baton Rouge)	15	4.60	ARKANSAS (Fayetteville)	38	4.12
COLORADO STATE	16	4.57	V.P.I. & STATE U.	39	4.10
NEBRASKA (Lincoln)	17	4.53	CLEMSON	40	4.09
MARYLAND (College Park)	18	4.52	NEW MEXICO STATE	41	4.08
OKLAHOMA STATE	19	4.51	MONTANA STATE	42	4.06
NORTH CAROLINA STATE	20	4.49	WEST VIRGINIA (Morgantown)	43	4.05
OREGON STATE	21	4.48	CONNECTICUT (Storrs)	44	4.04
TENNESSEE (Knoxville)	22	4.46	TEXAS TECH	45	4.02
UTAH STATE	23	4.43			

AMERICAN STUDIES
Leading Institutions – Rating of Undergraduate Program

Fourteen institutions with scores in the 4.0-5.0 range, in rank order

INSTITUTION	Rank	Score
YALE	1	4.81
PENNSYLVANIA	2	4.76
MICHIGAN (Ann Arbor)	3	4.65
CASE WESTERN RESERVE	4	4.60
IOWA (Iowa City)	5	4.58
MARYLAND (College Park)	6	4.54
MINNESOTA (Minneapolis)	7	4.46
BROWN	8	4.44
KANSAS	9	4.39
NORTH CAROLINA (Chapel Hill)	10	4.32
CORNELL (N.Y.)	11	4.26
BRANDEIS	12	4.15
TEXAS (Austin)	13	4.10
GEORGE WASHINGTON	14	4.07

Thirteen institutions with scores in the 3.0-3.4 range, in rank order

INSTITUTION	Rank	Score
NEW MEXICO	21	3.43
ST. LOUIS U.	22	3.39
STANFORD	23	3.31
SUNY (Buffalo)	24	3.27
NORTHWESTERN (Evanston)	25	3.22
TULANE	26	3.18
WILLIAMS (Massachusetts)	27	3.17
MIAMI (Florida)	28	3.13
HAWAII (Manoa)	29	3.10
PURDUE (Lafayette)	30	3.08
FLORIDA STATE	31	3.05
SMITH (Massachusetts)	32	3.04
PENN STATE (University Park)	33	3.02

Six institutions with scores in the 3.5-3.9 range, in rank order

INSTITUTION	Rank	Score
HARVARD & RADCLIFFE	15	3.87
CHICAGO	16	3.80
AMHERST	17	3.76
N.Y.U.	18	3.72
NOTRE DAME	19	3.66
MICHIGAN STATE	20	3.64

ANIMAL SCIENCE
Leading Institutions – Rating of Undergraduate Program

Thirty-five institutions with scores in the 4.0-5.0 range, in rank order

INSTITUTION	Rank	Score	INSTITUTION	Rank	Score
CORNELL (N.Y.)	1	4.91	OKLAHOMA STATE	19	4.41
CALIFORNIA, DAVIS	2	4.89	GEORGIA (Athens)	20	4.36
TEXAS A&M (College Station)	3	4.86	CLEMSON	21	4.30
IOWA STATE (Ames)	4	4.85	OREGON STATE	22	4.26
PURDUE (Lafayette)	5	4.82	NORTH CAROLINA STATE (Raleigh)	23	4.22
ILLINOIS (Urbana)	6	4.80	DELAWARE (Newark)	24	4.19
MINNESOTA (Minneapolis)	7	4.76	V.P.I. & STATE U.	25	4.16
WISCONSIN (Madison)	8	4.73	MASSACHUSETTS (Amherst)	26	4.12
KANSAS STATE	9	4.70	CONNECTICUT (Storrs)	27	4.10
COLORADO STATE	10	4.66	WEST VIRGINIA (Morgantown)	28	4.09
OHIO STATE (Columbus)	11	4.62	WASHINGTON STATE	29	4.08
MISSOURI (Columbia)	12	4.60	UTAH STATE	30	4.07
PENN STATE (University Park)	13	4.58	NORTH DAKOTA STATE	31	4.06
LOUISIANA STATE (Baton Rouge)	14	4.55	TEXAS TECH	32	4.05
FLORIDA (Gainesville)	15	4.50	HAWAII (Manoa)	33	4.04
WYOMING	16	4.47	TENNESSEE (Knoxville)	34	4.03
NEBRASKA (Lincoln)	17	4.46	MISSISSIPPI STATE	35	4.02
MARYLAND (College Park)	18	4.43			

ANTHROPOLOGY
Leading Institutions – Rating of Undergraduate Program

Fifty institutions with scores in the 4.0-5.0 range, in rank order

INSTITUTION	Rank	Score	INSTITUTION	Rank	Score
MICHIGAN (Ann Arbor)	1	4.92	INDIANA (Bloomington)	26	4.45
CHICAGO	2	4.91	HAWAII (Manoa)	27	4.42
CALIFORNIA, BERKELEY	3	4.90	CALIFORNIA, IRVINE	28	4.40
PENNSYLVANIA	4	4.88	NORTH CAROLINA (Chapel Hill)	29	4.37
ARIZONA	5	4.86	VIRGINIA	30	4.35
STANFORD	6	4.85	SUNY (Buffalo)	31	4.33
YALE	7	4.82	MICHIGAN STATE	32	4.32
UCLA	8	4.80	SUNY (Binghamton)	33	4.30
HARVARD & RADCLIFFE	9	4.79	ARIZONA STATE	34	4.27
NORTHWESTERN (Evanston)	10	4.77	BRANDEIS	35	4.26
TEXAS (Austin)	11	4.75	CALIFORNIA, DAVIS	36	4.23
NEW MEXICO	12	4.72	COLORADO (Boulder)	37	4.20
CORNELL (N.Y.)	13	4.70	TULANE	38	4.19
ILLINOIS (Urbana)	14	4.68	N.Y.U.	39	4.18
COLUMBIA (N.Y.)	15	4.67	PRINCETON	40	4.16
CALIFORNIA, SANTA BARBARA	16	4.64	WASHINGTON (St. Louis)	41	4.14
CALIFORNIA, SAN DIEGO	17	4.62	CONNECTICUT (Storrs)	42	4.12
WASHINGTON (Seattle)	18	4.60	BRYN MAWR	43	4.10
MASSACHUSETTS (Amherst)	19	4.59	OREGON (Eugene)	44	4.09
WISCONSIN (Madison)	20	4.56	CALIFORNIA, RIVERSIDE	45	4.08
FLORIDA (Gainesville)	21	4.52	MINNESOTA (Minneapolis)	46	4.07
PENN STATE (University Park)	22	4.51	BROWN	47	4.06
PITTSBURGH (Pittsburgh)	23	4.49	SOUTHERN METHODIST	48	4.05
DUKE	24	4.48	KANSAS	49	4.04
RUTGERS (New Brunswick)	25	4.46	MISSOURI (Columbia)	50	4.03

APPLIED MATHEMATICS
Leading Institutions – Rating of Undergraduate Program

Sixteen institutions with scores
in the 4.0-5.0 range, in rank order

INSTITUTION	Rank	Score
HARVARD & RADCLIFFE	1	4.87
CHICAGO	2	4.85
CALIFORNIA, BERKELEY	3	4.83
BROWN	4	4.80
WISCONSIN (Madison)	5	4.76
COLUMBIA (N.Y.)	6	4.74
YALE	7	4.70
UCLA	8	4.66
CAL TECH	9	4.63
PURDUE (Lafayette)	10	4.61
CALIFORNIA, SAN DIEGO	11	4.55
NORTHWESTERN (Evanston)	12	4.52
CARNEGIE-MELLON	13	4.48
JOHNS HOPKINS	14	4.43
VIRGINIA	15	4.37
COLORADO (Boulder)	16	4.32

Nine institutions with scores
in the 4.0-5.0 range, in rank order

INSTITUTION	Rank	Score
CHICAGO	1	4.84
MICHIGAN (Ann Arbor)	2	4.79
PENNSYLVANIA	3	4.73
HARVARD & RADCLIFFE	4	4.69
PRINCETON	5	4.61
N.Y.U.	6	4.50
JOHNS HOPKINS	7	4.40
COLUMBIA (N.Y.)	8	4.33
GEORGETOWN (D.C.)	9	4.27

ARCHITECTURAL ENGINEERING
Leading Institutions – Rating of Undergraduate Program

Eight institutions with scores
in the 4.0-5.0 range, in rank order

INSTITUTION	Rank	Score
TEXAS (Austin)	1	4.81
PENN STATE (University Park)	2	4.73
KANSAS	3	4.64
COLORADO (Boulder)	4	4.61
MIAMI (Florida)	5	4.54
KANSAS STATE	6	4.48
CALIFORNIA POLY. STATE (SLO)	7	4.40
OKLAHOMA STATE	8	4.32

ARCHITECTURE
Leading Institutions – Rating of Undergraduate Program

Thirteen institutions with scores in the 4.0-5.0 range, in rank order

INSTITUTION	Rank	Score
CALIFORNIA, BERKELEY	1	4.89
M.I.T.	2	4.76
CARNEGIE-MELLON	3	4.62
PRINCETON	4	4.58
CORNELL (N.Y.)	5	4.53
MICHIGAN (Ann Arbor)	6	4.49
ILLINOIS (Urbana)	7	4.38
RICE	8	4.32
GEORGIA TECH	9	4.27
SOUTHERN CALIFORNIA	10	4.19
TEXAS (Austin)	11	4.14
PRATT (N.Y.)	12	4.10
MINNESOTA (Minneapolis)	13	4.07

Sixteen institutions with scores in the 3.0-3.4 range, in rank order

INSTITUTION	Rank	Score
OREGON (Eugene)	24	3.42
OHIO STATE (Columbus)	25	3.40
COOPER (N.Y.)	26	3.38
HOUSTON (U. Park)	27	3.36
VIRGINIA	28	3.34
NOTRE DAME	29	3.32
MIAMI (Florida)	30	3.26
HAWAII (Manoa)	31	3.23
FLORIDA (Gainesville)	32	3.22
LOUISIANA STATE (Baton Rouge)	33	3.17
CITY (CUNY)	34	3.12
PENN STATE (University Park)	35	3.11
SYRACUSE	36	3.08
TULANE	37	3.06
WISCONSIN (Milwaukee)	38	3.04
NORTH CAROLINA STATE (Raleigh)	39	3.03

Ten institutions with scores in the 3.5-3.9 range, in rank order

INSTITUTION	Rank	Score
CINCINNATI	14	3.86
KANSAS	15	3.82
OKLAHOMA (Norman)	16	3.77
RENSSELAER (N.Y.)	17	3.74
ARIZONA (Tucson)	18	3.70
WASHINGTON (Seattle)	19	3.65
WASHINGTON (St. Louis)	20	3.62
V.P.I. & STATE U.	21	3.58
TEXAS A&M (College Station)	22	3.53
KANSAS STATE	23	3.52

ART
Leading Institutions – Rating of Undergraduate Program

Eighteen institutions with scores in the 4.0-5.0 range, in rank order

INSTITUTION	Rank	Score
N.Y.U.	1	4.90
HARVARD & RADCLIFFE	2	4.89
PRINCETON	3	4.83
YALE	4	4.76
CALIFORNIA, BERKELEY	5	4.67
COLUMBIA (N.Y.)	6	4.60
STANFORD	7	4.59
BRYN MAWR	8	4.54
MICHIGAN (Ann Arbor)	9	4.50
PENNSYLVANIA	10	4.48
CHICAGO	11	4.46
CORNELL (N.Y.)	12	4.41
JOHNS HOPKINS	13	4.39
BROWN	14	4.35
NORTH CAROLINA (Chapel Hill)	15	4.30
UCLA	16	4.27
PITTSBURGH (Pittsburgh)	17	4.25
INDIANA (Bloomington)	18	4.21

Twelve institutions with scores in the 3.0-3.4 range, in rank order

INSTITUTION	Rank	Score
WISCONSIN (Madison)	31	3.42
OHIO STATE (Columbus)	32	3.39
WASHINGTON (Seattle)	33	3.35
CASE WESTERN RESERVE	34	3.30
NEW MEXICO	35	3.29
ARIZONA (Tucson)	36	3.28
GEORGIA (Athens)	37	3.22
MISSOURI (Columbia)	38	3.19
SOUTHERN CALIFORNIA	39	3.12
FLORIDA STATE	40	3.10
OREGON (Eugene)	41	3.09
OHIO U. (Athens)	42	3.07

Twelve institutions with scores in the 3.5-3.9 range, in rank order

INSTITUTION	Rank	Score
DELAWARE (Newark)	19	3.89
VIRGINIA	20	3.87
BOSTON U.	21	3.80
MARYLAND (College Park)	22	3.79
NORTHWESTERN (Evanston)	23	3.72
MINNESOTA (Minneapolis)	24	3.69
RUTGERS (New Brunswick)	25	3.64
PENN STATE (University Park)	26	3.59
KANSAS	27	3.55
TEXAS (Austin)	28	3.54
IOWA (Iowa City)	29	3.53
WASHINGTON (St. Louis)	30	3.51

ART HISTORY
Leading Institutions – Rating of Undergraduate Program

Nineteen institutions with scores in the 4.0-5.0 range, in rank order

INSTITUTION	Rank	Score
N.Y.U.	1	4.92
HARVARD & RADCLIFFE	2	4.91
PRINCETON	3	4.89
YALE	4	4.86
COLUMBIA (N.Y.)	5	4.83
CALIFORNIA, BERKELEY	6	4.80
STANFORD	7	4.78
BRYN MAWR	8	4.75
MICHIGAN (Ann Arbor)	9	4.70
JOHNS HOPKINS	10	4.63
PENNSYLVANIA	11	4.60
UCLA	12	4.59
CHICAGO	13	4.55
BROWN	14	4.46
NORTH CAROLINA (Chapel Hill)	15	4.40
CORNELL (N.Y.)	16	4.33
PITTSBURGH (Pittsburgh)	17	4.27
INDIANA (Bloomington)	18	4.20
DELAWARE (Newark)	19	4.14

Eleven institutions with scores in the 3.0-3.4 range, in rank order

INSTITUTION	Rank	Score
WISCONSIN (Madison)	31	3.41
OHIO STATE (Columbus)	32	3.36
WASHINGTON (Seattle)	33	3.30
CASE WESTERN RESERVE	34	3.27
NEW MEXICO	35	3.20
OREGON (Eugene)	36	3.19
GEORGIA (Athens)	37	3.16
MISSOURI (Columbia)	38	3.15
FLORIDA STATE	39	3.13
SOUTHERN CALIFORNIA	40	3.11
OHIO U. (Athens)	41	3.05

Eleven institutions with scores in the 3.5-3.9 range, in rank order

INSTITUTION	Rank	Score
VIRGINIA	20	3.85
BOSTON U.	21	3.80
MARYLAND (College Park)	22	3.74
NORTHWESTERN (Evanston)	23	3.69
RUTGERS (New Brunswick)	24	3.64
MINNESOTA (Minneapolis)	25	3.60
PENN STATE (University Park)	26	3.54
KANSAS	27	3.51
IOWA (Iowa City)	28	3.50
TEXAS (Austin)	29	3.48
WASHINGTON (St. Louis)	30	3.46

ASIAN/ORIENTAL STUDIES
Leading Institutions – Rating of Undergraduate Program

Thirteen institutions with scores
in the 4.0-5.0 range, in rank order

INSTITUTION	Rank	Score
HARVARD	1	4.82
CALIFORNIA, BERKELEY	2	4.78
CHICAGO	3	4.73
CORNELL (N.Y.)	4	4.70
WASHINGTON (Seattle)	5	4.66
PENNSYLVANIA	6	4.62
MICHIGAN (Ann Arbor)	7	4.59
HAWAII (Manoa)	8	4.56
TEXAS (Austin)	9	4.51
ILLINOIS (Urbana)	10	4.45
YALE	11	4.41
STANFORD	12	4.37
WISCONSIN (Madison)	13	4.33

ASTRONOMY
Leading Institutions – Rating of Undergraduate Program

Twenty-five institutions with scores
in the 4.0-5.0 range, in rank order

INSTITUTION	Rank	Score
CAL TECH	1	4.92
CALIFORNIA, BERKELEY	2	4.86
HARVARD & RADCLIFFE	3	4.82
CORNELL (N.Y.)	4	4.75
WISCONSIN (Madison)	5	4.66
M.I.T.	6	4.62
ARIZONA	7	4.59
MARYLAND (College Park)	8	4.53
MICHIGAN (Ann Arbor)	9	4.50
UCLA	10	4.46
YALE	11	4.41
CASE WESTERN RESERVE	12	4.40
ILLINOIS (Urbana)	13	4.38
TEXAS (Austin)	14	4.35
VIRGINIA	15	4.32
WASHINGTON (Seattle)	16	4.29
KANSAS	17	4.28
INDIANA (Bloomington)	18	4.25
NORTHWESTERN (Evanston)	19	4.23
PENNSYLVANIA	20	4.22
OHIO STATE (Columbus)	21	4.21
PENN STATE (University Park)	22	4.20
MINNESOTA (Minneapolis)	23	4.18
OKLAHOMA	24	4.16
SOUTHERN CALIFORNIA	25	4.15

ASTROPHYSICS
Leading Institutions – Rating of Undergraduate Program

Ten institutions with scores
in the 4.0-5.0 range, in rank order

INSTITUTION	Rank	Score
M.I.T.	1	4.85
CAL TECH	2	4.81
PRINCETON	3	4.79
INDIANA (Bloomington)	4	4.72
MINNESOTA (Minneapolis)	5	4.66
HARVARD & RADCLIFFE	6	4.61
PURDUE (Lafayette)	7	4.53
PENNSYLVANIA	8	4.45
VIRGINIA	9	4.40
OKLAHOMA	10	4.34

ATMOSPHERIC SCIENCES
Leading Institutions – Rating of Undergraduate Program

Eight institutions with scores
in the 4.0-5.0 range, in rank order

INSTITUTION	Rank	Score
CORNELL (N.Y.)	1	4.90
ARIZONA (Tucson)	2	4.85
MICHIGAN (Ann Arbor)	3	4.81
KANSAS (Lawrence)	4	4.72
CALIFORNIA, DAVIS	5	4.69
PURDUE (Lafayette)	6	4.64
UCLA	7	4.59
MISSOURI (Columbia)	8	4.55

BACTERIOLOGY/MICROBIOLOGY
Leading Institutions – Rating of Undergraduate Program

Thirty-seven institutions with scores in the 4.0-5.0 range, in rank order

INSTITUTION	Rank	Score	INSTITUTION	Rank	Score
M.I.T.	1	4.92	NOTRE DAME	20	4.67
CALIFORNIA, SAN DIEGO	2	4.90	PITTSBURGH (Pittsburgh)	21	4.63
CALIFORNIA, BERKELEY	3	4.88	MASSACHUSETTS (Amherst)	22	4.58
WASHINGTON (Seattle)	4	4.86	OREGON STATE	23	4.55
UCLA	5	4.84	PENN STATE (University Park)	24	4.50
ILLINOIS (Urbana)	6	4.83	MARYLAND (College Park)	25	4.48
CALIFORNIA, DAVIS	7	4.82	WAYNE STATE (Michigan)	26	4.43
WISCONSIN (Madison)	8	4.81	NORTHWESTERN (Evanston)	27	4.38
MICHIGAN (Ann Arbor)	9	4.80	CONNECTICUT (Storrs)	28	4.35
STANFORD	10	4.79	GEORGIA (Athens)	29	4.31
RUTGERS (New Brunswick)	11	4.78	NORTH CAROLINA STATE (Raleigh)	30	4.26
CORNELL (N.Y.)	12	4.77	MISSOURI (Columbia)	31	4.24
MINNESOTA (Minneapolis)	13	4.75	TENNESSEE (Knoxville)	32	4.21
PURDUE (Lafayette)	14	4.73	IOWA STATE (Ames)	33	4.18
MICHIGAN STATE	15	4.72	KANSAS STATE	34	4.16
TEXAS (Austin)	16	4.71	KANSAS	35	4.11
ROCHESTER (N.Y.)	17	4.70	COLORADO STATE	36	4.08
IOWA (Iowa City)	18	4.69	OHIO STATE (Columbus)	37	4.06
INDIANA (Bloomington)	19	4.68			

BEHAVIORAL SCIENCES
Leading Institutions – Rating of Undergraduate Program

Nine institutions with scores
in the 4.0-5.0 range, in rank order

INSTITUTION	Rank	Score
CORNELL (N.Y.)	1	4.86
JOHNS HOPKINS	2	4.82
CARNEGIE-MELLON	3	4.79
CHICAGO	4	4.74
PENNSYLVANIA	5	4.70
N.Y.U.	6	4.67
NORTHWESTERN (Evanston)	7	4.60
U.S. AIR FORCE ACADEMY	8	4.57
U.S. MILITARY ACADEMY (West Point)	9	4.53

BIOCHEMISTRY
Leading Institutions – Rating of Undergraduate Program

Thirty-two institutions with scores in the 4.0-5.0 range, in rank order

INSTITUTION	Rank	Score	INSTITUTION	Rank	Score
HARVARD & RADCLIFFE	1	4.92	PRINCETON	17	4.46
M.I.T.	2	4.91	IOWA (Iowa City)	18	4.43
CALIFORNIA, BERKELEY	3	4.90	MICHIGAN STATE	19	4.40
WISCONSIN (Madison)	4	4.85	RICE	20	4.38
YALE	5	4.84	CASE WESTERN RESERVE	21	4.34
UCLA	6	4.81	PURDUE (Lafayette)	22	4.33
CORNELL (N.Y.)	7	4.79	OREGON STATE	23	4.28
CALIFORNIA, SAN DIEGO	8	4.75	N.Y.U.	24	4.25
CHICAGO	9	4.71	OREGON (Eugene)	25	4.23
ILLINOIS (Urbana)	10	4.70	RUTGERS (New Brunswick)	26	4.20
COLUMBIA (N.Y.)	11	4.63	SUNY (Stony Brook)	27	4.19
MICHIGAN (Ann Arbor)	12	4.58	TEXAS (Austin)	28	4.17
PENNSYLVANIA	13	4.55	IOWA STATE (Ames)	29	4.15
CALIFORNIA, DAVIS	14	4.53	CALIFORNIA, RIVERSIDE	30	4.14
BRANDEIS	15	4.50	PENN STATE (University Park)	31	4.13
NORTHWESTERN (Evanston)	16	4.49	SOUTHERN CALIFORNIA	32	4.10

BIOENGINEERING/BIOMEDICAL ENGINEERING
Leading Institutions – Rating of Undergraduate Program

Sixteen institutions with scores
in the 4.0-5.0 range, in rank order

INSTITUTION	Rank	Score
JOHNS HOPKINS[2]	1	4.90
PENNSYLVANIA[1]	2	4.88
BROWN[2]	3	4.87
DUKE[2]	4	4.84
NORTHWESTERN (Evanston)[2]	5	4.78
TULANE[2]	6	4.70
CASE WESTERN RESERVE[2]	7	4.62
TEXAS A&M (College Station)[1]	8	4.57
RENSSELAER (N.Y.)[2]	9	4.56
MARQUETTE[2]	10	4.46
CALIFORNIA, SAN DIEGO	11	4.44
LOUISIANA TECH[2]	12	4.28
BOSTON U.[2]	13	4.25
IOWA (Iowa City)	14	4.20
ARIZONA STATE	15	4.16
ILLINOIS (Chicago)[1]	16	4.02

Explanatory Note: Actual titles used by the institution to identify their curricula

[1]Bioengineering

[2]Biomedical Engineering

BIOLOGY
Leading Institutions – Rating of Undergraduate Program

Thirty-six institutions with scores in the 4.0-5.0 range, in rank order

INSTITUTION	Rank	Score
CAL TECH	1	4.92
M.I.T.	2	4.91
YALE	3	4.89
HARVARD & RADCLIFFE	4	4.88
WISCONSIN (Madison)	5	4.87
CALIFORNIA, SAN DIEGO	6	4.86
CALIFORNIA, BERKELEY	7	4.84
COLORADO (Boulder)	8	4.82
COLUMBIA (N.Y.)	9	4.80
STANFORD	10	4.76
WASHINGTON (Seattle)	11	4.72
CHICAGO	12	4.70
DUKE	13	4.69
WASHINGTON (St. Louis)	14	4.68
UCLA	15	4.67
MICHIGAN (Ann Arbor)	16	4.66
CORNELL (N.Y.)	17	4.64
PENNSYLVANIA	18	4.62
PURDUE (Lafayette)	19	4.59
INDIANA (Bloomington)	20	4.55
NORTH CAROLINA (Chapel Hill)	21	4.54
UTAH (Salt Lake City)	22	4.53
JOHNS HOPKINS	23	4.52
NORTHWESTERN (Evanston)	24	4.50
PRINCETON	25	4.45
CALIFORNIA, IRVINE	26	4.43
NOTRE DAME	27	4.42
CALIFORNIA, SANTA BARBARA	28	4.38
VIRGINIA	29	4.36
BROWN	30	4.35
ILLINOIS (Urbana)	31	4.32
PITTSBURGH (Pittsburgh)	32	4.29
VANDERBILT	33	4.28
ORREGON (Eugene)	34	4.25
SUNY (Stony Brook)	35	4.19
ROCHESTER (N.Y.)	36	4.11

Thirteen institutions with scores in the 3.5-3.9 range, in rank order

INSTITUTION	Rank	Score
TUFTS	37	3.90
MINNESOTA (Minneapolis)	38	3.88
SUNY (Buffalo)	39	3.85
TEXAS (Austin)	40	3.81
FLORIDA STATE	41	3.77
MICHIGAN STATE	42	3.74
SOUTHERN CALIFORNIA	43	3.71
CONNECTICUT (Storrs)	44	3.67
CALIFORNIA, RIVERSIDE	45	3.63
RICE	46	3.61
IOWA STATE (Ames)	47	3.58
SUNY (Albany)	48	3.55
CASE WESTERN RESERVE	49	3.53

Twelve institutions with scores in the 3.0-3.4 range, in rank order

INSTITUTION	Rank	Score
BOSTON U.	50	3.40
OHIO STATE (Columbus)	51	3.38
N.Y.U.	52	3.36
IOWA (Iowa City)	53	3.35
PENN STATE (University Park)	54	3.32
EMORY	55	3.27
BRANDEIS	56	3.25
KANSAS	57	3.20
RUTGERS (New Brunswick)	58	3.16
TULANE	59	3.15
U.S. AIR FORCE ACADEMY	60	3.12
MISSOURI (Columbia)	61	3.11

BIOPHYSICS
Leading Institutions – Rating of Undergraduate Program

Thirteen institutions with scores
in the 4.0-5.0 range, in rank order

INSTITUTION	Rank	Score
JOHNS HOPKINS	1	4.88
MICHIGAN (Ann Arbor)	2	4.87
CALIFORNIA, SAN DIEGO	3	4.85
YALE	4	4.82
ILLINOIS (Urbana)	5	4.77
PURDUE (Lafayette)	6	4.73
M.I.T.	7	4.71
PENNSYLVANIA	8	4.68
CORNELL (N.Y.)	9	4.61
CARNEGIE-MELLON	10	4.56
BROWN	11	4.51
IOWA STATE (Ames)	12	4.46
SUNY (Buffalo)	13	4.40

Thirty-one institutions with scores in the 4.0-5.0 range, in rank order

INSTITUTION	Rank	Score	INSTITUTION	Rank	Score
CALIFORNIA, DAVIS	1	4.90	WASHINTON (St. Louis)	17	4.45
CORNELL (N.Y.)	2	4.89	IOWA STATE (Ames)	18	4.40
TEXAS (Austin)	3	4.86	OHIO STATE (Columbus)	19	4.38
WISCONSIN (Madison)	4	4.82	KENTUCKY	20	4.36
MICHIGAN (Ann Arbor)	5	4.81	OREGON STATE	21	4.34
DUKE	6	4.78	FLORIDA (Gainesville)	22	4.32
MICHIGAN STATE	7	4.76	MASSACHUSETTS (Amherst)	23	4.30
ILLINOIS (Urbana)	8	4.73	NEBRASKA (Lincoln)	24	4.26
CALIFORNIA, RIVERSIDE	9	4.70	SUNY College Envir. Sci. & Forestry		
NORTH CAROLINA STATE (Raleigh)	10	4.66	(Syracuse)	25	4.25
PENN STATE (University Park)	11	4.63	OKLAHOMA (Norman)	26	4.20
INDIANA (Bloomington)	12	4.61	RUTGERS (New Brunswick)	27	4.17
MINNESOTA (Minneapolis)	13	4.59	WASHINGTON STATE	28	4.13
GEORGIA (Athens)	14	4.55	COLORADO STATE	29	4.12
WASHINGTON (Seattle)	15	4.50	HAWAII (Manoa)	30	4.10
PURDUE (Lafayette)	16	4.48	TENNESSEE (Knoxville)	31	4.08

BUSINESS ADMINISTRATION
Leading Institutions – Rating of Undergraduate Program

Forty-five institutions with scores in the 4.0-5.0 range, in rank order

INSTITUTION	Rank	Score	INSTITUTION	Rank	Score
PENNSYLVANIA	1	4.91	SUNY (Buffalo)	24	4.46
INDIANA (Bloomington)	2	4.89	UTAH (Salt Lake City)	25	4.43
MICHIGAN (Ann Arbor)	3	4.87	LEHIGH	26	4.42
CALIFORNIA, BERKELEY	4	4.85	OREGON (Eugene)	27	4.40
VIRGINIA (Charlottesville)	5	4.82	FLORIDA (Gainesville)	28	4.39
N.Y.U.	6	4.81	LOUISIANA STATE (Baton Rouge)	29	4.36
ILLINOIS (Urbana)	7	4.76	MASSACHUSETTS (Amherst)	30	4.34
WISCONSIN (Madison)	8	4.74	ARIZONA (Tucson)	31	4.33
PURDUE (Lafayette)	9	4.73	IOWA (Iowa City)	32	4.31
NORTH CAROLINA (Chapel Hill)	10	4.72	ARIZONA STATE	33	4.28
WASHINGTON (Seattle)	11	4.67	MARYLAND (College Park)	34	4.26
MICHIGAN STATE	12	4.66	GEORGIA STATE	35	4.25
TEXAS (Austin)	13	4.65	TEMPLE (Philadelphia)	36	4.23
CUNY (Bernard Baruch)	14	4.64	GEORGE WASHINGTON	37	4.21
MINNESOTA (Minneapolis)	15	4.62	SYRACUSE	38	4.20
WASHINGTON (St. Louis)	16	4.60	COLORADO (Boulder)	39	4.16
SOUTHERN CALIFORNIA (USC)	17	4.59	EMORY	40	4.14
HOUSTON (University Park)	18	4.58	MISSOURI (Columbia)	41	4.12
PENN STATE (University Park)	19	4.57	SOUTH CAROLINA (Columbia)	42	4.11
TEXAS A&M (College Station)	20	4.55	DENVER	43	4.08
NOTRE DAME	21	4.53	GEORGIA (Athens)	44	4.07
SOUTHERN METHODIST	22	4.51	NEBRASKA (Lincoln)	45	4.03
OHIO STATE (Columbus)	23	4.48			

CELL BIOLOGY
Leading Institutions – Rating of Undergraduate Program

Nineteen institutions with scores
in the 4.0-5.0 range, in rank order

INSTITUTION	Rank	Score
M.I.T.	1	4.91
CAL TECH	2	4.90
WISCONSIN (Madison)	3	4.83
CALIFORNIA, SAN DIEGO	4	4.81
CHICAGO	5	4.77
CALIFORNIA, BERKELEY	6	4.74
COLORADO (Boulder)	7	4.71
PURDUE (Lafayette)	8	4.67
BROWN	9	4.62
NORTHWESTERN (Evanston)	10	4.59
MICHIGAN (Ann Arbor)	11	4.52
CARNEGIE-MELLON	12	4.49
MINNESOTA (Minneapolis)	13	4.38
CORNELL (N.Y.)	14	4.37
PENN STATE (University Park)	15	4.30
ROCHESTER (N.Y.)	16	4.26
ARIZONA (Tucson)	17	4.24
KANSAS	18	4.18
SUNY (Buffalo)	19	4.16

CERAMIC ART/DESIGN
Leading Institutions – Rating of Undergraduate Program

Fourteen institutions with scores
in the 4.0-5.0 range, in rank order

INSTITUTION	Rank	Score
ALFRED (N.Y.)	1	4.86
CARNEGIE-MELLON	2	4.83
OHIO STATE (Columbus)	3	4.80
PRATT INSTITUTE (N.Y.)	4	4.72
IOWA (Iowa City)	5	4.69
KANSAS (Lawrence)	6	4.64
OKLAHOMA (Norman)	7	4.60
TEXAS (Austin)	8	4.56
PURDUE (Lafayette)	9	4.50
LOUISIANA STATE (Baton Rouge)	10	4.49
FLORIDA (Gainesville)	11	4.46
HOUSTON (Houston)	12	4.42
MICHIGAN (Ann Arbor)	13	4.39
MIAMI (Florida)	14	4.35

CERAMIC ENGINEERING
Leading Institutions – Rating of Undergraduate Program

Ten institutions with scores
in the 4.0-5.0 range, in rank order

INSTITUTION	Rank	Score
SUNY (Alfred)[1, 2, 4]	1	4.90
ILLINOIS (Urbana)[1]	2	4.88
OHIO STATE (Columbus)[1]	3	4.82
IOWA STATE (Ames)[1]	4	4.74
MISSOURI (Rolla)[1]	5	4.68
GEORGIA TECH[1]	6	4.57
WASHINGTON (Seattle)[1]	7	4.48
RUTGERS (New Brunswick)[1]	8	4.33
PENN STATE (University Park)[3]	9	4.28
CLEMSON[1]	10	4.24

***Explanatory Note: Actual titles used by the
institution to identify their curricula***

[1]Ceramic Engineering

[2]Ceramic Engineering Science

[3]Ceramic Science and Engineering

[4]Glass Engineering Science

CHEMICAL ENGINEERING
Leading Institutions – Rating of Undergraduate Program

Fifty-four institutions with scores in the 4.0-5.0 range, in rank order

INSTITUTION	Rank	Score	INSTITUTION	Rank	Score
MINNESOTA (Minneapolis)	1	4.91	CASE WESTERN RESERVE	28	4.44
WISCONSIN (Madison)	2	4.90	COLORADO (Boulder)	29	4.43
CALIFORNIA, BERKELEY	3	4.88	WASHINGTON (St. Louis)	30	4.40
CAL TECH	4	4.85	LEHIGH	31	4.39
STANFORD	5	4.82	TEXAS A&M (College Station)	32	4.37
DELAWARE (Newark)	6	4.80	CUNY (City College)	33	4.35
M.I.T.	7	4.79	OHIO STATE (Columbus)	34	4.33
ILLINOIS (Urbana)	8	4.75	GEORGIA TECH	35	4.31
PRINCETON	9	4.74	NORTH CAROLINA STATE (Raleigh)	36	4.29
HOUSTON (University Park)	10	4.73	YALE	37	4.25
PURDUE (Lafayette)	11	4.72	RENSSELAER (N.Y.)	38	4.23
NOTRE DAME	12	4.71	V.P.I. & State U.	39	4.21
NORTHWESTERN (Evanston)	13	4.68	TENNESSEE (Knoxville)	40	4.20
CORNELL (N.Y.)	14	4.65	VIRGINIA (Charlottesville)	41	4.19
TEXAS (Austin)	15	4.63	COLUMBIA (N.Y.)	42	4.18
STEVENS (N.J.)	16	4.62	ARIZONA (Tucson)	43	4.17
PENNSYLVANIA	17	4.61	SYRACUSE	44	4.16
CARNEGIE-MELLON	18	4.60	UTAH (Salt Lake City)	45	4.15
MICHIGAN (Ann Arbor)	19	4.58	UCLA	46	4.13
RICE	20	4.57	OKLAHOMA (Norman)	47	4.11
WASHINGTON (Seattle)	21	4.56	MARYLAND (College Park)	48	4.10
MASSACHUSETTS (Amherst)	22	4.55	OREGON STATE	49	4.09
IOWA STATE (Ames)	23	4.53	LOUISIANA STATE (Baton Rouge)	50	4.06
FLORIDA (Gainesville)	24	4.51	PITTSBURGH (Pittsburgh)	51	4.05
ROCHESTER (N.Y.)	25	4.50	IOWA (Iowa City)	52	4.04
SUNY (Buffalo)	26	4.48	OREGON STATE	53	4.03
PENN STATE (University Park)	27	4.47	CLARKSON (N.Y.)	54	4.02

CHEMISTRY
Leading Institutions – Rating of Undergraduate Program

Fifty-three institutions with scores in the 4.0-5.0 range, in rank order

INSTITUTION	Rank	Score	INSTITUTION	Rank	Score
CAL TECH	1	4.95	PENNSYLVANIA	28	4.48
CALIFORNIA, BERKELEY	2	4.94	RICE	29	4.47
HARVARD & RADCLIFFE	3	4.93	MICHIGAN (Ann Arbor)	30	4.46
M.I.T.	4	4.92	WASHINGTON (Seattle)	31	4.45
COLUMBIA (N.Y.)	5	4.91	COLORADO (Boulder)	32	4.44
STANFORD	6	4.90	TEXAS A&M (College Station)	33	4.43
ILLINOIS (Urbana)	7	4.88	SOUTHERN CALIFORNIA	34	4.41
CHICAGO	8	4.85	PITTSBURGH (Pittsburgh)	35	4.39
UCLA	9	4.82	FLORIDA (Gainesville)	36	4.37
WISCONSIN (Madison)	10	4.80	CALIFORNIA, RIVERSIDE	37	4.35
CORNELL (N.Y.)	11	4.78	DARTMOUTH	38	4.34
NORTHWESTERN (Evanston)	12	4.77	CALIFORNIA, SANTA BARBARA	39	4.32
PRINCETON	13	4.75	CALIFORNIA, IRVINE	40	4.30
YALE	14	4.74	JOHNS HOPKINS	41	4.28
PURDUE (Lafayette)	15	4.71	CALIFORNIA, DAVIS	42	4.27
NORTH CAROLINA (Chapel Hill)	16	4.69	UTAH (Salt Lake City)	43	4.25
OHIO STATE (Columbus)	17	4.66	OREGON (Eugene)	44	4.23
TEXAS (Austin)	18	4.63	DUKE	45	4.20
IOWA STATE (Ames)	19	4.61	MICHIGAN STATE	46	4.18
INDIANA (Bloomington)	20	4.59	RENSSELAER (N.Y.)	47	4.16
CALIFORNIA, SAN DIEGO	21	4.58	VIRGINIA	48	4.15
MINNESOTA (Minneapolis)	22	4.57	FLORIDA STATE	49	4.14
NOTRE DAME	23	4.56	VANDERBILT	50	4.10
PENN STATE (University Park)	24	4.53	CASE WESTERN RESERVE	51	4.09
BROWN	25	4.52	IOWA (Iowa City)	52	4.06
ROCHESTER (N.Y.)	26	4.51	GEORGIA TECH	53	4.05
CARNEGIE-MELLON	27	4.50			

CHILD PSYCHOLOGY
Leading Institutions – Rating of Undergraduate Program

Seventeen institutions with scores
in the 4.0-5.0 range, in rank order

INSTITUTION	Rank	Score
WAYNE STATE (Michigan)	1	4.59
NORTHWESTERN (Evanston)	2	4.55
CORNELL (N.Y.)	3	4.52
N.Y.U.	4	4.47
MICHIGAN (Ann Arbor)	5	4.44
IOWA (Iowa City)	6	4.40
CARNEGIE-MELLON	7	4.37
MINNESOTA (Minneapolis)	8	4.30
IOWA STATE (Ames)	9	4.28
PENNSYLVANIA	10	4.26
PITTSBURGH (Pittsburgh)	11	4.24
OHIO STATE (Columbus)	12	4.20
WISCONSIN (Madison)	13	4.16
SYRACUSE	14	4.14
TUFTS (Massachusetts)	15	4.09
FLORIDA STATE	16	4.05
UTAH (Salt Lake City)	17	4.04

Fourteen institutions with scores
in the 4.0-5.0 range, in rank order

INSTITUTION	Rank	Score
HARVARD & RADCLIFFE	1	4.87
CORNELL (N.Y.)	2	4.85
CHICAGO	3	4.82
PENNSYLVANIA	4	4.73
CALIFORNIA, BERKELEY	5	4.68
COLUMBIA (N.Y.)	6	4.67
STANFORD	7	4.65
WISCONSIN (Madison)	8	4.55
MICHIGAN (Ann Arbor)	9	4.54
HAWAII (Manoa)	10	4.48
WASHINGTON (Seattle)	11	4.46
YALE	12	4.42
INDIANA (Bloomington)	13	4.32
GEORGETOWN (D.C.)	14	4.27

Fifty-five institutions with scores in the 4.0-5.0 range, in rank order

INSTITUTION	Rank	Score	INSTITUTION	Rank	Score
CALIFORNIA, BERKELEY	1	4.92	MASSACHUSETTS (Amherst)	29	4.38
M.I.T.	2	4.90	V.P.I. & STATE U.	30	4.35
ILLINOIS (Urbana)	3	4.89	FLORIDA (Gainesville)	31	4.32
STANFORD	4	4.85	WASHINGTON (St. Louis)	32	4.30
TEXAS (Austin)	5	4.82	RICE	33	4.29
CORNELL (N.Y.)	6	4.80	RENSSELAER (N.Y.)	34	4.27
NORTHWESTERN (Evanston)	7	4.78	KANSAS	35	4.25
PURDUE (Lafayette)	8	4.77	DUKE	36	4.23
MICHIGAN (Ann Arbor)	9	4.74	SOUTHERN CALIFORNIA	37	4.22
COLORADO STATE	10	4.72	PENN STATE (University Park)	38	4.21
WASHINGTON (Seattle)	11	4.67	OREGON STATE	39	4.20
PRINCETON	12	4.66	MICHIGAN STATE	40	4.19
WISCONSIN (Madison)	13	4.64	VANDERBILT[1]	41	4.18
STEVENS (N.J.)	14	4.62	MARYLAND (College Park)	42	4.17
COLUMBIA (N.Y.)	15	4.60	MISSOURI (Rolla)	43	4.16
BROWN	16	4.59	PENNSYLVANIA[2]	44	4.15
LEHIGH	17	4.56	NOTRE DAME	45	4.13
UCLA	18	4.55	MISSOURI (Columbia)	46	4.12
GEORGIA TECH	19	4.52	SUNY (Buffalo)	47	4.11
CARNEGIE-MELLON	20	4.50	PITTSBURGH (Pittsburgh)	48	4.10
TEXAS A&M (College Station)	21	4.49	OKLAHOMA (Norman)	49	4.09
CALIFORNIA, DAVIS	22	4.48	UTAH STATE	50	4.08
COLORADO (Boulder)	23	4.47	TENNESSEE (Knoxville)	51	4.07
OHIO STATE (Columbus)	24	4.46	OKLAHOMA STATE	52	4.06
NORTH CAROLINA STATE (Raleigh)	25	4.45	ARIZONA (Tucson)	53	4.04
MINNESOTA (Minneapolis)	26	4.44	CUNY (City College)	54	4.03
IOWA STATE (Ames)	27	4.42	U.S. AIR FORCE ACADEMY	55	4.02
IOWA (Iowa City)	28	4.40			

Explanatory Note: Actual titles used by the institution to identify their curricula

[1]Civil and Environmental Engineering
[2]Civil Engineering Systems

CLASSICS
Leading Institutions – Rating of Undergraduate Program

Twenty-three institutions with scores
in the 4.0-5.0 range, in rank order

INSTITUTION	Rank	Score
HARVARD & RADCLIFFE	1	4.90
CALIFORNIA, BERKELEY	2	4.89
YALE	3	4.87
PRINCETON	4	4.82
MICHIGAN (Ann Arbor)	5	4.80
NORTH CAROLINA (Chapel Hill)	6	4.75
BRYN MAWR	7	4.71
TEXAS (Austin)	8	4.69
BROWN	9	4.64
COLUMBIA (N.Y.)	10	4.62
PENNSYLVANIA	11	4.59
CORNELL (N.Y.)	12	4.57
STANFORD	13	4.53
CHICAGO	14	4.47
ILLINOIS (Urbana)	15	4.41
DUKE	16	4.33
JOHNS HOPKINS	17	4.29
UCLA	18	4.23
INDIANA (Bloomington)	19	4.18
BOSTON U.	20	4.16
CATHOLIC U. (D.C.)	21	4.14
FORDHAM (N.Y.)	22	4.11
VANDERBILT	23	4.10

COMMUNICATION
Leading Institutions – Rating of Undergraduate Program

Nineteen institutions with scores
in the 4.0-5.0 range, in rank order

INSTITUTION	Rank	Score
NORTHWESTERN (Illinois)	1	4.86
STANFORD	2	4.84
PENNSYLVANIA	3	4.81
MICHIGAN (Ann Arbor)	4	4.77
SOUTHERN CALIFORNIA	5	4.71
IOWA (Iowa City)	6	4.67
MICHIGAN STATE	7	4.65
TEXAS (Austin)	8	4.63
SYRACUSE	9	4.60
FLORIDA STATE	10	4.54
WISCONSIN (Madison)	11	4.43
WASHINGTON (Seattle)	12	4.39
OHIO STATE (Columbus)	13	4.37
MINNESOTA (Minneapolis)	14	4.33
PURDUE (Lafayette)	15	4.25
SUNY (Buffalo)	16	4.20
MASSACHUSETTS (Amherst)	17	4.16
OHIO U. (Athens)	18	4.11
WAYNE STATE (Michigan)	19	4.10

COMPARATIVE LITERATURE
Leading Institutions – Rating of Undergraduate Program

Twenty-eight institutions with scores in the 4.0-5.0 range, in rank order

INSTITUTION	Rank	Score	INSTITUTION	Rank	Score
CALIFORNIA, BERKELEY	1	4.81	WASHINGTON (Seattle)	15	4.41
HARVARD & RADCLIFFE	2	4.78	NORTH CAROLINA (Chapel Hill)	16	4.39
COLUMBIA (N.Y.)	3	4.76	CALIFORNIA, IRVINE	17	4.35
YALE	4	4.73	N.Y.U.	18	4.32
CHICAGO	5	4.71	JOHNS HOPKINS	19	4.27
PENNSYLVANIA	6	4.69	IOWA (Iowa City)	20	4.25
ILLINOIS (Urbana)	7	4.68	BRANDEIS	21	4.24
PRINCETON	8	4.63	TEXAS (Austin)	22	4.23
STANFORD	9	4.61	WASHINGTON (St. Louis)	23	4.20
MICHIGAN (Ann Arbor)	10	4.57	WISCONSIN (Madison)	24	4.18
CORNELL (N.Y.)	11	4.54	MASSACHUSETTS (Amherst)	25	4.15
INDIANA (Bloomington)	12	4.52	DUKE	26	4.13
BROWN	13	4.47	DENVER	27	4.12
NORTHWESTERN (Evanston)	14	4.42	CALIFORNIA, SANTA BARBARA	28	4.08

COMPUTER ENGINEERING
Leading Institutions – Rating of Undergraduate Program

Twenty-two institutions with scores
in the 4.0-5.0 range, in rank order

INSTITUTION	Rank	Score
M.I.T.[5]	1	4.91
CALIFORNIA, BERKELEY[4]	2	4.90
ILLINOIS (Urbana)[1]	3	4.87
MICHIGAN (Ann Arbor)[1]	4	4.83
PURDUE (Lafayette)[2]	5	4.77
CASE WESTERN RESERVE[1]	6	4.74
RENSSELAER (N.Y.)[4]	7	4.68
CARNEGIE-MELLON[1]	8	4.60
IOWA STATE (Ames)[1]	9	4.59
FLORIDA (Gainesville)[1]	10	4.54
MISSOURI (Columbia)[1]	11	4.48
ARIZONA STATE[6]	12	4.46
STEVENS (N.J.)[1]	13	4.41
SYRACUSE[1]	14	4.35
UCLA[5]	15	4.31
GEORGIA TECH[1]	16	4.25
ARIZONA (Tucson)[1]	17	4.21
CINCINNATI[1]	18	4.17
BOSTON U.[1]	19	4.13
LEHIGH[1]	20	4.12
PENN STATE (University Park)[1]	21	4.11
TEXAS (Austin)[1]	22	4.10

Explanatory Note: Actual titles used by the institution to identify their curricula

[1]Computer Engineering

[2]Computer and Electrical Engineering

[3]Computer and Systems Engineering

[4]Computer Science

[5]Computer Science and Engineering

[6]Computer Systems Engineering

COMPUTER SCIENCE
Leading Institutions – Rating of Undergraduate Program

Thirty-two institutions with scores in the 4.0-5.0 range, in rank order

INSTITUTION	Rank	Score
M.I.T.	1	4.92
CARNEGIE-MELLON	2	4.91
CALIFORNIA, BERKELEY	3	4.89
CORNELL (N.Y.)	4	4.87
ILLINOIS (Urbana)	5	4.85
UCLA	6	4.82
YALE	7	4.80
CAL TECH	8	4.79
TEXAS (Austin)	9	4.75
WISCONSIN (Madison)	10	4.73
MARYLAND (College Park)	11	4.70
PRINCETON	12	4.69
WASHINGTON (Seattle)	13	4.67
SOUTHERN CALIFORNIA	14	4.65
SUNY (Stony Brook)	15	4.63
BROWN	16	4.61
GEORGIA TECH	17	4.60
PENNSYLVANIA	18	4.58
ROCHESTER (N.Y.)	19	4.55
N.Y.U.	20	4.52
MINNESOTA (Minneapolis)	21	4.50
UTAH (Salt Lake City)	22	4.48
COLUMBIA (N.Y.)	23	4.42
OHIO STATE (Columbus)	24	4.39
RICE	25	4.33
DUKE	26	4.28
NORTHWESTERN (Evanston)	27	4.22
SUNY (Buffalo)	28	4.18
PITTSBURGH (Pittsburgh)	29	4.14
CALIFORNIA, IRVINE	30	4.11
CALIFORNIA, SAN DIEGO	31	4.08
MASSACHUSETTS (Amherst)	32	4.05

Twelve institutions with scores in the 3.5-3.9 range, in rank order

INSTITUTION	Rank	Score
RUTGERS (New Brunswick)	33	3.90
INDIANA (Bloomington)	34	3.86
PENN STATE (University Park)	35	3.85
CALIFORNIA, SANTA BARBARA	36	3.81
SYRACUSE	37	3.80
IOWA STATE (Ames)	38	3.75
RENSSELAER (N.Y.)	39	3.70
VIRGINIA (Charlottesville)	40	3.66
MICHIGAN (Ann Arbor)	41	3.62
IOWA (Iowa City)	42	3.58
CONNECTICUT (Storrs)	43	3.54
SOUTHERN METHODIST	44	3.53

Thirteen institutions with scores in the 3.0-3.4 range, in rank order

INSTITUTION	Rank	Score
U.S. NAVAL ACADEMY	45	3.40
U.S. MILITARY ACADEMY	46	3.39
HOUSTON (University Park)	47	3.38
KANSAS	48	3.36
WASHINGTON (St. Louis)	49	3.34
MICHIGAN STATE	50	3.32
STEVENS INST. OF TECH. (N.J.)	51	3.28
CASE WESTERN RESERVE	52	3.26
TEXAS A&M (College Station)	53	3.24
OKLAHOMA (Norman)	54	3.22
KANSAS STATE	55	3.20
VANDERBILT	56	3.18
WASHINGTON STATE	57	3.14

DAIRY SCIENCES
Leading Institutions – Rating of Undergraduate Program

Eleven institutions with scores
in the 4.0-5.0 range, in rank order

INSTITUTION	Rank	Score
WISCONSIN (Madison)	1	4.91
CORNELL (N.Y.)	2	4.90
KANSAS STATE	3	4.82
PENN STATE (University Park)	4	4.76
IOWA STATE (Ames)	5	4.72
MARYLAND (College Park)	6	4.68
ILLINOIS (Urbana)	7	4.67
MISSOURI (Columbia)	8	4.63
NEBRASKA (Lincoln)	9	4.62
OHIO STATE (Columbus)	10	4.58
TEXAS A&M (College Station)	11	4.55

DIETETICS
Leading Institutions – Rating of Undergraduate Program

Fifteen institutions with scores
in the 4.0-5.0 range, in rank order

INSTITUTION	Rank	Score
CORNELL (N.Y.)	1	4.90
MICHIGAN STATE	2	4.89
CALIFORNIA, DAVIS	3	4.85
PURDUE (Lafayette)	4	4.82
COLORADO STATE	5	4.80
IOWA STATE (Ames)	6	4.76
KANSAS STATE	7	4.71
CALIFORNIA, BERKELEY	8	4.69
ILLINOIS (Urbana)	9	4.67
WISCONSIN (Madison)	10	4.61
OHIO STATE (Columbus)	11	4.55
ALABAMA (Tuscaloosa)	12	4.50
FLORIDA STATE	13	4.46
MISSOURI (Columbia)	14	4.40
OKLAHOMA STATE	15	4.35

DRAMA/THEATRE
Leading Institutions – Rating of Undergraduate Program

Nineteen institutions with scores in the 4.0-5.0 range, in rank order

INSTITUTION	Rank	Score
NORTHWESTERN (Evanston)	1	4.91
UCLA	2	4.90
CORNELL (N.Y.)	3	4.88
WASHINGTON (Seattle)	4	4.85
SOUTHERN CALIFORNIA	5	4.83
INDIANA (Bloomington)	6	4.80
STANFORD	7	4.75
IOWA (Iowa City)	8	4.70
CARNEGIE-MELLON	9	4.66
N.Y.U.	10	4.62
MINNESOTA (Minneapolis)	11	4.60
PENN STATE (University Park)	12	4.58
MICHIGAN STATE	13	4.51
TUFTS	14	4.46
CALIFORNIA, BERKELEY	15	4.39
WISCONSIN (Madison)	16	4.30
CATHOLIC U. (D.C.)	17	4.25
YALE[1]	18	4.20
FLORIDA STATE	19	4.18

Explanatory Note: Actual title used by the institution to identify their curricula

[1]Theatre Studies

Eleven institutions with scores in the 3.5-3.9 range, in rank order

INSTITUTION	Rank	Score
BAYLOR	20	3.90
NORTH CAROLINA (Chapel Hill)	21	3.83
TULANE	22	3.78
MICHIGAN (Ann Arbor)	23	3.74
ILLINOIS (Urbana)	24	3.68
CALIFORNIA, SANTA BARBARA	25	3.66
OHIO STATE (Columbus)	26	3.64
BOSTON U.	27	3.60
BRANDEIS	28	3.55
CASE WESTERN RESERVE	29	3.53
SOUTHERN METHODIST	30	3.51

Sixteen institutions with scores in the 3.0-3.4 range, in rank order

INSTITUTION	Rank	Score
SYRACUSE	31	3.40
SAN FRANCISCO STATE	32	3.38
BOWLING GREEN	33	3.37
ARIZONA (Tucson)	34	3.30
FLORIDA (Gainesville)	35	3.23
OHIO U.	36	3.22
TEMPLE (Philadelphia)	37	3.21
PITTSBURGH (Pittsburgh)	38	3.18
MIAMI (Florida)	39	3.16
ARIZONA STATE	40	3.13
CUNY (City)	41	3.11
DARTMOUTH	42	3.09
OCCIDENTAL (California)	43	3.08
KANSAS	44	3.07
TEXAS (Austin)	45	3.04
WAYNE STATE (Michigan)	46	3.03

EARTH SCIENCE
Leading Institutions – Rating of Undergraduate Program

Twelve institutions with scores
in the 4.0-5.0 range, in rank order

INSTITUTION	Rank	Score
JOHNS HOPKINS	1	4.86
MICHIGAN (Ann Arbor)	2	4.83
WISCONSIN (Madison)	3	4.79
MICHIGAN STATE	4	4.73
DARTMOUTH COLLEGE	5	4.70
IOWA STATE (Ames)	6	4.64
OHIO STATE (Columbus)	7	4.59
PENN STATE (University Park)	8	4.57
PURDUE (Lafayette)	9	4.52
ARIZONA (Tucson)	10	4.49
MINNESOTA (Minneapolis)	11	4.42
STANFORD	12	4.41

EAST ASIAN STUDIES
Leading Institutions – Rating of Undergraduate Program

Eleven institutions with scores
in the 4.0-5.0 range, in rank order

INSTITUTION	Rank	Score
HARVARD	1	4.86
CALIFORNIA, BERKELEY	2	4.83
PENNSYLVANIA	3	4.79
COLUMBIA (N.Y.)	4	4.77
CHICAGO	5	4.73
STANFORD	6	4.70
CORNELL (N.Y.)	7	4.68
INDIANA (Bloomington)	8	4.64
PRINCETON	9	4.61
MICHIGAN (Ann Arbor)	10	4.56
YALE	11	4.53

ECOLOGY/ENVIRONMENTAL STUDIES
Leading Institutions – Rating of Undergraduate Program

Thirteen institutions with scores
in the 4.0-5.0 range, in rank order

INSTITUTION	Rank	Score
HARVARD	1	4.89
CORNELL (N.Y.)	2	4.87
CALIFORNIA, BERKELEY	3	4.84
ILLINOIS (Urbana)	4	4.79
MICHIGAN (Ann Arbor)	5	4.78
PENNSYLVANIA	6	4.76
WISCONSIN (Madison)	7	4.72
INDIANA (Bloomington)	8	4.69
RICE	9	4.65
COLORADO (Boulder)	10	4.60
ARIZONA (Tucson)	11	4.57
N.Y. COLLEGE OF ENVIR. SCI. (SUNY)	12	4.52
PURDUE (Lafayette)	13	4.49

ECONOMICS
Leading Institutions – Rating of Undergraduate Program

Forty-six institutions with scores in the 4.0-5.0 range, in rank order

INSTITUTION	Rank	Score	INSTITUTION	Rank	Score
M.I.T.	1	4.92	CALIFORNIA, DAVIS	24	4.58
CHICAGO	2	4.91	WASHINGTON (Seattle)	25	4.57
STANFORD	3	4.90	MARYLAND (College Park)	26	4.56
PRINCETON	4	4.89	MICHIGAN STATE	27	4.54
HARVARD & RADCLIFFE	5	4.87	NORTH CAROLINA (Chapel Hill)	28	4.52
YALE	6	4.85	ILLINOIS (Urbana)	29	4.50
MINNESOTA (Minneapolis)	7	4.84	TEXAS A&M (College Station)	30	4.48
PENNSYLVANIA	8	4.83	BOSTON U.	31	4.44
WISCONSIN (Madison)	9	4.82	WASHINGTON (St. Louis)	32	4.42
CALIFORNIA, BERKELEY	10	4.81	PURDUE (Lafayette)	33	4.40
NORTHWESTERN (Evanston)	11	4.79	SOUTHERN CALIFORNIA	34	4.38
ROCHESTER (N.Y.)	12	4.76	TEXAS (Austin)	35	4.35
COLUMBIA (N.Y.)	13	4.75	VANDERBILT	36	4.31
UCLA	14	4.74	OHIO STATE (Columbus)	37	4.27
MICHIGAN (Ann Arbor)	15	4.73	IOWA STATE (Ames)	38	4.24
JOHNS HOPKINS	16	4.72	SUNY (Stony Brook)	39	4.20
CARNEGIE-MELLON	17	4.71	IOWA (Iowa City)	40	4.17
BROWN	18	4.69	MASSACHUSETTS (Amherst)	41	4.15
CALIFORNIA, SAN DIEGO	19	4.67	CALIFORNIA, SANTA BARBARA	42	4.13
DUKE	20	4.66	PITTSBURGH (Pittsburgh)	43	4.12
CORNELL (N.Y.)	21	4.65	V.P.I. & STATE U.	44	4.10
N.Y.U.	22	4.63	CLAREMONT McKENNA COLLEGE	45	4.08
VIRGINIA	23	4.60	RUTGERS (New Brunswick)	46	4.06

ELECTRICAL ENGINEERING
Leading Institutions – Rating of Undergraduate Program

Sixty-two institutions with scores in the 4.0-5.0 range, in rank order

INSTITUTION	Rank	Score	INSTITUTION	Rank	Score
M.I.T.[3]	1	4.92	PENNSYLVANIA	32	4.40
STANFORD	2	4.91	YALE	33	4.38
CALIFORNIA, BERKELEY[2]	3	4.88	V.P.I. & STATE U.	34	4.37
ILLINOIS (Urbana)	4	4.86	PENN STATE (University Park)	35	4.36
UCLA	5	4.82	CASE WESTERN RESERVE	36	4.35
CORNELL (N.Y.)	6	4.81	MISSOURI (Rolla)	37	4.34
PURDUE (Lafayette)	7	4.79	MASSACHUSETTS (Amherst)	38	4.32
SOUTHERN CALIFORNIA	8	4.77	SYRACUSE	39	4.30
PRINCETON	9	4.76	MICHIGAN STATE	40	4.28
MICHIGAN (Ann Arbor)	10	4.75	NOTRE DAME	41	4.27
CARNEGIE-MELLON	11	4.74	PITTSBURGH (Pittsburgh)	42	4.26
POLYTECHNIC U. (Brooklyn, N.Y.)	12	4.73	IOWA STATE (Ames)	43	4.25
TEXAS (Austin)	13	4.70	NORTH CAROLINA STATE (Raleigh)	44	4.24
COLUMBIA (N.Y.)	14	4.66	WASHINGTON (Seattle)	45	4.22
GEORGIA TECH	15	4.65	TEXAS A&M (College Station)	46	4.21
MARYLAND (College Park)	16	4.64	SOUTHERN METHODIST	47	4.20
OHIO STATE (Columbus)	17	4.63	CALIFORNIA, DAVIS	48	4.18
STEVENS (N.J.)	18	4.62	DUKE	49	4.17
MINNESOTA (Minneapolis)	19	4.60	SUNY (Stony Brook)	50	4.15
NORTHWESTERN (Evanston)	20	4.58	TENNESSEE (Knoxville)	51	4.13
CALIFORNIA, SANTA BARBARA	21	4.57	ARIZONA STATE	52	4.11
FLORIDA (Gainesville)	22	4.56	KANSAS	53	4.10
RENSSELAER (N.Y.)[1]	23	4.54	HAWAII (Manoa)	54	4.08
JOHNS HOPKINS	24	4.53	TEXAS TECH	55	4.07
RICE	25	4.52	COLORADO STATE	56	4.06
BROWN	26	4.50	SUNY (Buffalo)	57	4.05
WISCONSIN (Madison)	27	4.49	UTAH (Salt Lake City)	58	4.04
ARIZONA (Tucson)	28	4.46	U.S. AIR FORCE ACADEMY	59	4.03
CALIFORNIA, SAN DIEGO	29	4.45	IOWA (Iowa City)	60	4.02
COLORADO (Boulder)[2]	30	4.43	CUNY (City College)	61	4.01
WASHINGTON (St. Louis)	31	4.42	CONNECTICUT (Storrs)	62	4.00

Explanatory Note: Actual titles used by the institution to identify their curricula

[1] Electric Power Engineering

[2] Electrical and Computer Engineering

[3] Electrical Science and Engineering

Ten institutions with scores
in the 4.0-5.0 range, in rank order

INSTITUTION	Rank	Score
ILLINOIS (Urbana)	1	4.85
OKLAHOMA (Norman)	2	4.80
MARYLAND (College Park)	3	4.78
CARNEGIE-MELLON[1]	4	4.76
COLORADO (Mines)	5	4.75
HARVEY MUDD	6	4.72
STEVENS (N.J.)	7	4.70
DARTMOUTH COLLEGE	8	4.66
OKLAHOMA STATE	9	4.62
MICHIGAN TECH	10	4.58

ENGINEERING MECHANICS
Leading Institutions – Rating of Undergraduate Program

Six institutions with scores
in the 4.0-5.0 range, in rank order

INSTITUTION	Rank	Score
ILLINOIS (Urbana)	1	4.82
WISCONSIN (Madison)	2	4.74
U.S. AIR FORCE ACADEMY	3	4.72
JOHNS HOPKINS	4	4.69
V.P.I. & STATE U.[1]	5	4.64
CINCINNATI	6	4.61

Explanatory Note: Actual titles used by the institution to identify their curricula

[1]Engineering Science and Mechanics

ENGINEERING PHYSICS
Leading Institutions – Rating of Undergraduate Program

Eight institutions with scores
in the 4.0-5.0 range, in rank order

INSTITUTION	Rank	Score
PRINCETON	1	4.82
CORNELL (N.Y.)	2	4.77
KANSAS	3	4.53
OKLAHOMA (Norman)	4	4.49
COLORADO (Mines)	5	4.44
TEXAS TECH	6	4.33
STEVENS (New Jersey)	7	4.27
TULSA	8	4.23

ENGINEERING SCIENCE
Leading Institutions – Rating of Undergraduate Program

Ten institutions with scores
in the 4.0-5.0 range, in rank order

INSTITUTION	Rank	Score
HARVARD	1	4.85
U.S. AIR FORCE ACADEMY	2	4.79
IOWA STATE (Ames)	3	4.70
FLORIDA (Gainesville)	4	4.68
PENN STATE (University Park)	5	4.63
COLORADO STATE	6	4.61
CASE WESTERN RESERVE[1]	7	4.58
TENNESSEE (Knoxville)	8	4.53
MONTANA TECH	9	4.49
SUNY (Stony Brook)	10	4.16

***Explanatory Note: Actual titles used by the
institution to identify their curricula***

[1]Fluid and Thermal Engineering Science

ENGLISH
Leading Institutions – Rating of Undergraduate Program

Forty-one institutions with scores in the 4.0-5.0 range, in rank order

INSTITUTION	Rank	Score	INSTITUTION	Rank	Score
YALE	1	4.92	N.Y.U.	22	4.57
CALIFORNIA, BERKELEY	2	4.91	NOTRE DAME	23	4.53
HARVARD & RADCLIFFE	3	4.90	ILLINOIS (Urbana)	24	4.51
CHICAGO	4	4.87	WASHINGTON (Seattle)	25	4.48
STANFORD	5	4.86	DUKE	26	4.45
CORNELL (N.Y.)	6	4.84	TEXAS (Austin)	27	4.44
PRINCETON	7	4.83	SUNY (Stony Brook)	28	4.43
COLUMBIA (N.Y.)	8	4.81	ROCHESTER (N.Y.)	29	4.40
JOHNS HOPKINS	9	4.79	EMORY	30	4.38
PENNSYLVANIA	10	4.78	WASHINGTON (St. Louis)	31	4.35
UCLA	11	4.76	DARTMOUTH COLLEGE	32	4.32
BROWN	12	4.74	MINNESOTA (Minneapolis)	33	4.31
INDIANA (Bloomington)	13	4.73	CALIFORNIA, SAN DIEGO	34	4.28
MICHIGAN (Ann Arbor)	14	4.71	VANDERBILT	35	4.26
CALIFORNIA, IRVINE	15	4.69	POMONA (California)	36	4.23
NORTHWESTERN (Evanston)	16	4.68	BRANDEIS	37	4.20
WISCONSIN (Madison)	17	4.65	SWARTHMORE	38	4.19
RUTGERS (New Brunswick)	18	4.64	HAVERFORD	39	4.17
NORTH CAROLINA (Chapel Hill)	19	4.63	AMHERST	40	4.15
IOWA (Iowa City)	20	4.61	CALIFORNIA, SANTA BARBARA	41	4.12
VIRGINIA	21	4.59			

ENTOMOLOGY
Leading Institutions – Rating of Undergraduate Program

Twenty-six institutions with scores
in the 4.0-5.0 range, in rank order

INSTITUTION	Rank	Score
CALIFORNIA, BERKELEY	1	4.91
CORNELL (N.Y.)	2	4.90
ILLINOIS (Urbana)	3	4.87
CALIFORNIA, DAVIS	4	4.82
WISCONSIN (Madison)	5	4.81
CALIFORNIA, RIVERSIDE	6	4.76
KANSAS	7	4.73
MINNESOTA (Minneapolis)	8	4.72
PURDUE (Lafayette)	9	4.69
OHIO STATE (Columbus)	10	4.66
IOWA STATE (Ames)	11	4.63
MICHIGAN STATE	12	4.60
OREGON STATE	13	4.58
LOUISIANA STATE (Baton Rouge)	14	4.55
NORTH CAROLINA STATE (Raleigh)	15	4.53
TEXAS A&M (College Station)	16	4.51
FLORIDA (Gainesville)	17	4.49
ARIZONA (Tucson)	18	4.47
MARYLAND (College Park)	19	4.44
MASSACHUSETTS (Amherst)	20	4.43
PENN STATE (University Park)	21	4.41
COLORADO STATE	22	4.39
AUBURN (Auburn)	23	4.36
GEORGIA (Athens)	24	4.32
RUTGERS (New Brunswick)	25	4.28
NEBRASKA (Lincoln)	26	4.23

ENVIRONMENTAL DESIGN
Leading Institutions – Rating of Undergraduate Program

Fourteen institutions with scores
in the 4.0-5.0 range, in rank order

INSTITUTION	Rank	Score
M.I.T.	1	4.91
HARVARD	2	4.89
CORNELL (N.Y.)	3	4.85
MICHIGAN (Ann Arbor)	4	4.83
CALIFORNIA, DAVIS	5	4.78
PENNSYLVANIA	6	4.74
TEXAS A&M (College Station)	7	4.71
COLORADO (Boulder)	8	4.67
NORTH CAROLINA STATE (Raleigh)	9	4.64
NEW MEXICO (Albuquerque)	10	4.60
OKLAHOMA (Norman)	11	4.58
HOUSTON (Houston)	12	4.55
N.Y. COLLEGE OF ENVIRONMENTAL SCIENCE AND FORESTRY (SUNY)	13	4.53
MINNESOTA (Minneapolis)	14	4.52

Eleven institutions with scores
in the 4.0-5.0 range, in rank order

INSTITUTION	Rank	Score
RENSSELAER (N.Y.)	1	4.86
NORTHWESTERN (Illinois)	2	4.81
M.I.T.[2]	3	4.83
FLORIDA (Gainesville)	4	4.80
MICHIGAN (Ann Arbor)[1]	5	4.75
OHIO STATE (Columbus)[3]	6	4.73
MICHIGAN TECH	7	4.72
MONTANA (Mineral Sci. & Tech.)	8	4.69
OKLAHOMA STATE[1]	9	4.66
CALIFORNIA POLY STATE U. (SLO)	10	4.62
SYRACUSE	11	4.58

***Explanatory Note: Actual title used by the
institution to identify their curricula***

[1]Civil and Environmental Engineering
[2]Environmental Engineering Science
[3]Environmental Engineering option in Civil
   Engineering

ENVIRONMENTAL SCIENCES
Leading Institutions – Rating of Undergraduate Program

Twelve institutions with scores
in the 4.0-5.0 range, in rank order

INSTITUTION	Rank	Score
HARVARD	1	4.89
M.I.T.	2	4.88
CORNELL (N.Y.)	3	4.85
CALIFORNIA, BERKELEY	4	4.82
CALIFORNIA, DAVIS	5	4.79
MICHIGAN (Ann Arbor)	6	4.74
PENNSYLVANIA	7	4.70
VIRGINIA (Charlottesville)	8	4.65
N.Y. COLLEGE OF ENVIRONMENTAL SCIENCE AND FORESTRY (SUNY)	9	4.62
JOHNS HOPKINS	10	4.58
PURDUE (Lafayette)	11	4.53
MINNESOTA (Minneapolis)	12	4.52

Nine institutions with scores
in the 4.0-5.0 range, in rank order

INSTITUTION	Rank	Score
CORNELL (N.Y.)	1	4.85
COLORADO STATE	2	4.80
KANSAS STATE	3	4.74
TEXAS TECH	4	4.71
CALIFORNIA, DAVIS	5	4.65
WISCONSIN (Madison)	6	4.61
ARIZONA (Tucson)	7	4.59
IOWA STATE (Ames)	8	4.55
PURDUE (Lafayette)	9	4.52

FILM
Leading Institutions – Rating of Undergraduate Program

Ten institutions with scores
in the 4.0-5.0 range, in rank order

INSTITUTION	Rank	Score
UCLA	1	4.86
SOUTHERN CALIFORNIA (Los Angeles)	2	4.83
N.Y.U.	3	4.81
NORTHWESTERN (Evanston)	4	4.77
SYRACUSE	5	4.73
CALIFORNIA, BERKELEY	6	4.65
NORTH CAROLINA (Chapel Hill)	7	4.61
MICHIGAN (Ann Arbor)	8	4.52
TEXAS (Austin)	9	4.51
FLORIDA STATE	10	4.49

FINANCE
Leading Institutions – Rating of Undergraduate Program

Forty-four institutions with scores in the 4.0-5.0 range, in rank order

INSTITUTION	Rank	Score	INSTITUTION	Rank	Score
PENNSYLVANIA	1	4.92	ARIZONA (Tucson)	23	4.47
INDIANA (Bloomington)	2	4.91	UTAH (Salt Lake City)	24	4.45
MICHIGAN (Ann Arbor)	3	4.88	EMORY	25	4.44
CALIFORNIA, BERKELEY	4	4.86	LOUISIANA STATE (Baton Rouge)	26	4.42
N.Y.U.	5	4.85	MASSACHUSETTS (Amherst)	27	4.40
TEXAS (Austin)	6	4.84	MINNESOTA (Minneapolis)	28	4.39
ILLINOIS (Urbana)	7	4.82	SOUTHERN METHODIST	29	4.38
WISCONSIN (Madison)	8	4.80	OREGON (Eugene)	30	4.36
PURDUE (Lafayette)	9	4.79	MARYLAND (College Park)	31	4.33
WASHINGTON (Seattle)	10	4.77	LEHIGH	32	4.31
MICHIGAN STATE	11	4.75	ARIZONA STATE	33	4.28
VIRGINIA (Charlottesville)	12	4.72	MISSOURI (Columbia)	34	4.27
CUNY (Baruch College)	13	4.70	GEORGE WASHINGTON	35	4.26
WASHINGTON (St. Louis)	14	4.68	SYRACUSE	36	4.25
CASE WESTERN RESERVE	15	4.66	GEORGIA STATE	37	4.24
SOUTHERN CALIFORNIA (USC)	16	4.65	COLORADO (Boulder)	38	4.20
HOUSTON (University Park)	17	4.64	TEMPLE (Philadelphia)	39	4.15
PENN STATE (University Park)	18	4.63	IOWA (Iowa City)	40	4.14
TEXAS A&M (College Station)	19	4.62	DENVER	41	4.12
NOTRE DAME	20	4.60	SOUTH CAROLINA (Columbia)	42	4.09
OHIO STATE (Columbus)	21	4.57	NEBRASKA (Lincoln)	43	4.03
FLORIDA (Gainesville)	22	4.54	GEORGIA (Athens)	44	4.02

FISH/GAME MANAGEMENT
Leading Institutions – Rating of Undergraduate Program

Twelve institutions with scores
in the 4.0-5.0 range, in rank order

INSTITUTION	Rank	Score
CALIFORNIA, DAVIS	1	4.83
COLORADO STATE	2	4.82
MICHIGAN STATE	3	4.77
TEXAS A&M (Galveston)	4	4.73
MINNESOTA (Minneapolis)	5	4.69
IOWA STATE (Ames)	6	4.64
KANSAS STATE	7	4.62
OHIO STATE (Columbus)	8	4.56
MICHIGAN (Ann Arbor)	9	4.55
AUBURN (Auburn)	10	4.48
WYOMING	11	4.46
MONTANA STATE (Bozeman)	12	4.42

Eighteen institutions with scores
in the 4.0-5.0 range, in rank order

INSTITUTION	Rank	Score
CORNELL (N.Y.)	1	4.91
MICHIGAN STATE	2	4.88
IOWA STATE (Ames)	3	4.87
M.I.T.	4	4.86
KANSAS STATE	5	4.82
CALIFORNIA, DAVIS	6	4.76
PURDUE (Lafayette)	7	4.72
ILLINOIS (Urbana)	8	4.68
PENN STATE (University Park)	9	4.63
MINNESOTA (Minneapolis)	10	4.61
OREGON STATE	11	4.59
TENNESSEE (Knoxville)	12	4.55
ALABAMA (Tuscaloosa)	13	4.51
OHIO STATE (Columbus)	14	4.47
GEORGIA (Athens)	15	4.40
OKLAHOMA STATE	16	4.34
MISSOURI (Columbia)	17	4.32
WISCONSIN (Madison)	18	4.30

FOOD SERVICES MANAGEMENT
Leading Institutions – Rating of Undergraduate Program

Twelve institutions with scores
in the 4.0-5.0 range, in rank order

INSTITUTION	Rank	Score
CORNELL (N.Y.)	1	4.86
NEVADA (Las Vegas)	2	4.85
MICHIGAN STATE	3	4.79
KANSAS STATE	4	4.73
IOWA STATE (Ames)	5	4.67
PURDUE (Lafayette)	6	4.66
ILLINOIS (Urbana)	7	4.62
PENN STATE (University Park)	8	4.60
CALIFORNIA, DAVIS	9	4.57
OREGON STATE	10	4.55
ALABAMA (Tuscaloosa)	11	4.51
GEORGIA (Athens)	12	4.45

Thirty institutions with scores
in the 4.0-5.0 range, in rank order

INSTITUTION	Rank	Score
MINNESOTA (Minneapolis)	1	4.88
SUNY College of Envir. Sci. & Forestry (Syracuse)	2	4.87
PENN STATE (University Park)	3	4.75
NORTH CAROLINA STATE (Raleigh)	4	4.72
MISSOURI (Columbia)	5	4.71
WISCONSIN (Madison)	6	4.70
WASHINGTON (Seattle)	7	4.69
OREGON STATE	8	4.68
PURDUE (Lafayette)	9	4.67
MICHIGAN STATE	10	4.66
GEORGIA (Athens)	11	4.64
VPI & STATE U.	12	4.61
COLORADO STATE	13	4.60
IOWA STATE (Ames)	14	4.59
AUBURN (Auburn)	15	4.55
TEXAS A&M (College Station)	16	4.53
UTAH STATE	17	4.50
CALIFORNIA, BERKELEY	18	4.47
MONTANA (Missoula)	19	4.46
IDAHO (Moscow)	20	4.43
MICHIGAN (Ann Arbor)	21	4.41
MAINE (Orono)	22	4.35
FLORIDA (Gainesville)	23	4.33
CLEMSON	24	4.26
LOUISIANA STATE (Baton Rouge)	25	4.22
TENNESSEE (Knoxville)	26	4.20
WEST VIRGINIA (Morgantown)	27	4.19
ILLINOIS (Urbana)	28	4.17
KENTUCKY (Lexington)	29	4.14
OKLAHOMA STATE	30	4.12

FRENCH
Leading Institutions – Rating of Undergraduate Program

Thirty institutions with scores
in the 4.0-5.0 range, in rank order

INSTITUTION	Rank	Score
YALE	1	4.92
PRINCETON	2	4.91
COLUMBIA (N.Y.)	3	4.90
N.Y.U.	4	4.88
CORNELL (N.Y.)	5	4.86
INDIANA (Bloomington)	6	4.85
MICHIGAN (Ann Arbor)	7	4.83
PENNSYLVANIA	8	4.80
CALIFORNIA, BERKELEY	9	4.77
STANFORD	10	4.74
VIRGINIA	11	4.71
ILLINOIS (Urbana)	12	4.68
WISCONSIN (Madison)	13	4.67
DUKE	14	4.64
CHICAGO	15	4.62
NORTH CAROLINA (Chapel Hill)	16	4.59
CALIFORNIA, IRVINE	17	4.53
TEXAS (Austin)	18	4.50
HARVARD & RADCLIFFE	19	4.46
BROWN	20	4.42
CALIFORNIA, SANTA BARBARA	21	4.40
RICE	22	4.36
BRYN MAWR	23	4.33
JOHNS HOPKINS	24	4.32
TULANE	25	4.29
NORTHWESTERN (Evanston)	26	4.28
WASHINGTON (Seattle)	27	4.25
IOWA (Iowa City)	28	4.22
SUNY (Buffalo)	29	4.19
UCLA	30	4.17

Thirteen institutions with scores
in the 4.0-5.0 range, in rank order

INSTITUTION	Rank	Score
CALIFORNIA, DAVIS	1	4.91
CORNELL (N.Y.)	2	4.90
M.I.T.	3	4.88
WISCONSIN (Madison)	4	4.82
ILLINOIS (Urbana)	5	4.79
OHIO STATE (Columbus)	6	4.73
PURDUE (Lafayette)	7	4.69
ROCHESTER (N.Y.)	8	4.66
MINNESOTA (Minneapolis)	9	4.62
RUTGERS (New Brunswick)	10	4.58
GEORGIA (Athens)	11	4.55
KANSAS	12	4.52
TEXAS A&M (College Station)	13	4.49

Thirty institutions with scores
in the 4.0-5.0 range, in rank order

INSTITUTION	Rank	Score
MINNESOTA (Minneapolis)	1	4.90
WISCONSIN (Madison)	2	4.89
PENN STATE (University Park)	3	4.86
CALIFORNIA, BERKELEY	4	4.82
OHIO STATE (Columbus)	5	4.75
ILLINOIS (Urbana)	6	4.71
MICHIGAN (Ann Arbor)	7	4.70
WASHINGTON (Seattle)	8	4.65
UCLA	9	4.62
SYRACUSE	10	4.59
IOWA (Iowa City)	11	4.58
COLORADO (Boulder)	12	4.53
KANSAS	13	4.51
LOUISIANA STATE (Baton Rouge)	14	4.50
GEORGIA (Athens)	15	4.48
WISCONSIN (Milwaukee)	16	4.47
SUNY (Buffalo)	17	4.46
HAWAII (Manoa)	18	4.44
MICHIGAN STATE	19	4.41
ARIZONA (Tucson)	20	4.37
RUTGERS (New Brunswick)	21	4.35
NEBRASKA (Lincoln)	22	4.34
NORTH CAROLINA (Chapel Hill)	23	4.31
TEXAS (Austin)	24	4.30
CLARK	25	4.28
MARYLAND (College Park)	26	4.25
FLORIDA (Gainesville)	27	4.23
OKLAHOMA (Norman)	28	4.20
OREGON (Eugene)	29	4.16
UTAH (Salt Lake City)	30	4.14

GEOLOGICAL ENGINEERING
Leading Institutions – Rating of Undergraduate Program

Twelve institutions with scores
in the 4.0-5.0 range, in rank order

INSTITUTION	Rank	Score
COLORADO (Mines)[1]	1	4.91
MISSOURI (Rolla)	2	4.87
MINNESOTA (Minneapolis)	3	4.79
ARIZONA (Tucson)	4	4.73
UTAH (Salt Lake City)	5	4.68
SOUTH DAKOTA (Mines & Tech.)	6	4.62
PRINCETON	7	4.56
MICHIGAN TECH	8	4.51
IDAHO (Moscow)	9	4.47
ALASKA (Fairbanks)	10	4.43
MONTANA TECH[1]	11	4.42
NEVADA (Reno)	12	4.36

Explanatory Note: Actual titles used by the institution to identify their curricula

[1]Geophysical Engineering

Note: Majors
Colorado School of Mines
Geological Engineering
Geophysical Engineering

Montana College of Mineral Science and Technology
Geological Engineering
Geophysical Engineering

GEOLOGY/GEOSCIENCE
Leading Institutions – Rating of Undergraduate Program

Fifty institutions with scores in the 4.0-5.0 range, in rank order

INSTITUTION	Rank	Score	INSTITUTION	Rank	Score
CAL TECH	1	4.92	CALIFORNIA , DAVIS	26	4.45
M.I.T.	2	4.91	COLORADO (Boulder)	27	4.42
PRINCETON	3	4.89	ILLINOIS (Urbana)	28	4.41
COLUMBIA (N.Y.)	4	4.87	SOUTHERN CALIFORNIA	29	4.39
STANFORD	5	4.85	ARIZONA STATE	30	4.37
HARVARD & RADCLIFFE	6	4.82	CALIFORNIA, SANTA CRUZ	31	4.36
CHICAGO	7	4.80	MIAMI (Florida)	32	4.34
UCLA	8	4.79	UTAH (Salt Lake City)	33	4.32
YALE	9	4.76	MASSACHUSETTS (Amherst)	34	4.31
CALIFORNIA, BERKELEY	10	4.74	NORTH CAROLINA (Chapel Hill)	35	4.30
CORNELL (N.Y.)	11	4.72	OREGON (Eugene)	36	4.28
PENN STATE (University Park)	12	4.70	TEXAS A&M (College Station)	37	4.26
TEXAS (Austin)	13	4.69	SUNY (Albany)	38	4.25
WISCONSIN (Madison)	14	4.68	OHIO STATE (Columbus)	39	4.24
ARIZONA (Tucson)	15	4.66	KANSAS	40	4.20
CALIFORNIA, SANTA BARBARA	16	4.64	SOUTH CAROLINA (Columbia)	41	4.19
BROWN	17	4.62	WYOMING	42	4.17
V.P.I. & STATE U.	18	4.61	CINCINNATI	43	4.16
SUNY (Stony Brook)	19	4.58	NEW MEXICO	44	4.14
MICHIGAN (Ann Arbor)	20	4.57	RICE	45	4.12
JOHNS HOPKINS	21	4.55	IOWA (Iowa City)	46	4.10
NORTHWESTERN (Evanston)	22	4.53	LOUISIANA STATE (Baton Rouge)	47	4.08
WASHINGTON (Seattle)	23	4.51	OREGON STATE	48	4.07
INDIANA (Bloomington)	24	4.49	HAWAII (Manoa)	49	4.06
MINNESOTA (Minneapolis)	25	4.48	MICHIGAN STATE	50	4.05

Twenty-eight institutions with scores
in the 4.0-5.0 range, in rank order

INSTITUTION	Rank	Score
CAL TECH	1	4.92
M.I.T.	2	4.90
CALIFORNIA, BERKELEY	3	4.89
STANFORD	4	4.83
UCLA	5	4.82
YALE	6	4.80
CHICAGO	7	4.78
PRINCETON	8	4.76
BROWN	9	4.75
MINNESOTA (Minneapolis)	10	4.73
CALIFORNIA, SANTA CRUZ	11	4.71
HARVARD & RADCLIFFE	12	4.70
COLUMBIA (N.Y.)	13	4.68
PURDUE (Lafayette)	14	4.65
WISCONSIN (Madison))	15	4.63
LEHIGH	16	4.62
V.P.I. & STATE U.	17	4.61
TEXAS A&M (College Station)	18	4.59
KANSAS	19	4.57
UTAH (Salt Lake City)	20	4.55
HAWAII (Manoa)	21	4.53
SUNY (Binghamton)	22	4.51
NEW MEXICO (Tech)	23	4.49
OKLAHOMA (Norman)	24	4.48
SAINT LOUIS U.	25	4.46
HOUSTON (University Park)	26	4.43
MISSOURI (Rolla)	27	4.42
TULSA	28	4.40

GERMAN
Leading Institutions – Rating of Undergraduate Program

Thirty institutions with scores
in the 4.0-5.0 range, in rank order

INSTITUTION	Rank	Score
YALE	1	4.90
WISCONSIN (Madison)	2	4.88
PRINCETON	3	4.86
INDIANA (Bloomington)	4	4.84
CALIFORNIA, BERKELEY	5	4.82
TEXAS (Austin)	6	4.80
STANFORD	7	4.77
CORNELL (N.Y.)	8	4.73
VIRGINIA	9	4.71
HARVARD & RADCLIFFE	10	4.69
ILLINOIS (Urbana)	11	4.68
UCLA	12	4.67
JOHNS HOPKINS	13	4.64
MICHIGAN (Ann Arbor)	14	4.63
PENNSYLVANIA	15	4.62
MASSACHUSETTS (Amherst)	16	4.60
WASHINGTON (St. Louis)	17	4.59
OHIO STATE (Columbus)	18	4.58
NORTH CAROLINA (Chapel Hill)	19	4.56
MINNESOTA (Minneapolis)	20	4.55
RICE	21	4.53
PENN STATE (University Park)	22	4.52
PITTSBURGH (Pittsburgh)	23	4.51
CALIFORNIA, IRVINE	24	4.49
WASHINGTON (Seattle)	25	4.47
BROWN	26	4.45
KANSAS	27	4.44
CALIFORNIA, SANTA BARBARA	28	4.43
DUKE	29	4.39
NORTHWESTERN (Evanston)	30	4.36

Sixteen institutions with scores
in the 4.0-5.0 range, in rank order

INSTITUTION	Rank	Score
HARVARD	1	4.87
CALIFORNIA, BERKELEY	2	4.85
BROWN	3	4.80
COLUMBIA (N.Y.)	4	4.77
PENNSYLVANIA	5	4.72
YALE	6	4.66
INDIANA (Bloomington)	7	4.61
WISCONSIN (Madison)	8	4.59
BRYN MAWR (Pennsylvania)	9	4.56
MINNESOTA (Minneapolis)	10	4.52
NORTH CAROLINA (Chapel Hill)	11	4.49
CORNELL (N.Y.)	12	4.42
CHICAGO	13	4.40
N.Y.U.	14	4.38
ILLINOIS (Urbana)	15	4.36
MICHIGAN (Ann Arbor)	16	4.32

Twenty institutions with scores
in the 4.0-5.0 range, in rank order

INSTITUTION	Rank	Score
PENNSYLVANIA	1	4.91
WISCONSIN (Madison)	2	4.90
COLUMBIA (N.Y.)	3	4.86
CALIFORNIA, BERKELEY	4	4.85
N.Y.U.	5	4.82
YESHIVA (N.Y.)	6	4.81
HARVARD & RADCLIFFE	7	4.79
BRANDEIS	8	4.76
TEXAS (Austin)	9	4.73
CHICAGO	10	4.70
INDIANA (Bloomington)	11	4.68
MICHIGAN (Ann Arbor)	12	4.65
MINNESOTA (Minneapolis)	13	4.63
TEMPLE (Philadelphia)	14	4.62
OHIO STATE (Columbus)	15	4.59
UCLA	16	4.55
CORNELL (N.Y.)	17	4.53
PRINCETON	18	4.52
BROWN	19	4.51
WASHINGTON (Seattle)	20	4.48

HISTORY
Leading Institutions – Rating of Undergraduate Program

Forty-six institutions with scores in the 4.0-5.0 range, in rank order

INSTITUTION	Rank	Score	INSTITUTION	Rank	Score
YALE	1	4.93	MINNESOTA (Minneapolis)	24	4.53
CALIFORNIA, BERKELEY	2	4.92	IOWA (Iowa City)	25	4.52
PRINCETON	3	4.91	DUKE	26	4.51
HARVARD & RADCLIFFE	4	4.90	RUTGERS (New Brunswick)	27	4.50
STANFORD	5	4.88	CALIFORNIA, SANTA BARBARA	28	4.48
MICHIGAN (Ann Arbor)	6	4.86	CALIFORNIA, SAN DIEGO	29	4.47
COLUMBIA (N.Y.)	7	4.84	N.Y.U.	30	4.46
CHICAGO	8	4.81	VANDERBILT	31	4.45
JOHNS HOPKINS	9	4.80	WASHINGTON (St. Louis)	32	4.44
WISCONSIN (Madison)	10	4.77	MARYLAND (College Park)	33	4.42
CORNELL (N.Y.)	11	4.75	OHIO STATE (Columbus)	34	4.40
INDIANA (Bloomington)	12	4.73	MISSOURI (Columbia)	35	4.38
PENNSYLVANIA	13	4.70	EMORY	36	4.35
BROWN	14	4.68	PITTSBURGH (Pittsburgh)	37	4.34
NORTH CAROLINA (Chapel Hill)	15	4.67	RICE	38	4.33
UCLA	16	4.66	SUNY (Stony Brook)	39	4.32
NORTHWESTERN (Evanston)	17	4.62	DARTMOUTH	40	4.27
VIRGINIA	18	4.61	BRANDEIS	41	4.23
TEXAS (Austin)	19	4.58	KANSAS	42	4.20
ROCHESTER (N.Y.)	20	4.57	BOSTON U.	43	4.18
ILLINOIS (Urbana)	21	4.56	CALIFORNIA, DAVIS	44	4.15
NOTRE DAME	22	4.55	SUNY (Buffalo)	45	4.14
WASHINGTON (Seattle)	23	4.54	MICHIGAN STATE	46	4.10

Thirty institutions with scores
in the 4.0-5.0 range, in rank order

INSTITUTION	Rank	Score
OHIO STATE (Columbus)	1	4.87
MINNESOTA (Minneapolis)	2	4.83
WISCONSIN (Madison)	3	4.81
PURDUE (Lafayette)	4	4.79
ILLINOIS (Urbana)	5	4.75
IOWA STATE (Ames)	6	4.73
FLORIDA STATE	7	4.71
MICHIGAN STATE	8	4.68
MARYLAND (College Park)	9	4.66
COLORADO STATE	10	4.65
HOUSTON (Houston)	11	4.63
GEORGIA (Athens)	12	4.61
TEXAS TECH	13	4.58
AUBURN (Auburn)	14	4.56
NEBRASKA (Lincoln)	15	4.53
V.P.I. & STATE U.	16	4.52
ARIZONA STATE	17	4.50
OKLAHOMA STATE	18	4.48
OREGON STATE	19	4.46
ALABAMA (Tuscaloosa)	20	4.43
TEXAS (Austin)	21	4.41
MASSACHUSETTS (Amherst)	22	4.39
TEXAS WOMAN'S U.	23	4.37
WASHINGTON STATE	24	4.35
B.Y.U.	25	4.33
ARKANSAS (Fayetteville)	26	4.32
IDAHO (Moscow)	27	4.29
OHIO U. (Athens)	28	4.26
ARIZONA (Tucson)	29	4.23
HAWAII (Manoa)	30	4.21

Thirty-six institutions with scores
in the 4.0-5.0 range, in rank order

INSTITUTION	Rank	Score
CORNELL (N.Y.)	1	4.92
TEXAS A&M (College Station)	2	4.90
IOWA STATE (Ames)	3	4.88
PURDUE (Lafayette)	4	4.85
ILLINOIS (Urbana)	5	4.83
MICHIGAN STATE	6	4.81
WISCONSIN (Madison)	7	4.79
MINNESOTA (Minneapolis)	8	4.77
OHIO STATE (Columbus)	9	4.75
KANSAS STATE	10	4.73
MISSOURI (Columbia)	11	4.72
PENN STATE (University Park)	12	4.71
COLORADO STATE	13	4.69
LOUISIANA STATE (Baton Rouge)	14	4.67
MARYLAND (College Park)	15	4.65
OKLAHOMA STATE	16	4.63
GEORGIA (Athens)	17	4.62
NORTH CAROLINA STATE (Raleigh)	18	4.60
OREGON STATE	19	4.58
TENNESSEE (Knoxville)	20	4.55
NEBRASKA (Lincoln)	21	4.53
FLORIDA (Gainesville)	22	4.52
AUBURN (Auburn)	23	4.50
WASHINGTON STATE	24	4.48
VERMONT	25	4.46
KENTUCKY	26	4.44
ARIZONA (Tucson)	27	4.42
ARKANSAS (Fayetteville)	28	4.40
MISSISSIPPI STATE	29	4.38
V.P.I. & STATE U.	30	4.36
NEW HAMPSHIRE	31	4.33
NORTH DAKOTA STATE	32	4.32
MONTANTA STATE (Bozeman)	33	4.31
SOUTH DAKOTA STATE	34	4.29
TEXAS TECH	35	4.27
CONNECTICUT (Storrs)	36	4.26

HOTEL, RESTAURANT, INSTITUTIONAL MANAGEMENT
Leading Institutions – Rating of Undergraduate Program

Twenty-three institutions with scores in the 4.0-5.0 range, in rank order

INSTITUTION	Rank	Score
CORNELL (N.Y.)	1	4.90
NEVADA (Las Vegas)	2	4.87
MICHIGAN STATE	3	4.83
MASSACHUSETTS (Amherst)	4	4.78
HOUSTON (Houston)	5	4.74
ILLINOIS (Urbana)	6	4.70
PURDUE (Lafayette)	7	4.67
DENVER	8	4.62
IOWA STATE (Ames)	9	4.53
MARYLAND (College Park)	10	4.52
TENNESSEE (Knoxville)	11	4.48
PENN STATE (University Park)	12	4.46
FLORIDA STATE	13	4.43
KANSAS STATE	14	4.41
FAIRLEIGH DICKINSON U. (Rutherford)	15	4.38
OHIO STATE (Columbus)	16	4.36
DREXEL	17	4.33
GOLDEN GATE U. (California)	18	4.31
SYRACUSE	19	4.27
SOUTH CAROLINA (Columbia)	20	4.24
V.P.I. & STATE U.	21	4.20
WASHINGTON STATE	22	4.18
FLORIDA INTERNATIONAL U.	23	4.16

INDUSTRIAL ENGINEERING
Leading Institutions – Rating of Undergraduate Program

Thirty-four institutions with scores in the 4.0-5.0 range, in rank order

INSTITUTION	Rank	Score	INSTITUTION	Rank	Score
STANFORD	1	4.90	MISSOURI (Columbia)	18	4.50
MICHIGAN (Ann Arbor)[2]	2	4.88	LEHIGH	19	4.47
CALIFORNIA, BERKELEY	3	4.85	OKLAHOMA (Norman)	20	4.46
PURDUE (Lafayette)	4	4.81	SOUTHERN CALIFORNIA[3]	21	4.42
NORTHWESTERN (Evanston)	5	4.78	SUNY (Buffalo)	22	4.40
GEORGIA TECH	6	4.74	V.P.I. & STATE U.[3]	23	4.37
CORNELL (N.Y.)[6]	7	4.72	RENSSELAER (N.Y.)[1]	24	4.35
OHIO STATE (Columbus)[3]	8	4.70	NORTH CAROLINA STATE (Raleigh)	25	4.33
COLUMBIA (N.Y.)	9	4.68	AUBURN (Auburn)	26	4.30
TEXAS A&M (College Station)	10	4.66	MASSACHUSETTS (Amherst)[5]	27	4.28
WISCONSIN (Madison)	11	4.64	CINCINNATI	28	4.26
IOWA (Iowa City)	12	4.62	LOUISIANA STATE (Baton Rouge)	29	4.25
IOWA STATE (Ames)	13	4.59	FLORIDA (Gainesville)[3]	30	4.24
PITTSBURGH (Pittsburgh)	14	4.57	TEXAS TECH	31	4.23
ILLINOIS (Urbana)	15	4.55	POLYTECHNIC U. (Brooklyn, N.Y.)	32	4.20
KANSAS STATE	16	4.53	OKLAHOMA STATE[4]	33	4.19
PENN STATE (University Park)	17	4.52	ARIZONA (Tucson)	34	4.18

***Explanatory Note: Actual titles used by the
institution to identify their curricula***

[1]Industrial and Management Engineering

[2]Industrial and Operations Engineering

[3]Industrial and Systems Engineering

[4]Industrial Engineering and Management

[5]Industrial Engineering and Operations Research

[6]Operations Research and Industrial Engineering

Ten institutions with scores
in the 4.0-5.0 range, in rank order

INSTITUTION	Rank	Score
M.I.T.	1	4.86
CALIFORNIA, SAN DIEGO	2	4.83
MICHIGAN (Ann Arbor)	3	4.77
PITTSBURGH (Pittsburgh)	4	4.73
OHIO STATE (Columbus)	5	4.70
CARNEGIE-MELLON	6	4.66
ALABAMA (Birmingham)	7	4.63
HARVARD	8	4.59
CALIFORNIA, IRVINE	9	4.55
MARYLAND (College Park)	10	4.52

INTERNATIONAL RELATIONS
Leading Institutions – Rating of Undergraduate Program

Fifteen institutions with scores
in the 4.0-5.0 range, in rank order

INSTITUTION	Rank	Score
TUFTS (Massachusetts)	1	4.88
PRINCETON	2	4.85
JOHNS HOPKINS	3	4.83
GEORGETOWN (D.C.)	4	4.79
PENNSYLVANIA	5	4.78
HARVARD	6	4.75
CORNELL (N.Y.)	7	4.72
WISCONSIN (Madison)	8	4.69
M.I.T.	9	4.64
STANFORD	10	4.62
VIRGINIA (Charlottesville)	11	4.60
NOTRE DAME (Indiana)	12	4.58
U.S. AIR FORCE ACADEMY	13	4.57
U.S. MILITARY ACADEMY (West Point)	14	4.55
CLAREMONT McKENNA COLLEGE	15	4.50

Leading Institutions – Rating of Undergraduate Program

Twenty-two institutions with scores
in the 4.0-5.0 range, in rank order

INSTITUTION	Rank	Score
COLUMBIA (N.Y.)	1	4.82
N.Y.U.	2	4.80
YALE	3	4.75
JOHNS HOPKINS	4	4.66
INDIANA (Bloomington)	5	4.61
CALIFORNIA, BERKELEY	6	4.58
MICHIGAN (Ann Arbor)	7	4.55
WISCONSIN (Madison)	8	4.53
BROWN	9	4.50
ILLINOIS (Urbana)	10	4.48
CATHOLIC (D.C.)	11	4.46
HARVARD & RADCLIFFE	12	4.42
NORTHWESTERN (Evanston)	13	4.40
VIRGINIA	14	4.38
BRYN MAWR	15	4.35
UCLA	16	4.33
CHICAGO	17	4.30
CALIFORNIA, SANTA CRUZ	18	4.27
TEXAS (Austin)	19	4.25
MINNESOTA (Minneapolis)	20	4.24
NORTH CAROLINA (Chapel Hill)	21	4.23
WASHINGTON (Seattle)	22	4.21

JAPANESE
Leading Institutions – Rating of Undergraduate Program

Fourteen institutions with scores
in the 4.0-5.0 range, in rank order

INSTITUTION	Rank	Score
HARVARD & RADCLIFFE	1	4.84
CHICAGO	2	4.80
PENNSYLVANIA	3	4.73
COLUMBIA (N.Y.)	4	4.71
CALIFORNIA, BERKELEY	5	4.64
CORNELL (N.Y.)	6	4.62
MICHIGAN (Ann Arbor)	7	4.54
WASHINGTON (Seattle)	8	4.51
WISCONSIN (Madison)	9	4.48
HAWAII (Manoa)	10	4.44
STANFORD	11	4.40
OHIO STATE (Columbus)	12	4.38
YALE	13	4.35
INDIANA (Bloomington)	14	4.32

Thirty-one institutions with scores
in the 4.0-5.0 range, in rank order

INSTITUTION	Rank	Score
MISSOURI (Columbia)	1	4.87
NORTHWESTERN (Evanston)	2	4.84
SYRACUSE	3	4.82
MINNESOTA (Minneapolis)	4	4.79
ILLINOIS (Urbana)	5	4.77
NORTH CAROLINA (Chapel Hill)	6	4.76
WISCONSIN (Madison)	7	4.73
OHIO STATE (Columbus)	8	4.71
MICHIGAN STATE	9	4.68
SOUTHERN CALIFORNIA	10	4.66
N.Y.U.	11	4.63
INDIANA (Bloomington)	12	4.62
WASHINGTON (Seattle)	13	4.59
KANSAS	14	4.55
TEXAS (Austin)	15	4.53
KANSAS STATE	16	4.50
MARQUETTE	17	4.48
IOWA (Iowa City)	18	4.47
COLORADO (Boulder)	19	4.45
OHIO U. (Athens)	20	4.43
PENN STATE (University Park)	21	4.40
FLORIDA (Gainesville)	22	4.38
MONTANA (Missoula)	23	4.37
ARIZONA (Tucson)	24	4.35
OREGON (Eugene)	25	4.34
IOWA STATE (Ames)	26	4.32
OKLAHOMA (Norman)	27	4.30
GEORGIA (Athens)	28	4.27
UTAH (Salt Lake City)	29	4.25
ARIZONA STATE	30	4.20
MARYLAND	31	4.18

LABOR AND INDUSTRIAL RELATIONS
Leading Institutions – Rating of Undergraduate Program

Ten institutions with scores
in the 4.0-5.0 range, in rank order

INSTITUTION	Rank	Score
CORNELL (N.Y.)	1	4.91
PENNSYLVANIA	2	4.85
CARNEGIE-MELLON	3	4.82
SYRACUSE	4	4.73
MICHIGAN (Ann Arbor)	5	4.71
TEMPLE (Philadelphia)	6	4.67
PURDUE (Lafayette)	7	4.61
IOWA (Iowa City)	8	4.56
WAYNE STATE (Michigan)	9	4.52
MARYLAND (College Park)	10	4.47

LANDSCAPE ARCHITECTURE
Leading Institutions – Rating of Undergraduate Program

Thirty-three institutions with scores
in the 4.0-5.0 range, in rank order

INSTITUTION	Rank	Score
CORNELL (N.Y.)	1	4.90
TEXAS A&M (College Station)	2	4.89
KANSAS STATE	3	4.82
CALIFORNIA, DAVIS	4	4.81
ILLINOIS (Urbana)	5	4.80
OHIO STATE (Columbus)	6	4.78
MINNESOTA (Minneapolis)	7	4.77
WISCONSIN (Madison)	8	4.76
IOWA STATE (Ames)	9	4.74
LOUISIANA STATE (Baton Rouge)	10	4.72
GEORGIA (Athens)	11	4.69
FLORIDA (Gainesville)	12	4.68
V.P.I. & STATE U.	13	4.65
SUNY College Envir. & Sci. Forestry (Syracuse)	14	4.63
WASHINGTON (Seattle)	15	4.61
ARIZONA	16	4.60
PENN STATE (University Park)	17	4.58
MICHIGAN STATE	18	4.56
PURDUE (Lafayette)	19	4.53
COLORADO STATE	20	4.50
UTAH STATE	21	4.48
MASSACHUSETTS (Amherst)	22	4.46
WASHINGTON STATE	23	4.43
CUNY (City College)	24	4.41
CALIFORNIA POLY. STATE (SLO)	25	4.39
OKLAHOMA STATE	26	4.38
WEST VIRGINIA (Morgantown)	27	4.37
OREGON (Eugene)	28	4.36
MISSISSIPPI STATE	29	4.33
IDAHO (Moscow)	30	4.32
TEXAS TECH	31	4.31
KENTUCKY	32	4.29
CALIFORNIA POLY. STATE (Pomona)	33	4.27

Eleven institutions with scores
in the 4.0-5.0 range, in rank order

INSTITUTION	Rank	Score
COLUMBIA (N.Y.)	1	4.89
INDIANA (Bloomington)	2	4.86
BRYN MAWR (Pennsylvania)	3	4.83
MINNESOTA (Minneapolis)	4	4.80
CATHOLIC U. (D.C.)	5	4.75
NORTH CAROLINA (Chapel Hill)	6	4.71
MICHIGAN (Ann Arbor)	7	4.67
CALIFORNIA, BERKELEY	8	4.61
YALE	9	4.56
CHICAGO	10	4.51
HARVARD	11	4.49

LATIN AMERICAN STUDIES
Leading Institutions – Rating of Undergraduate Program

Sixteen institutions with scores
in the 4.0-5.0 range, in rank order

INSTITUTION	Rank	Score
TEXAS (Austin)	1	4.83
TULANE	2	4.80
CALIFORNIA, BERKELEY	3	4.74
NORTH CAROLINA (Chapel Hill)	4	4.71
STANFORD	5	4.66
COLUMBIA (N.Y.)	6	4.60
NEW MEXICO	7	4.55
VANDERBILT	8	4.52
MIAMI (Florida)	9	4.49
UCLA	10	4.44
CHICAGO	11	4.38
YALE	12	4.36
ARIZONA (Tucson)	13	4.30
N.Y.U.	14	4.26
GEORGE WASHINGTON	15	4.20
PITTSBURGH (Pittsburgh)	16	4.17

Thirty institutions with scores
in the 4.0-5.0 range, in rank order

INSTITUTION	Rank	Score
UCLA	1	4.91
CHICAGO	2	4.90
CALIFORNIA, BERKELEY	3	4.88
PENNSYLVANIA	4	4.85
CORNELL (N.Y.)	5	4.83
CALIFORNIA, SAN DIEGO	6	4.81
YALE	7	4.79
ILLINOIS (Urbana)	8	4.76
STANFORD	9	4.74
M.I.T.	10	4.72
MICHIGAN (Ann Arbor)	11	4.71
INDIANA (Bloomington)	12	4.69
WISCONSIN (Madison)	13	4.68
WASHINGTON (Seattle)	14	4.66
N.Y.U.	15	4.64
OHIO STATE (Columbus)	16	4.63
ROCHESTER (N.Y.)	17	4.62
HARVARD & RADCLIFFE	18	4.61
HAWAII (Manoa)	19	4.59
KANSAS	20	4.52
RICE	21	4.50
TEXAS (Austin)	22	4.48
PITTSBURGH (Pittsburgh)	23	4.45
ARIZONA (Tucson)	24	4.41
MINNESOTA (Minneapolis)	25	4.37
CALIFORNIA, IRVINE	26	4.35
FLORIDA (Gainesville)	27	4.32
IOWA (Iowa City)	28	4.28
MASSACHUSETTS (Amherst)	29	4.26
CALIFORNIA, SANTA BARBARA	30	4.22

MANAGEMENT
Leading Institutions – Rating of Undergraduate Program

Forty-seven institutions with scores in the 4.0-5.0 range, in rank order

INSTITUTION	Rank	Score	INSTITUTION	Rank	Score
PENNSYLVANIA	1	4.91	OHIO STATE (Columbus)	25	4.47
M.I.T.	2	4.90	FLORIDA (Gainesville)	26	4.44
INDIANA (Bloomington)	3	4.88	OREGON (Eugene)	27	4.40
MICHIGAN (Ann Arbor)	4	4.86	SOUTHERN METHODIST	28	4.39
CALIFORNIA, BERKELEY	5	4.84	UTAH (Salt Lake City)	29	4.38
CARNEGIE-MELLON	6	4.82	GEORGIA STATE	30	4.36
N.Y.U.	7	4.81	LOUISIANA STATE (Baton Rouge)	31	4.35
ILLINOIS (Urbana)	8	4.80	MASSACHUSETTS (Amherst)	32	4.34
VIRGINIA (Charlottesville)	9	4.78	LEHIGH	33	4.33
WISCONSIN (Madison)	10	4.76	ARIZONA (Tucson)	34	4.32
MICHIGAN STATE	11	4.74	MARYLAND (College Park)	35	4.30
WASHINGTON (Seattle)	12	4.73	ARIZONA STATE	36	4.28
PURDUE (Lafayette)	13	4.71	SOUTH CAROLINA (Columbia)	37	4.25
TEXAS (Austin)	14	4.70	GEORGE WASHINGTON	38	4.21
CUNY (Baruch College)	15	4.66	EMORY	39	4.20
MINNESOTA (Minneapolis)	16	4.65	SUNY (Buffalo)	40	4.18
WASHINGTON (St. Louis)	17	4.62	COLORADO (Boulder)	41	4.16
CASE WESTERN RESERVE	18	4.60	MISSOURI (Columbia)	42	4.15
SOUTHERN CALIFORNIA	19	4.59	IOWA (Iowa City)	43	4.12
HOUSTON (University Park)	20	4.57	SYRACUSE	44	4.10
PENN STATE (University Park)	21	4.55	DENVER	45	4.08
NOTRE DAME	22	4.52	NEBRASKA (Lincoln)	46	4.07
NORTH CAROLINA (Chapel Hill)	23	4.51	GEORGIA (Athens)	47	4.05
TEXAS A&M (College Station)	24	4.50			

Six institutions with scores
in the 4.0-5.0 range, in rank order

INSTITUTION	Rank	Score
CALIFORNIA, BERKELEY	1	4.42
BOSTON U.	2	4.38
UTAH STATE[1]	3	4.32
OREGON STATE[2]	4	4.29
KANSAS STATE[3]	5	4.24
MIAMI (Florida)	6	4.20

***Explanatory Note: Actual titles used by the
institution to identify their curricula***

[1]Manufacturing Engineering option
  in Mechanical Engineering

[2]Manufacturing Engineering option
  in Industrial Engineering

[3]Manufacturing Systems Engineering

MARINE BIOLOGY
Leading Institutions – Rating of Undergraduate Program

Seven institutions with scores
in the 4.0-5.0 range, in rank order

INSTITUTION	Rank	Score
M.I.T.	1	4.80
CALIFORNIA, SANTA BARBARA	2	4.75
TEXAS A&M (College Station)	3	4.67
MIAMI (Florida)	4	4.59
NORTH CAROLINA (Wilmington)	5	4.51
BROWN	6	4.50
FLORIDA INST. OF TECHNOLOGY	7	4.48

Six institutions with scores
in the 4.0-5.0 range, in rank order

INSTITUTION	Rank	Score
CORNELL (N.Y.)	1	4.82
U.S. COAST GUARD ACADEMY	2	4.76
TEXAS A&M (College Station)	3	4.65
MIAMI (Florida)	4	4.60
SOUTH CAROLINA (Columbia)	5	4.55
LONG ISLAND U. (Southampton)	6	4.52

MARKETING
Leading Institutions – Rating of Undergraduate Program

Forty-one institutions with scores in the 4.0-5.0 range, in rank order

INSTITUTION	Rank	Score	INSTITUTION	Rank	Score
PENNSYLVANIA	1	4.90	NOTRE DAME	22	4.48
INDIANA (Bloomington)	2	4.88	SOUTHERN METHODIST	23	4.45
MICHIGAN (Ann Arbor)	3	4.85	LEHIGH	24	4.41
CALIFORNIA, BERKELEY	4	4.83	UTAH (Salt Lake City)	25	4.40
N.Y.U.	5	4.81	EMORY	26	4.39
ILLINOIS (Urbana)	6	4.79	LOUISIANA STATE (Baton Rouge)	27	4.38
MICHIGAN STATE	7	4.76	MASSACHUSETTS (Amherst)	28	4.36
PURDUE (Lafayette)	8	4.72	OREGON (Eugene)	29	4.33
WASHINGTON (Seattle)	9	4.71	ARIZONA (Tucson)	30	4.32
WISCONSIN (Madison)	10	4.68	MARYLAND (College Park)	31	4.30
VIRGINIA (Charlottesville)	11	4.66	IOWA (Iowa City)	32	4.29
CUNY (Baruch College)	12	4.63	GEORGIA STATE	33	4.27
MINNESOTA (Minneapolis)	13	4.61	ARIZONA STATE	34	4.25
WASHINGTON (St. Louis)	14	4.60	SYRACUSE	35	4.23
CASE WESTERN RESERVE	15	4.58	GEORGE WASHINGTON	36	4.21
HOUSTON (University Park)	16	4.57	COLORADO (Boulder)	37	4.16
PENN STATE (University Park)	17	4.55	DENVER	38	4.13
SOUTHERN CALIFORNIA	18	4.54	SOUTH CAROLINA (Columbia)	39	4.11
TEXAS A&M (College Station)	19	4.52	GEORGIA (Athens)	40	4.08
FLORIDA (Gainesville)	20	4.50	NEBRASKA (Lincoln)	41	4.06
OHIO STATE (Columbus)	21	4.49			

Thirty-two institutions with scores
in the 4.0-5.0 range, in rank order

INSTITUTION	Rank	Score
CORNELL (N.Y.)[2]	1	4.91
NORTHWESTERN[2]	2	4.90
MINNESOTA (Minneapolis)[2]	3	4.87
M.I.T.[2]	4	4.85
RICE[2]	5	4.83
RENSSELAER (N.Y.)[1]	6	4.81
PENNSYLVANIA[2]	7	4.80
BROWN[1]	8	4.77
JOHNS HOPKINS[2]	9	4.76
CASE WESTERN RESERVE[2]	10	4.74
NORTH CAROLINA STATE (Raleigh)[2]	11	4.72
FLORIDA (Gainesville)[2]	12	4.69
LEHIGH[2]	13	4.65
V.P.I. & STATE U.[1]	14	4.62
UCLA[1]	15	4.60
COLUMBIA (N.Y.)[2]	16	4.58
MICHIGAN (Ann Arbor)[2]	17	4.55
UTAH[2]	18	4.53
MICHIGAN STATE[2]	19	4.50
GEORGIA TECH[1]	20	4.47
DREXEL[1]	21	4.45
OHIO STATE (Columbus)[2]	22	4.44
PITTSBURGH (Pittsburgh)[2]	23	4.40
CALIFORNIA, DAVIS[2]	24	4.38
PURDUE (West Lafayette)[2]	25	4.36
AUBURN (Auburn)[1]	26	4.34
CINNCINNATI[1]	27	4.30
ALABAMA (Birmingham)[1]	28	4.28
ARIZONA (Tucson)[2]	29	4.25
TENNESSEE (Knoxville)[2]	30	4.23
NEW MEXICO INSTITUTE[1]	31	4.22
KENTUCKY[2]	32	4.19

Explanatory Note: Actual titles used by the institution to identify their curricula

[1]Materials Engineering

[2]Materials Science and Engineering

MATHEMATICS
Leading Institutions – Rating of Undergraduate Program

Fifty-eight institutions with scores in the 4.0-5.0 range, in rank order

INSTITUTION	Rank	Score	INSTITUTION	Rank	Score
PRINCETON	1	4.92	CARNEGIE-MELLON	30	4.47
CALIFORNIA, BERKELEY	2	4.91	JOHNS HOPKINS	31	4.46
HARVARD & RADCLIFFE	3	4.88	WASHINGTON (St. Louis)	32	4.44
M.I.T.	4	4.86	OHIO STATE (Columbus)	33	4.43
CHICAGO	5	4.85	SUNY (Stony Brook)	34	4.41
STANFORD	6	4.84	PENN STATE (University Park)	35	4.40
N.Y.U.	7	4.82	VIRGINIA	36	4.38
YALE	8	4.80	RENSSELAER (N.Y.)	37	4.37
WISCONSIN (Madison)	9	4.78	ILLINOIS (Chicago Circle)	38	4.36
COLUMBIA (N.Y.)	10	4.76	COLORADO (Boulder)	39	4.34
MICHIGAN (Ann Arbor)	11	4.75	KENTUCKY	40	4.32
BROWN	12	4.73	NORTH CAROLINA (Chapel Hill)	41	4.31
CORNELL (N.Y.)	13	4.71	DARTMOUTH	42	4.30
UCLA	14	4.69	ROCHESTER (N.Y.)	43	4.28
ILLINOIS (Urbana)	15	4.68	UTAH (Salt Lake City)	44	4.26
CAL TECH	16	4.66	SUNY (Buffalo)	45	4.25
MINNESOTA (Minneapolis)	17	4.65	TULANE	46	4.23
PENNSYLVANIA	18	4.63	SOUTHERN CALIFORNIA	47	4.22
NOTRE DAME	19	4.62	CALIFORNIA, SANTA BARBARA	48	4.20
GEORGIA TECH	20	4.61	MASSACHUSETTS (Amherst)	49	4.19
WASHINGTON (Seattle)	21	4.60	OREGON (Eugene)	50	4.18
PURDUE (Lafayette)	22	4.58	DUKE	51	4.17
RUTGERS (New Brunswick)	23	4.57	LOUISIANA STATE (Baton Rouge)	52	4.16
INDIANA (Bloomington)	24	4.55	ARIZONA (Tucson)	53	4.15
MARYLAND (College Park)	25	4.54	CASE WESTERN RESERVE	54	4.14
RICE	26	4.52	MICHIGAN STATE	55	4.13
CALIFORNIA, SAN DIEGO	27	4.51	PITTSBURGH (Pittsburgh)	56	4.12
NORTHWESTERN (Evanston)	28	4.50	BRANDEIS	57	4.11
TEXAS (Austin)	29	4.48	U.S. AIR FORCE ACADEMY	58	4.09

MECHANICAL ENGINEERING
Leading Institutions – Rating of Undergraduate Program

Fifty-eight institutions with scores in the 4.0-5.0 range, in rank order

INSTITUTION	Rank	Score	INSTITUTION	Rank	Score
M.I.T.	1	4.93	WASHINGTON (Seattle)	30	4.50
STANFORD	2	4.92	YALE	31	4.48
CALIFORNIA, BERKELEY	3	4.91	RICE	32	4.47
MINNESOTA (Minneapolis)	4	4.89	HOUSTON (University Park)	33	4.45
PRINCETON	5	4.86	MARYLAND (College Park)	34	4.44
PURDUE (Lafayette)	6	4.85	NOTRE DAME	35	4.42
BROWN	7	4.83	SYRACUSE	36	4.40
CORNELL (N.Y.)	8	4.81	IOWA (Iowa City)	37	4.39
MICHIGAN (Ann Arbor)	9	4.79	VIRGINIA (Charlottesville)	38	4.38
UCLA	10	4.77	MICHIGAN STATE	39	4.37
ILLINOIS (Urbana)	11	4.76	OKLAHOMA STATE	40	4.35
WISCONSIN (Madison)	12	4.75	ROCHESTER (N.Y.)	41	4.33
NORTHWESTERN (Evanston)	13	4.74	JOHNS HOPKINS	42	4.32
RENSSELAER (N.Y.)	14	4.72	FLORIDA (Gainesville)	43	4.30
TEXAS (Austin)	15	4.71	RUTGERS (New Brunswick)	44	4.28
STEVENS (New Jersey)	16	4.70	POLYTECHNIC U. (Brooklyn, N.Y.)	45	4.26
COLUMBIA (N.Y.)	17	4.68	DELAWARE (Newark)	46	4.25
PENNSYLVANIA[1]	18	4.67	OREGON STATE	47	4.24
CARNEGIE-MELLON	19	4.66	DREXEL	48	4.23
LEHIGH	20	4.65	CINCINNATI	49	4.20
CASE WESTERN RESERVE	21	4.63	SUNY (Buffalo)	50	4.19
GEORGIA TECH	22	4.62	MISSOURI (Rolla)	51	4.18
CALIFORNIA, DAVIS	23	4.60	SUNY (Stony Brook)	52	4.16
V.P.I. & STATE U.	24	4.59	ARIZONA (Tucson)	53	4.15
IOWA STATE (Ames)	25	4.58	WASHINGTON (St. Louis)	54	4.13
OHIO STATE (Columbus)	26	4.57	ARIZONA STATE	55	4.12
PENN STATE (University Park)	27	4.55	COLORADO STATE	56	4.11
SOUTHERN CALIFORNIA	28	4.53	OKLAHOMA (Norman)	57	4.10
NORTH CAROLINA STATE (Raleigh)	29	4.52	VANDERBILT	58	4.09

Explanatory Note: Actual titles used by the institution to identify their curricula

[1]Mechanical Engineering and Applied Mechanics

MEDIEVAL STUDIES
Leading Institutions – Rating of Undergraduate Program

Ten institutions with scores
in the 4.0-5.0 range, in rank order

INSTITUTION	Rank	Score
COLUMBIA (N.Y.)	1	4.83
CORNELL (N.Y.)	2	4.80
N.Y.U.	3	4.77
CHICAGO	4	4.74
NOTRE DAME (Indiana)	5	4.72
ILLINOIS (Urbana)	6	4.70
MICHIGAN (Ann Arbor)	7	4.68
WASHINGTON (St. Louis)	8	4.65
DUKE	9	4.63
CATHOLIC U. (D.C.)	10	4.60

Eighteen institutions with scores
in the 4.0-5.0 range, in rank order

INSTITUTION	Rank	Score
ILLINOIS (Urbana)	1	4.91
OHIO STATE (Columbus)	2	4.87
CARNEGIE-MELLON[3]	3	4.85
PENN STATE (University Park)[4]	4	4.83
COLORADO (Mines)	5	4.81
WISCONSIN (Madison)	6	4.78
IOWA STATE (Ames)	7	4.77
MISSOURI (Rolla)	8	4.75
PITTSBURGH (Pittsburgh)	9	4.73
MICHIGAN TECH[2]	10	4.68
UTAH (Salt Lake City)	11	4.66
STEVENS (New Jersey)[1]	12	4.62
SOUTH DAKOTA (Mines & Tech.)	13	4.60
MONTANA TECH	14	4.56
TEXAS (El Paso)	15	4.53
IDAHO (Moscow)	16	4.51
ALABAMA (Tuscaloosa)	17	4.48
ILLINOIS INSTITUTE OF TECH.	18	4.45

***Explanatory Note: Actual titles used by the
institution to identify their curricula***

[1]Materials and Metallurgical Engineering

[2]Materials Science and Engineering
  Option in Metallurgical Engineering

[3]Material Science and Engineering

[4]Metals Science and Engineering

METEOROLOGY
Leading Institutions – Rating of Undergraduate Program

Ten institutions with scores
in the 4.0-5.0 range, in rank order

INSTITUTION	Rank	Score
CORNELL (N.Y.)	1	4.89
M.I.T.	2	4.87
IOWA STATE (Ames)	3	4.83
PENN STATE (University Park)	4	4.80
KANSAS (Lawrence)	5	4.75
MICHIGAN (Ann Arbor)	6	4.71
PURDUE (Lafayette)	7	4.67
NORTH CAROLINA STATE (Raleigh)	8	4.64
OKLAHOMA (Norman)	9	4.58
TEXAS A&M (College Station)	10	4.56

Eighteen institutions with scores
in the 4.0-5.0 range, in rank order

INSTITUTION	Rank	Score
COLORADO (Mines)[1]	1	4.89
ARIZONA (Tucson)[1]	2	4.87
MISSOURI (Rolla)[1]	3	4.84
V.P.I. & STATE U.[3]	4	4.82
PENN STATE (University Park)[4]	5	4.79
PENN STATE (University Park)[5]	6	4.78
COLUMBIA (N.Y.)[1]	7	4.75
WEST VIRGINIA (Morgantown)[1]	8	4.72
UTAH (Salt Lake City)[1]	9	4.69
IDAHO (Moscow)[1]	10	4.66
SOUTH DAKOTA (Mines & Tech.)[1]	11	4.63
MICHIGAN TECH[2]	12	4.60
MONTANA TECH[1]	13	4.57
ALASKA (Fairbanks)[1]	14	4.53
NEVADA (Reno)	15	4.51
KENTUCKY[1]	16	4.49
ALABAMA (Tuscaloosa)	17	4.45
SOUTHERN ILLINOIS (Carbondale)[1]	18	4.41

***Explanatory Note: Actual titles used by the
institution to identify their curricula***

[1]Mining Engineering

[2]Mineral Processing Engineering

[3]Mining and Minerals Engineering

[4]Mining Engineering – Mineral Processing Option

[5]Mining Engineering – Mining Option

MOLECULAR BIOLOGY
Leading Institutions – Rating of Undergraduate Program

Twenty-two institutions with scores
in the 4.0-5.0 range, in rank order

INSTITUTION	Rank	Score
M.I.T.	1	4.90
CAL TECH	2	4.88
WISCONSIN (Madison)	3	4.84
CALIFORNIA, BERKELEY	4	4.82
COLORADO (Boulder)	5	4.79
NORTHWESTERN (Evanston)	6	4.75
CALIFORNIA, SAN DIEGO	7	4.73
MICHIGAN (Ann Arbor)	8	4.72
HARVARD	9	4.71
PRINCETON	10	4.68
CARNEGIE-MELLON	11	4.66
CORNELL (N.Y.)	12	4.62
PENNSYLVANIA	13	4.60
PURDUE (Lafayette)	14	4.58
RENSSELAR POLYTECHNIC	15	4.57
SUNY (Buffalo)	16	4.53
ARIZONA (Tucson)	17	4.52
TEXAS (Austin)	18	4.50
WASHINGTON (Seattle)	19	4.48
PENN STATE (University Park)	20	4.45
VANDERBILT	21	4.43
CALIFORNIA, SANTA CRUZ	22	4.42

Thirty institutions with scores
in the 4.0-5.0 range, in rank order

INSTITUTION	Rank	Score
CALIFORNIA, BERKELEY	1	4.92
CHICAGO	2	4.91
PRINCETON	3	4.90
YALE	4	4.89
CORNELL (N.Y.)	5	4.87
MICHIGAN (Ann Arbor)	6	4.84
ILLINOIS (Urbana)	7	4.82
COLUMBIA (N.Y.)	8	4.80
HARVARD & RADCLIFFE	9	4.79
UCLA	10	4.78
ROCHESTER (N.Y.)	11	4.77
NORTH CAROLINA (Chapel Hill)	12	4.76
STANFORD	13	4.71
OBERLIN	14	4.70
INDIANA (Bloomington)	15	4.69
N.Y.U.	16	4.65
PENNSYLVANIA	17	4.63
BRANDEIS	18	4.61
SOUTHERN CALIFORNIA	19	4.58
IOWA (Iowa City)	20	4.55
NORTHWESTERN (Evanston)	21	4.53
TEXAS (Austin)	22	4.52
RUTGERS (New Brunswick)	23	4.49
OHIO STATE (Columbus)	24	4.46
NORTH TEXAS, U. OF	25	4.44
WASHINGTON (Seattle)	26	4.42
CALIFORNIA STATE, NORTHRIDGE	27	4.41
FLORIDA STATE	28	4.40
BOSTON U.	29	4.36
CINCINNATI	30	4.33

NATURAL RESOURCE MANAGEMENT
Leading Institutions – Rating of Undergraduate Program

Fifteen institutions with scores
in the 4.0-5.0 range, in rank order

INSTITUTION	Rank	Score
CORNELL (N.Y.)	1	4.84
COLORADO STATE	2	4.80
MICHIGAN STATE	3	4.74
ARIZONA	4	4.72
PURDUE (Lafayette)	5	4.65
CALIFORNIA, DAVIS	6	4.61
MINNESOTA (Minneapolis)	7	4.57
OHIO STATE (Columbus)	8	4.52
KANSAS STATE	9	4.46
MICHIGAN (Ann Arbor)	10	4.41
WISCONSIN (Madison)	11	4.40
MONTANA (Missoula)	12	4.36
MAINE (Orono)	13	4.33
IDAHO (Moscow)	14	4.31
MARYLAND (College Park)	15	4.29

NAVAL ARCHITECTURE AND MARINE ENGINEERING
Leading Institutions – Rating of Undergraduate Program

Eight institutions with scores
in the 4.0-5.0 range, in rank order

INSTITUTION	Rank	Score
MICHIGAN (Ann Arbor)[5]	1	4.90
U.S. NAVAL ACADEMY[1]	2	4.87
U.S. NAVAL ACADEMY[4]	3	4.85
SUNY (New York Maritime)[1]	4	4.83
SUNY (New York Maritime)[4]	5	4.82
U.S. COAST GUARD[5]	6	4.81
WEBB INST. OF NAVAL ARCHITECTURE (N.Y.)[5]	7	4.77
U.S. MERCHANT MARINE ACADEMY[2]	8	4.75

Explanatory Note: Actual titles used by the institution to identify their curricula

[1]Marine Engineering

[2]Marine Engineering Systems

[3]Marine Systems Engineering

[4]Naval Architecture

[5]Naval Architecture and Marine Engineering

NEAR/MIDDLE EASTERN STUDIES
Leading Institutions – Rating of Undergraduate Program

Seventeen institutions with scores
in the 4.0-5.0 range, in rank order

INSTITUTION	Rank	Score
CHICAGO	1	4.82
HARVARD & RADCLIFFE	2	4.80
PRINCETON	3	4.79
COLUMBIA (N.Y.)	4	4.77
PENNSYLVANIA	5	4.75
CALIFORNIA, BERKELEY	6	4.72
MICHIGAN (Ann Arbor)	7	4.70
INDIANA (Bloomington)	8	4.68
JOHNS HOPKINS	9	4.66
N.Y.U.	10	4.64
WASHINGTON (Seattle)	11	4.62
UCLA	12	4.60
YALE	13	4.58
CORNELL (N.Y.)	14	4.56
BROWN	15	4.55
MINNESOTA (Minneapolis)	16	4.53
U.S. MILITARY ACADEMY	17	4.51

Twenty-two institutions with scores
in the 4.0-5.0 range, in rank order

INSTITUTION	Rank	Score
M.I.T.	1	4.91
MICHIGAN (Ann Arbor)	2	4.87
CALIFORNIA, BERKELEY	3	4.83
WISCONSIN (Madison)	4	4.80
VIRGINIA (Charlottesville)	5	4.79
RENSSELAER (N.Y.)	6	4.75
ILLINOIS (Urbana)	7	4.72
ARIZONA (Tucson)	8	4.70
PENN STATE (University Park)	9	4.68
CINCINNATI[1]	10	4.65
FLORIDA (Gainesville)	11	4.63
PURDUE (Lafayette)	12	4.61
MARYLAND (College Park)	13	4.60
GEORGIA TECH	14	4.58
KANSAS STATE	15	4.56
TENNESSEE (Knoxville)	16	4.53
TEXAS A&M (College Station)	17	4.52
NORTH CAROLINA STATE (Raleigh)	18	4.50
MISSOURI (Rolla)	19	4.48
CALIFORNIA, SANTA BARBARA	20	4.46
OREGON STATE	21	4.43
NEW MEXICO (Albuquerque)	22	4.40

Explanatory Note: Actual title used by the institution to identify their curricula

[1]Nuclear and Power Engineering

NURSING
Leading Institutions – Rating of Undergraduate Program

Thirty-nine institutions with scores in the 4.0-5.0 range, in rank order

INSTITUTION	Rank	Score	INSTITUTION	Rank	Score
N.Y.U.	1	4.90	IOWA (Iowa City)	21	4.40
MICHIGAN (Ann Arbor)	2	4.89	EMORY (Atlanta)	22	4.39
PENNSYLVANIA	3	4.87	UTAH (Salt Lake City)	23	4.38
WASHINGTON (Seattle)	4	4.86	VIRGINIA (Charlottesville)	24	4.37
NORTHWESTERN (Chicago)	5	4.85	ARIZONA (Tucson)	25	4.36
PITTSBURGH (Pittsburgh)	6	4.83	TENNESSEE (Knoxville)	26	4.35
WAYNE STATE (Michigan)	7	4.78	FLORIDA (Gainesville)	27	4.34
CATHOLIC U. (D.C.)	8	4.75	LOMA LINDA (California)	28	4.33
CALIFORNIA (San Francisco)	9	4.72	SUNY (Stony Brook)	29	4.32
WISCONSIN (Madison)	10	4.68	INDIANA (Indianapolis)	30	4.30
MARYLAND (Baltimore)	11	4.66	SUNY (Buffalo)	31	4.28
MINNESOTA (Minneapolis)	12	4.61	GEORGETOWN (D.C.)	32	4.26
COLUMBIA (N.Y.)	13	4.59	PENN STATE (University Park)	33	4.25
ST. LOUIS U.	14	4.57	LOYOLA (Chicago)	34	4.23
ROCHESTER (N.Y.)	15	4.55	MISSOURI (Columbia)	35	4.21
OHIO STATE (Columbus)	16	4.53	TEXAS WOMAN'S U.	36	4.19
NORTH CAROLINA (Chapel Hill)	17	4.50	MARQUETTE	37	4.18
ILLINOIS (Chicago)	18	4.49	CINCINNATI	38	4.17
ALABAMA (Birmingham)	19	4.44	SOUTH CAROLINA (Columbia)	39	4.15
KANSAS (Kansas City)	20	4.42			

Twenty-eight institutions with scores
in the 4.0-5.0 range, in rank order

INSTITUTION	Rank	Score
CORNELL (N.Y.)	1	4.89
IOWA STATE (Ames)	2	4.86
MICHIGAN STATE	3	4.84
CALIFORNIA, DAVIS	4	4.83
COLORADO STATE	5	4.81
PURDUE (Lafayette)	6	4.80
OHIO STATE (Columbus)	7	4.78
ILLINOIS (Urbana)	8	4.76
CALIFORNIA, BERKELEY	9	4.75
ARIZONA (Tucson)	10	4.73
MINNESOTA (Minneapolis)	11	4.71
MISSOURI (Columbia)	12	4.69
MICHIGAN (Ann Arbor)	13	4.67
GEORGIA (Athens)	14	4.65
WISCONSIN (Madison)	15	4.64
PENN STATE (University Park)	16	4.63
ALABAMA (Tuscaloosa)	17	4.61
FLORIDA STATE	18	4.60
OKLAHOMA STATE	19	4.58
PITTSBURGH (Pittsburgh)	20	4.55
TEXAS (Health Science Ctr – Houston)	21	4.53
FLORIDA (Gainesville)	22	4.50
TEXAS WOMAN'S U.	23	4.48
WAYNE STATE (Detroit)	24	4.47
INDIANA (Bloomington)	25	4.46
TEXAS A&M (College Station)	26	4.43
OREGON STATE	27	4.41
OKLAHOMA (Health Science Center Oklahoma City)	28	4.38

OCCUPATIONAL THERAPY
Leading Institutions – Rating of Undergraduate Program

Thirty-two institutions with scores
in the 4.0-5.0 range, in rank order

INSTITUTION	Rank	Score
N.Y.U.	1	4.91
BOSTON U.	2	4.88
WAYNE STATE (Detroit)	3	4.85
TEMPLE (Philadelphia)	4	4.83
MINNESOTA (Minneapolis)	5	4.81
SUNY (Buffalo)	6	4.79
COLORADO STATE	7	4.78
FLORIDA (Gainesville)	8	4.76
OKLAHOMA (Health Science Center)	9	4.74
SOUTHERN CALIFORNIA (California)	10	4.72
OHIO STATE (Columbus)	11	4.70
WISCONSIN (Madison)	12	4.68
WASHINGTON (Seattle)	13	4.66
MISSOURI (Columbia)	14	4.65
TEXAS (San Antonio)	15	4.63
INDIAN (Indianapolis)	16	4.61
LOUISIANA STATE (New Orleans)	17	4.60
KANSAS (Medical Center)	18	4.58
SUNY (Brooklyn)	19	4.56
PITTSBURGH (Pittsburgh)	20	4.55
WASHINGTON (St. Louis)	21	4.52
ALABAMA (Birmingham)	22	4.50
MEDICAL U. OF SOUTH CAROLINA (Charleston)	23	4.46
MEDICAL COLLEGE OF GEORGIA	24	4.43
TEXAS TECH	25	4.41
ILLINOIS (Chicago)	26	4.40
TEXAS (Galveston)	27	4.38
WESTERN MICHIGAN	28	4.37
VIRGINIA COMMONWEALTH	29	4.35
LOMA LINDA (California)	30	4.34
THOMAS JEFFERSON (Pennsylvania)	31	4.32
UTICA College of Syracuse U.	32	4.29

OCEAN ENGINEERING
Leading Institutions – Rating of Undergraduate Program

Six institutions with scores
in the 4.0-5.0 range, in rank order

INSTITUTION	Rank	Score
M.I.T.	1	4.91
U.S. NAVAL ACADEMY	2	4.87
TEXAS A&M (College Station)	3	4.85
FLORIDA INSTITUTE OF TECHNOLOGY	4	4.82
FLORIDA ATLANTIC	5	4.79
V.P.I. & STATE U.	6	4.75

OPERATIONS RESEARCH
Leading Institutions – Rating of Undergraduate Program

Ten institutions with scores
in the 4.0-5.0 range, in rank order

INSTITUTION	Rank	Score
CORNELL (N.Y.)	1	4.87
COLUMBIA (School of Engineering and Applied Science) (N.Y.)	2	4.83
CARNEGIE-MELLON	3	4.79
PENN STATE (University Park)	4	4.76
U.S. AIR FORCE ACADEMY	5	4.73
U.S. MILITARY ACADEMY (West Point)	6	4.70
CASE WESTERN RESERVE	7	4.65
PURDUE (Lafayette)	8	4.61
GEORGIA TECH	9	4.58
COLORADO (Boulder)	10	4.56

Seven institutions with scores
in the 4.0-5.0 range, in rank order

INSTITUTION	Rank	Score
CORNELL (N.Y.)	1	4.87
IOWA STATE (Ames)	2	4.83
TEXAS A&M (College Station)	3	4.80
NORTH CAROLINA STATE (Raleigh)	4	4.77
ILLINOIS (Urbana)	5	4.74
TEXAS TECH	6	4.72
AUBURN (Auburn)	7	4.69

PARKS MANAGEMENT
Leading Institutions – Rating of Undergraduate Program

Seventeen institutions with scores
in the 4.0-5.0 range, in rank order

INSTITUTION	Rank	Score
MICHIGAN STATE	1	4.85
COLORADO STATE	2	4.81
PENN STATE (University Park)	3	4.78
TEXAS TECH	4	4.73
ILLINOIS (Urbana)	5	4.70
OHIO STATE (Columbus)	6	4.66
OREGON STATE	7	4.61
KANSAS STATE	8	4.59
TEXAS A&M (College Station)	9	4.54
CLEMSON	10	4.52
MAINE (Orono)	11	4.50
MINNESOTA (Minneapolis)	12	4.48
ARIZONA (Tucson)	13	4.46
MISSOURI (Columbia)	14	4.45
PURDUE (West Lafayette)	15	4.43
NORTH CAROLINA STATE (Raleigh)	16	4.40
MONTANA (Missoula)	17	4.38

PETROLEUM ENGINEERING
Leading Institutions – Rating of Undergraduate Program

Twenty-two institutions with scores
in the 4.0-5.0 range, in rank order

INSTITUTION	Rank	Score
TEXAS A&M (College Station)	1	4.91
TEXAS (Austin)	2	4.89
TULSA	3	4.86
LOUISIANA STATE (Baton Rouge)	4	4.83
STANFORD	5	4.81
OKLAHOMA (Norman)	6	4.78
PENN STATE (University Park)[2]	7	4.75
COLORADO (Mines)	8	4.73
TEXAS TECH	9	4.70
KANSAS	10	4.66
MISSOURI (Rolla)	11	4.65
NEW MEXICO TECH	12	4.63
WYOMING	13	4.61
MISSISSIPPI STATE	14	4.59
SOUTHWESTERN LOUISIANA	15	4.57
LOUISIANA TECH	16	4.56
MARIETTA (Ohio)	17	4.52
MONTANA TECH	18	4.50
TEXAS A&I[1]	19	4.48
WEST VIRGINIA[2]	20	4.45
ALABAMA (Tuscaloosa)	21	4.42
ALASKA (Fairbanks)	22	4.40

Explanatory Note: Actual titles used by the institution to identify their curricula

[1]Natural Gas Engineering

[2]Petroleum and Natural Gas Engineering

PHILOSOPHY
Leading Institutions – Rating of Undergraduate Program

Twenty-one institutions with scores
in the 4.0-5.0 range, in rank order

INSTITUTION	Rank	Score
PRINCETON	1	4.90
PITTSBURGH (Pittsburgh)	2	4.89
HARVARD & RADCLIFFE	3	4.87
CALIFORNIA, BERKELEY	4	4.83
CHICAGO	5	4.80
STANFORD	6	4.78
MICHIGAN (Ann Arbor)	7	4.76
UCLA	8	4.73
M.I.T.	9	4.70
CORNELL (N.Y.)	10	4.68
YALE	11	4.67
BROWN	12	4.65
COLUMBIA (N.Y.)	13	4.62
NOTRE DAME	14	4.60
BOSTON U.	15	4.58
NORTH CAROLINA (Chapel Hill)	16	4.57
WISCONSIN (Madison)	17	4.55
INDIANA (Bloomington)	18	4.53
MASSACHUSETTS (Amherst)	19	4.50
MINNESOTA (Minneapolis)	20	4.47
JOHNS HOPKINS	21	4.44

PHYSICAL THERAPY
Leading Institutions – Rating of Undergraduate Program

Twenty-four institutions with scores
in the 4.0-5.0 range, in rank order

INSTITUTION	Rank	Score
N.Y.U.	1	4.91
NORTH CAROLINA (Chapel Hill)	2	4.88
MINNESOTA (Minneapolis)	3	4.86
WISCONSIN (Madison)	4	4.83
WASHINGTON (Seattle)	5	4.80
SUNY (Buffalo)	6	4.77
SUNY (Stony Brook)	7	4.75
OKLAHOMA (Oklahoma City)	8	4.73
OHIO STATE (Columbus)	9	4.71
TENNESSEE (Memphis)	10	4.69
TEXAS (Dallas)	11	4.66
SUNY (Brooklyn)	12	4.64
ILLINOIS (Chicago)	13	4.61
INDIANA (Indianapolis)	14	4.59
TEXAS (San Antonio)	15	4.58
MISSOURI (Columbia)	16	4.57
WAYNE STATE (Detroit)	17	4.53
LOUISIANA STATE U. (New Orleans)	18	4.50
UTAH (Salt Lake City)	19	4.48
MEDICAL COLLEGE OF GEORGIA	20	4.46
FLORIDA (Gainesville)	21	4.40
MEDICAL UNIVERSITY OF SOUTH CAROLINA (Charleston)	22	4.39
UNIVERSITY OF MEDICINE & DENTISTRY/KEAN COLLEGE OF N.J./SETON HALL U.	23	4.38
CONNECTICUT (Storrs)	24	4.35

PHYSICS
Leading Institutions – Rating of Undergraduate Program

Thirty-five institutions with scores
in the 4.0-5.0 range, in rank order

INSTITUTION	Rank	Score
CAL TECH	1	4.92
HARVARD & RADCLIFFE	2	4.91
CORNELL (N.Y.)	3	4.90
PRINCETON	4	4.89
M.I.T.	5	4.88
CALIFORNIA, BERKELEY	6	4.87
STANFORD	7	4.85
CHICAGO	8	4.83
ILLINOIS (Urbana)	9	4.81
COLUMBIA (N.Y.)	10	4.80
YALE	11	4.79
GEORGIA TECH	12	4.78
CALIFORNIA, SAN DIEGO	13	4.77
UCLA	14	4.76
PENNSYLVANIA	15	4.74
WISCONSIN (Madison)	16	4.73
WASHINGTON (Seattle)	17	4.72
MICHIGAN (Ann Arbor)	18	4.71
MARYLAND (College Park)	19	4.69
CALIFORNIA, SANTA BARBARA	20	4.68
TEXAS (Austin)	21	4.67
CARNEGIE-MELLON	22	4.64
MINNESOTA (Minneapolis)	23	4.63
RENSSELAER (N.Y.)	24	4.61
BROWN	25	4.60
JOHNS HOPKINS	26	4.59
MICHIGAN STATE	27	4.58
NOTRE DAME	28	4.57
SUNY (Stony Brook)	29	4.56
CASE WESTERN RESERVE	30	4.55
NORTHWESTERN (Evanston)	31	4.54
ROCHESTER (N.Y.)	32	4.53
PITTSBURGH (Pittsburgh)	33	4.52
PENN STATE (University Park)	34	4.51
COLORADO (Boulder)	35	4.50

POLITICAL SCIENCE
Leading Institutions – Rating of Undergraduate Program

Fifty institutions with scores in the 4.0-5.0 range, in rank order

INSTITUTION	Rank	Score	INSTITUTION	Rank	Score
YALE	1	4.92	WASHINGTON (Seattle)	26	4.56
HARVARD & RADCLIFFE	2	4.91	PITTSBURGH (Pittsburgh)	27	4.55
CALIFORNIA, BERKELEY	3	4.90	ROCHESTER (N.Y.)	28	4.54
MICHIGAN (Ann Arbor)	4	4.89	RUTGERS (New Brunswick)	29	4.53
CHICAGO	5	4.87	BRANDEIS	30	4.52
M.I.T.	6	4.86	VANDERBILT	31	4.51
STANFORD	7	4.84	ILLINOIS (Urbana)	32	4.50
WISCONSIN (Madison)	8	4.83	OREGON (Eugene)	33	4.48
MINNESOTA (Minneapolis)	9	4.82	MARYLAND (College Park)	34	4.47
CORNELL (N.Y.)	10	4.80	IOWA (Iowa City)	35	4.45
PRINCETON	11	4.78	CALIFORNIA, SANTA BARBARA	36	4.44
UCLA	12	4.76	SUNY (Buffalo)	37	4.42
NORTHWESTERN (Evanston)	13	4.75	MASSACHUSETTS (Amherst)	38	4.40
NORTH CAROLINA (Chapel Hill)	14	4.74	N.Y.U.	39	4.38
COLUMBIA (N.Y.)	15	4.73	MICHIGAN STATE	40	4.36
INDIANA (Bloomington)	16	4.71	SYRACUSE	41	4.34
DUKE	17	4.70	WASHINGTON (St. Louis)	42	4.33
JOHNS HOPKINS	18	4.68	U.S. AIR FORCE ACADEMY	43	4.32
NOTRE DAME	19	4.67	U.S. MILITARY ACADEMY	44	4.30
TUFTS	20	4.66	DARTMOUTH	45	4.28
OHIO STATE (Columbus)	21	4.65	POMONA (California)	46	4.26
PENNSYLVANIA	22	4.63	EMORY	47	4.25
VIRGINIA	23	4.61	CALIFORNIA, DAVIS	48	4.23
GEORGETOWN (D.C.)	24	4.60	BOSTON U.	49	4.21
TEXAS (Austin)	25	4.57	TULANE	50	4.18

PORTUGUESE
Leading Institutions – Rating of Undergraduate Program

Twelve institutions with scores
in the 4.0-5.0 range, in rank order

INSTITUTION	Rank	Score
HARVARD	1	4.86
N.Y.U.	2	4.82
STANFORD	3	4.80
ILLINOIS (Urbana)	4	4.75
GEORGETOWN (D.C.)	5	4.71
NEW MEXICO (Albuquerque)	6	4.69
NORTH CAROLINA (Chapel Hill)	7	4.63
PENNSYLVANIA	8	4.61
WISCONSIN (Madison)	9	4.59
INDIANA (Bloomington)	10	4.54
TULANE	11	4.52
TEXAS (Austin)	12	4.50

POULTRY SCIENCES
Leading Institutions – Rating of Undergraduate Program

Thirteen institutions with scores
in the 4.0-5.0 range, in rank order

INSTITUTION	Rank	Score
CORNELL (N.Y.)	1	4.89
CALIFORNIA, DAVIS	2	4.85
WISCONSIN (Madison)	3	4.83
V.P.I. & STATE U.	4	4.82
OHIO STATE (Columbus)	5	4.79
NORTH CAROLINA STATE (Raleigh)	6	4.77
FLORIDA (Gainesville)	7	4.73
MARYLAND (College Park)	8	4.74
PENN STATE (University Park)	9	4.72
OREGON STATE	10	4.69
AUBURN (Auburn)	11	4.68
PURDUE (Lafayette)	12	4.66
TEXAS A&M (College Station)	13	4.63

PSYCHOLOGY
Leading Institutions – Rating of Undergraduate Program

Thirty institutions with score
in the 4.0-5.0 range, in rank order

INSTITUTION	Rank	Score
STANFORD	1	4.66
YALE	2	4.65
PENNSYLVANIA	3	4.64
MICHIGAN (Ann Arbor)	4	4.63
MINNESOTA (Minneapolis)	5	4.62
CALIFORNIA, BERKELEY	6	4.61
HARVARD & RADCLIFFE	7	4.59
ILLINOIS (Urbana)	8	4.57
CHICAGO	9	4.56
COLUMBIA (N.Y.)	10	4.55
CALIFORNIA, SAN DIEGO	11	4.54
UCLA	12	4.52
INDIANA (Bloomington)	13	4.51
COLORADO (Boulder)	14	4.49
CARNEGIE MELLON	15	4.48
WISCONSIN (Madison)	16	4.47
M.I.T.	17	4.46
PRINCETON	18	4.45
WASHINGTON (Seattle)	19	4.44
OREGON (Eugene)	20	4.42
CORNELL (N.Y.)	21	4.41
TEXAS (Austin)	22	4.40
NORTH CAROLINA (Chapel Hill)	23	4.39
BROWN	24	4.38
NORTHWESTERN (Evanston)	25	4.37
SUNY (Stony Brook)	26	4.36
JOHNS HOPKINS	27	4.35
DUKE	28	4.34
PENN STATE (University Park)	29	4.32
N.Y.U.	30	4.30

RADIO/TELEVISION STUDIES
Leading Institutions – Rating of Undergraduate Program

Ten institutions with scores
in the 4.0-5.0 range, in rank order

INSTITUTION	Rank	Score
SOUTHERN CALIFORNIA (Los Angeles)	1	4.89
UCLA	2	4.86
N.Y.U.	3	4.82
NORTHWESTERN (Evanston)	4	4.80
ARIZONA STATE (Tempe)	5	4.77
FLORIDA STATE	6	4.75
SYRACUSE	7	4.73
MICHIGAN (Ann Arbor)	8	4.71
INDIANA (Bloomington)	9	4.70
NORTH CAROLINA (Chapel Hill)	10	4.66

Twenty-one institutions with scores
in the 4.0-5.0 range, in rank order

INSTITUTION	Rank	Score
INDIANA (Bloomington)	1	4.84
VIRGINIA (Charlottesville)	2	4.82
NORTH CAROLINA (Chapel Hill)	3	4.80
PRINCETON	4	4.78
YALE	5	4.76
DUKE	6	4.74
SOUTHERN METHODIST	7	4.72
DARTMOUTH	8	4.70
CALIFORNIA, SANTA BARBARA	9	4.68
SYRACUSE	10	4.67
IOWA (Iowa City)	11	4.65
VANDERBILT	12	4.63
NORTHWESTERN (Evanston)	13	4.61
ARIZONA STATE	14	4.59
PENNSYLVANIA	15	4.56
STANFORD	16	4.53
TEMPLE (Philadelphia)	17	4.52
COLORADO (Boulder)	18	4.50
HARVARD & RADCLIFFE	19	4.48
BROWN	20	4.46
OBERLIN	21	4.43

Twenty institutions with scores
in the 4.0-5.0 range, in rank order

INSTITUTION	Rank	Score
COLUMBIA (N.Y.)	1	4.89
YALE	2	4.87
CHICAGO	3	4.85
PENNSYLVANIA	4	4.83
MICHIGAN (Ann Arbor)	5	4.81
HARVARD & RADCLIFFE	6	4.79
INDIANA (Bloomington)	7	4.76
WASHINGTON (Seattle)	8	4.73
STANDFORD	9	4.70
WISCONSIN (Madison)	10	4.68
BROWN	11	4.64
CORNELL (N.Y.)	12	4.60
N.Y.U.	13	4.58
NORTH CAROLINA (Chapel Hill)	14	4.55
TEXAS (Austin)	15	4.53
ILLINOIS (Urbana)	16	4.50
UCLA	17	4.48
MICHIGAN STATE	18	4.46
NORTHWESTERN (Evanston)	19	4.45
SYRACUSE	20	4.42

RUSSIAN/SLAVIC STUDIES
Leading Institutions – Rating of Undergraduate Program

Eighteen institutions with scores
in the 4.0-5.0 range, in rank order

INSTITUTION	Rank	Score
CHICAGO	1	4.85
YALE	2	4.83
PRINCETON	3	4.81
HARVARD & RADCLIFFE	4	4.78
MICHIGAN (Ann Arbor)	5	4.75
COLUMBIA (N.Y.)	6	4.73
CALIFORNIA, BERKELEY	7	4.71
CORNELL (N.Y.)	8	4.69
PENNSYLVANIA	9	4.67
NORTHWESTERN (Evanston)	10	4.65
N.Y.U.	11	4.62
INDIANA (Bloomington)	12	4.60
BROWN	13	4.58
SYRACUSE	14	4.57
NORTH CAROLINA (Chapel Hill)	15	4.53
OHIO STATE (Columbus)	16	4.48
BOSTON U.	17	4.47
WASHINGTON (Seattle)	18	4.46

Eight institutions with scores
in the 4.0-5.0 range, in rank order

INSTITUTION	Rank	Score
MINNESOTA (Minneapolis)	1	4.88
WASHINGTON (Seattle)	2	4.85
CALIFORNIA, BERKELEY	3	4.82
HARVARD & RADCLIFFE	4	4.79
WISCONSIN (Madison)	5	4.76
MICHIGAN (Ann Arbor)	6	4.73
TEXAS (Austin)	7	4.70
PENNSYLVANIA	8	4.66

Seventeen institutions with scores
in the 4.0-5.0 range, in rank order

INSTITUTION	Rank	Score
CHICAGO	1	4.85
PRINCETON	2	4.82
INDIANA (Bloomington)	3	4.80
CALIFORNIA, BERKELEY	4	4.78
HARVARD & RADCLIFFE	5	4.73
WASHINGTON (Seattle)	6	4.70
WISCONSIN (Madison)	7	4.68
BROWN	8	4.66
N.Y.U.	9	4.64
PENNSYLVANIA	10	4.63
NORTHWESTERN (Evanston)	11	4.60
SYRACUSE	12	4.58
VIRGINIA (Charlottesville)	13	4.55
OHIO STATE (Columbus)	14	4.53
COLUMBIA (N.Y.)	15	4.50
TEXAS (Austin)	16	4.48
DUKE	17	4.44

Seventeen institutions with scores
in the 4.0-5.0 range, in rank order

INSTITUTION	Rank	Score
WAYNE STATE (Detroit)	1	4.71
WISCONSIN (Madison)	2	4.70
N.Y.U.	3	4.66
WASHINGTON (Seattle)	4	4.63
PITTSBURGH (Pittsburgh)	5	4.60
ILLINOIS (Urbana)	6	4.58
MICHIGAN STATE	7	4.54
PENNSYLVANIA	8	4.52
TEMPLE (Philadelphia)	9	4.49
SYRACUSE	10	4.46
LOYOLA (Chicago)	11	4.41
FLORIDA STATE	12	4.38
PENN STATE (University Park)	13	4.33
CATHOLIC U. (D.C.)	14	4.28
CALIFORNIA, BERKELEY	15	4.26
ILLINOIS (Chicago)	16	4.25
INDIANA (Bloomington)	17	4.22

SOCIOLOGY
Leading Institutions – Rating of Undergraduate Program

Thirty institutions with scores
in the 4.0-5.0 range, in rank order

INSTITUTION	Rank	Score
WISCONSIN (Madison)	1	4.81
MICHIGAN (Ann Arbor)	2	4.79
CHICAGO	3	4.78
NORTH CAROLINA (Chapel Hill)	4	4.76
COLUMBIA (N.Y.)	5	4.74
HARVARD & RADCLIFFE	6	4.72
STANFORD	7	4.71
WASHINGTON (Seattle)	8	4.69
UCLA	9	4.68
YALE	10	4.67
INDIANA (Bloomington)	11	4.65
PENNSYLVANIA	12	4.63
WAYNE STATE (Detroit)	13	4.62
TEXAS (Austin)	14	4.60
MINNESOTA (Minneapolis)	15	4.59
MICHIGAN STATE	16	4.57
CORNELL (N.Y.)	17	4.55
PRINCETON	18	4.53
ILLINOIS (Urbana)	19	4.50
N.Y.U.	20	4.49
DUKE	21	4.47
MASSACHUSETTS (Amherst)	22	4.45
NORTHWESTERN (Evanston)	23	4.43
CATHOLIC U.	24	4.40
ARIZONA (Tucson)	25	4.38
SUNY (Buffalo)	26	4.35
BOSTON U.	27	4.32
BRANDEIS	28	4.30
PITTSBURGH (Pittsburgh)	29	4.27
CALIFORNIA, BERKELEY	30	4.26

SOUTH ASIAN STUDIES
Leading Institutions – Rating of Undergraduate Program

Nine institutions with scores
in the 4.0-5.0 range, in rank order

INSTITUTION	Rank	Score
HARVARD	1	4.86
PENNSYLVANIA	2	4.84
WASHINGTON (Seattle)	3	4.81
CALIFORNIA, BERKELEY	4	4.79
CHICAGO	5	4.78
BROWN	6	4.74
MINNESOTA (Minneapolis)	7	4.72
OHIO STATE (Columbus)	8	4.69
SYRACUSE	9	4.66

Nine institutions with scores
in the 4.0-5.0 range, in rank order

INSTITUTION	Rank	Score
HARVARD	1	4.87
CALIFORNIA, BERKELEY	2	4.85
PENNSYLVANIA	3	4.83
CHICAGO	4	4.81
MICHIGAN (Ann Arbor)	5	4.79
CORNELL (N.Y.)	6	4.76
WISCONSIN (Madison)	7	4.74
TUFTS	8	4.72
OHIO STATE (Columbus)	9	4.68

Thirty-six institutions with scores
in the 4.0-5.0 range, in rank order

INSTITUTION	Rank	Score
PENNSYLVANIA	1	4.91
HARVARD & RADCLIFFE	2	4.89
TEXAS (Austin)	3	4.86
CALIFORNIA, BERKELEY	4	4.84
YALE	5	4.83
MICHIGAN (Ann Arbor)	6	4.82
WISCONSIN (Madison)	7	4.80
UCLA	8	4.77
STANFORD	9	4.75
KANSAS	10	4.73
INDIANA (Bloomington)	11	4.72
ILLINOIS (Urbana)	12	4.69
CORNELL (N.Y.)	13	4.66
BROWN	14	4.63
CALIFORNIA, SAN DIEGO	15	4.62
PRINCETON	16	4.60
COLUMBIA (N.Y.)	17	4.58
MINNESOTA (Minneapolis)	18	4.57
N.Y.U.	19	4.55
CALIFORNIA, IRVINE	20	4.53
ARIZONA (Tucson)	21	4.52
NEW MEXICO (Albuquerque)	22	4.50
NORTH CAROLINA (Chapel Hill)	23	4.48
VIRGINIA (Charlottesville)	24	4.46
SUNY (Buffalo)	25	4.43
CALIFORNIA, SANTA BARBARA	26	4.41
WASHINGTON (Seattle)	27	4.40
PENN STATE (University Park)	28	4.38
KENTUCKY	29	4.36
MARYLAND (College Park)	30	4.35
PITTSBURGH (Pittsburgh)	31	4.33
DUKE	32	4.31
ARIZONA STATE	33	4.29
SOUTHERN CALIFORNIA	34	4.26
VANDERBILT	35	4.23
GEORGETOWN (D.C.)	36	4.20

Fourteen institutions with scores
in the 4.0-5.0 range, in rank order

INSTITUTION	Rank	Score
NORTHWESTERN (Evanston)	1	4.90
IOWA (Iowa City)	2	4.88
MICHIGAN (Ann Arbor)	3	4.84
INDIANA (Bloomington)	4	4.82
ILLINOIS (Urbana)	5	4.79
PENN STATE (University Park)	6	4.77
CALIFORNIA, BERKELEY	7	4.74
MISSOURI (Columbia)	8	4.72
WAYNE STATE (Michigan)	9	4.69
BAYLOR	10	4.66
OHIO U. (Athens)	11	4.63
ARIZONA (Tucson)	12	4.60
LOUISIANA STATE (Baton Rouge)	13	4.59
UTAH (Salt Lake City)	14	4.57

SPEECH PATHOLOGY/AUDIOLOGY
Leading Institutions – Rating of Undergraduate Program

Twenty-eight institutions with scores
in the 4.0-5.0 range, in rank order

INSTITUTION	Rank	Score
IOWA (Iowa City)	1	4.91
NORTHWESTERN (Evanston)	2	4.90
MINNESOTA (Minneapolis)	3	4.87
PURDUE (Lafayette)	4	4.86
MICHIGAN (Ann Arbor)	5	4.83
INDIANA (Bloomington)	6	4.82
KANSAS	7	4.80
MICHIGAN STATE	8	4.78
BOSTON U.	9	4.76
ILLINOIS (Urbana)	10	4.74
N.Y.U.	11	4.72
WAYNE STATE (Detroit)	12	4.70
COLORADO (Boulder)	13	4.68
MARQUETTE	14	4.67
BAYLOR	15	4.66
UTAH (Salt Lake City)	16	4.64
SYRACUSE	17	4.61
SUNY (Buffalo)	18	4.59
LOUISIANA STATE (Baton Rouge)	19	4.58
ARIZONA (Tucson)	20	4.55
WASHINGTON (Seattle)	21	4.53
OREGON (Eugene)	22	4.51
MISSOURI (Columbia)	23	4.49
FLORIDA STATE	24	4.46
MASSACHUSETTS (Amherst)	25	4.43
OHIO U. (Athens)	26	4.41
MARYLAND (College Park)	27	4.38
CASE WESTERN RESERVE	28	4.36

Twenty-five institutions with scores
in the 4.0-5.0 range, in rank order

INSTITUTION	Rank	Score
CALIFORNIA, BERKELEY	1	4.91
STANFORD	2	4.90
COLUMBIA (N.Y.)	3	4.84
WISCONSIN (Madison)	4	4.83
PURDUE (Lafayette)	5	4.81
IOWA STATE (Ames)	6	4.79
CHICAGO	7	4.78
MINNESOTA (Minneapolis)	8	4.76
ILLINOIS (Urbana)	9	4.74
V.P.I. & STATE U.	10	4.72
ROCHESTER (N.Y.)	11	4.70
IOWA (Iowa City)	12	4.68
NORTH CAROLINA STATE (Raleigh)	13	4.65
RUTGERS (New Brunswick)	14	4.63
CALIFORNIA, SANTA BARBARA	15	4.62
MICHIGAN (Ann Arbor)	16	4.60
PENNSYLVANIA	17	4.59
RICE	18	4.57
CALIFORNIA, DAVIS	19	4.56
FLORIDA STATE	20	4.53
NORTH CAROLINA (Chapel Hill)	21	4.52
MICHIGAN STATE	22	4.50
SUNY (Buffalo)	23	4.49
OHIO STATE (Columbus)	24	4.47
CORNELL (N.Y.)	25	4.45

Twelve institutions with scores
in the 4.0-5.0 range, in rank order

INSTITUTION	Rank	Score
U.S. NAVAL ACADEMY	1	4.85
CASE WESTERN RESERVE[3]	2	4.82
WASHINGTON (St. Louis)[4]	3	4.78
PENNSYLVANIA[4]	4	4.75
ARIZONA (Tucson)	5	4.71
VIRGINIA (Charlottesville)	6	4.68
CALIFORNIA, SAN DIEGO[3]	7	4.65
GEORGE WASHINGTON[2]	8	4.60
BOSTON U.	9	4.57
OAKLAND U.	10	4.52
TEXAS A&M (Galveston)[1]	11	4.48
WEST FLORIDA[3]	12	4.40

***Explanatory Note: Actual titles used by the
institution to identify their curricula***

[1]Maritime Systems Engineering

[2]Systems Analysis and Engineering

[3]Systems and Control Engineering

[4]Systems Science and Engineering

URBAN AND REGIONAL PLANNING
Leading Institutions – Rating of Undergraduate Program

Thirteen institutions with scores
in the 4.0-5.0 range, in rank order

INSTITUTION	Rank	Score
SOUTHERN CALIFORNIA (USC)	1	4.83
RUTGERS (New Brunswick)	2	4.81
M.I.T.	3	4.80
ILLINOIS (Urbana)	4	4.76
CORNELL (N.Y.)	5	4.74
IOWA STATE (Ames)	6	4.72
MICHIGAN STATE	7	4.71
CINCINNATI	8	4.68
COLORADO (Boulder)	9	4.66
PITTSBURGH (Pittsburgh)	10	4.64
VIRGINIA (Charlottesville)	11	4.61
ARIZONA STATE (Tempe)	12	4.58
OREGON (Eugene)	13	4.56

WILDLIFE BIOLOGY
Leading Institutions – Rating of Undergraduate Program

Sixteen institutions with scores
in the 4.0-5.0 range, in rank order

INSTITUTION	Rank	Score
PURDUE (Lafayette)	1	4.82
CALIFORNIA, DAVIS	2	4.80
COLORADO STATE	3	4.79
MICHIGAN (Ann Arbor)	4	4.76
IOWA STATE (Ames)	5	4.73
NORTH CAROLINA STATE (Raleigh)	6	4.71
SUNY (Envir. Sci. & Forestry)	7	4.68
MONTANA (Missoula)	8	4.66
NORTH DAKOTA STATE	9	4.65
SOUTH DAKOTA STATE	10	4.63
NEW HAMPSHIRE (Durham)	11	4.61
VERMONT	12	4.59
NEW MEXICO STATE	13	4.57
GEORGIA (Athens)	14	4.55
WASHINGTON STATE	15	4.53
CLEMSON	16	4.50

ZOOLOGY
Leading Institutions – Rating of Undergraduate Program

Nineteen institutions with scores
in the 4.0-5.0 range, in rank order

INSTITUTION	Rank	Score
WISCONSIN (Madison)	1	4.88
WASHINGTON (Seattle)	2	4.86
TEXAS (Austin)	3	4.82
CORNELL (N.Y.)	4	4.80
GEORGIA (Athens)	5	4.76
CALIFORNIA, DAVIS	6	4.73
MICHIGAN STATE	7	4.71
FLORIDA (Gainesville)	8	4.69
OHIO STATE (Columbus)	9	4.66
WASHINGTON STATE	10	4.64
ARIZONA STATE	11	4.59
IOWA STATE (Ames)	12	4.58
OREGON STATE	13	4.57
COLORADO STATE	14	4.54
NORTH CAROLINA STATE (Raleigh)	15	4.52
LOUISIANA STATE (Baton Rouge)	16	4.49
SUNY (Envir. Sci. & Forestry)	17	4.47
TEXAS A&M (College Station)	18	4.43
MARYLAND (University Park)	19	4.40

The GOURMAN REPORT
PART II

A RATING OF CANADIAN ENGINEERING SCHOOLS

Canadian Engineering

A RATING OF CANADIAN ENGINEERING PROGRAMS
Leading Institutions

INSTITUTION	Rank	Score
TORONTO	1	4.85
McGILL	2	4.83
BRITISH COLUMBIA	3	4.80
McMASTER	4	4.78
POLYTECHNIQUE ECOLE (University of Montreal)	5	4.75
SASKATCHEWAN	6	4.72
ALBERTA	7	4.70
MANITOBA	8	4.67
LAVAL	9	4.65
QUEEN'S	10	4.61
NOVA SCOTIA TECHNICAL UNIVERSITY	11	4.58
CALGARY	12	4.56
OTTAWA	13	4.53
NEW BRUNSWICK	14	4.50
ROYAL MILITARY	15	4.47
MEMORIAL U.	16	4.45
WINDSOR	17	4.42
WESTERN ONTARIO	18	4.40
WATERLOO	19	4.34
CARLETON	20	4.30
SHERBROOKE	21	4.26
GUELPH	22	4.20
MONCTON	23	4.15
CONCORDIA	24	4.10
LAKEHEAD	25	4.04
QUEBEC (Trois-Riveres)	26	3.80
REGINA	27	3.50
QUEBEC (Chicoutimi)	28	3.40
LAURENTIAN	29	3.37
SIMON FRASER UNIVERSITY	30	3.15
VICTORIA, UNIVERSITY OF	31	3.06

A RATING OF CANADIAN PROGRAMS IN ENGINEERING
Leading Institutions

INSTITUTION	CURRICULUM	Score
ALBERTA, UNIVERSITY OF	Agricultural	4.76
Edmonton, Alberta	Chemical	4.69
	Civil	4.70
	Computer	4.67
	Electrical	4.72
	Engineering Physics	4.30
	Mechanical	4.75
	Metallurgical	4.80
	Mineral	4.81
	Mineral Process	4.78
	Mining	4.79
	Petroleum	4.83
BRITISH COLUMBIA, UNIVERSITY OF	Agriculture	4.84
Vancouver, British Columbia	Bio-Resource	4.77
	Chemical	4.82
	Civil	4.80
	Electrical	4.81
	Engineering Physics	4.83
	Geological	4.86
	Mechanical	4.79
	Metallurgical	4.84
	Metals and Materials	4.76
	Mineral	4.88
	Mining and Mineral Process	4.87
CALGARY, UNIVERSITY OF	Chemical	4.62
Calgary, Alberta	Civil	4.72
	Electrical	4.71
	Geomatics	3.80
	Mechanical	4.70
	Surveying	4.66
CARLETON UNIVERSITY	Aerospace	4.27
Ottawa, Ontario	Civil	4.54
	Computer Systems	4.53
	Electrical	4.55
	Mecahnical	4.50
CONCORDIA UNIVERSITY	Building	4.47
Montreal, Quebec	Civil	4.30
	Computer	4.46
	Electrical	4.44
	Mechanical	4.40

A RATING OF CANADIAN PROGRAMS IN ENGINEERING (Continued)
Leading Institutions

INSTITUTION	CURRICULUM	Score
GUELPH, UNIVERSITY OF Guelph, Ontario	Agricultural	4.50
	Biological	4.46
	Engineering Systems & Computing	3.88
	Environmental	3.82
	Food	
LAKEHEAD UNIVERSITY Thunder Bay, Ontario	Chemical	4.49
	Civil	4.40
	Electrical	4.46
	Mechanical	4.42
LAURENTIAN UNIVERSITY Sudbury, Ontario	Extractive Metallurgical	3.39
	Extractive Metallurgy	3.35
	Mining	3.32
LAVAL UNIVERSITE Québec, Québec	Génie Chimique	4.65
	Génie Civil	4.68
	Génie des Materiaux et de la métallurgie	4.69
	Génie des mines et de minéralurgie	4.61
	Génie Électrique	4.69
	Génie Géologique	4.80
	Génie Informatique	4.55
	Génie Mécanique	4.75
	Génie Métallurgique	4.81
	Génie Minier	4.76
	Génie Physique.	4.70
	Génie Rural	4.63
MANITOBA, UNIVERSITY OF Winnipeg, Manitoba	Agricultural	4.85
	Civil	4.65
	Computer	4.64
	Electrical	4.70
	Geological	4.77
	Industrial	4.63
	Mechanical	4.76
McGILL UNIVERSITY Montreal, Quebec	Agricultural (MacDonald College)	4.82
	Chemical	4.88
	Civil	4.83
	Computer Engineering	4.66
	Electrical	4.82
	Mechanical	4.85
	Metallurgical	4.86
	Mining	4.87

INSTITUTION	CURRICULUM	Score
McMASTER UNIVERSITY	Ceramic Engineering	4.81
	Ceramic Engineering & Management	4.87
	Chemical Engineering	4.73
	Chemical Engineering & Management	4.70
	Civil Engineering	4.79
	Civil Engineering & Computer Systems	4.68
	Civil Engineering & Engineering Mechanics	4.78
	Civil Engineering & Management	4.75
	Computer Engineering	4.71
	Computer Engineering & Management	4.66
	Electrical Engineering	4.80
	Electrical Engineering & Management	4.76
	Engineering Physics	4.65
	Engineering Physics & Management	4.74
	Manufacturing Engineering	4.67
	Materials Engineering	4.45
	Materials Engineering & Management	4.72
	Mechanical Engineering	4.84
	Mechanical Engineering & Management	4.83
	Metallurgical Engineering	4.86
	Metallurgical Engineering & Management	4.77
MEMORIAL UNIVERSITY OF NEWFOUNDLAND St. John's Newfoundland	Civil	4.61
	Electrical	4.58
	Mechanical	4.57
	Naval Architecture Engineering	4.50
	Shipbuilding	4.59
MONCTON, UNIVERSITE DE Moncton, Nouveau-Brunswick	Génie Civil	3.48
	Génie Industriel	3.50
	Génie Méchanique	3.10
NEW BRUNSWICK, UNIVERSITY OF Fredericton, New Brunswick	Chemical	4.67
	Civil	4.64
	Electrical	4.68
	Forest	4.60
	Geological	4.61
	Mechanical	4.66
	Surveying	4.63

INSTITUTION	CURRICULUM	Score
NOVA SCOTIA TECHNICAL, UNIVERSITY OF Halifax, Nova Scotia	Agricultural	4.76
	Chemical	4.65
	Civil	4.67
	Electrical	4.66
	Engineering Physics	4.62
	Industrial	4.77
	Mechanical	4.69
	Metallurgical	4.68
	Mining	4.78
OTTAWA, UNIVERSITY OF Ottawa, Ontario	Chemical	4.68
	Civil	4.65
	Computer	4.10
	Electrical	4.66
	Mechanical	4.67
POLYTECHNIQUE ECOLE (Université de Montréal) Montréal, Québec	Génie Chimique	4.71
	Génie Civil	4.66
	Génie des Matériaux	4.50
	Génie des Mines	4.83
	Génie Électrique	4.70
	Génie Géologique	4.75
	Génie Industriel	4.79
	Génie Informatique	4.16
	Génie Méchanique	4.72
	Génie Métallurgique	4.81
	Génie Minier	4.82
	Génie Physique	4.80
QUEBEC, UNIVERSITE DU Chicoutimi, Québec	Génie Geologique	3.40
	Génie Informatique	3.14
	Génie Unififé	3.38
QUEBEC, UNIVERSITE DU Trois-Rivières	Génie Chimique	3.26
	GénieElectrique	3.81
	Génie Industriel	3.80
	Génie Mécanique Manfacturier	3.79
QUEEN'S UNIVERSITY Kingston, Ontario	Chemical	4.61
	Civil	4.74
	Electrical	4.72
	Engineering Chemistry	4.63
	Engineering Physics	4.70
	Geological	4.81
	Materials and Metallurgical Engineering	4.68
	Mathematics and Engineering	4.76
	Mechanical	4.69
	Metallurgical	4.75
	Mining	4.78

INSTITUTION	CURRICULUM	Score
REGINA, UNIVERSITY OF Regina, Saskatchewan	Electronic Information Systems Industrial Systems Environmental Systems Systems Engineering	3.49 3.48 3.46 3.51
ROYAL MILITARY COLLEGE Kingston, Ontario	Chemical and Materials Engineering Chemical Engineering Civil Computer Electrical Engineering and Management Engineering Physics Fuels and Materials Mechanical	4.57 4.60 4.63 4.59 4.65 4.62 4.66 4.58 4.64
SASKATCHEWAN, UNIVERSITY OF Saskatoon, Saskatchewan	Agriculture Chemical Civil Electrical Engineering Physics Geological Geological Engineering (Geophysics) Mechanical Mining	4.85 4.69 4.71 4.70 4.77 4.80 4.83 4.66 4.78
SHERBROOKE, UNIVERSITE DE Sherbrooke, Québec	Génie Chimique Génie Civil Génie Electrique Génie Mécanique	4.55 4.50 4.46 4.45
SIMON FRASER UNIVERSITY	Engineering Science	3.06
TORONTO, UNIVERSITY OF Toronto, Ontario	Chemical Civil Computer Electrical Engineering Science Geo-Engineering Geological and Mineral Geological Engineering Geological Engr. & Applied Earth Science Industrial Mechanical Metallurgy and Materials Science Metallurgical Engr. & Materials Science	4.81 4.85 4.73 4.86 4.84 4.83 4.81 4.80 4.87 4.77 4.82 4.79 4.76
VICTORIA, UNIVERSITY OF	Computer Electrical Mechanical	2.98 2.99 2.84

INSTITUTION	CURRICULUM	Score
WATERLOO, UNIVERSITY OF Waterloo, Ontario	Chemical	4.59
	Civil	4.53
	Computer	4.08
	Electrical	4.55
	Geological	4.50
	Mechanical	4.51
	Systems Design	4.52
WESTERN ONTARIO, UNIVERSITY OF London, Ontario	Chemical	4.53
	Chemical and Biochemical	4.58
	Civil	4.55
	Electrical	4.56
	Materials	4.54
	Mechanical	4.50
WINDSOR, UNIVERSITY OF Windsor, Ontario	Chemical	4.56
	Civil	4.53
	Electrical	4.50
	Engineering Materials	4.57
	Environmental Engineering	4.49
	Geological	4.62
	Industrial	4.59
	Mechanical	4.51

The GOURMAN REPORT
PART III

**A RATING OF CANADIAN COLLEGES
AND UNIVERSITIES**

A RATING OF CANADIAN COLLEGES AND UNIVERSITIES
Leading Institutions

INSTITUTION	Rank	Score
McGILL UNIVERSITY	1	4.64
UNIVERSITY OF TORONTO	2	4.61
THE UNIVERSITY OF BRITISH COLUMBIA	3	4.22
McMASTER UNIVERSITY	4	3.89
UNIVERSITY OF ALBERTA	5	3.63
YORK UNIVERSITY	6	3.61
CARLETON UNIVERSITY	7	3.58
SIMON FRASER UNIVERSITY	8	3.55
THE UNIVERSITY OF MANITOBA	9	3.50
UNIVERSITY OF OTTAWA	10	3.45
THE UNIVERSITY OF CALGARY	11	3.39
UNIVERSITÉ DE MONTRÉAL	12	3.38
UNIVERSITY OF NEW BRUNSWICK	13	3.37
UNIVERSITÉ LAVAL	14	3.36
UNIVERSITY OF WINDSOR	15	3.34
THE UNIVERSITY OF WESTERN ONTARIO	16	3.32
THE UNIVERSITY OF WINNIPEG	17	3.31
MEMORIAL UNIVERSITY OF NEWFOUNDLAND	18	3.30
UNIVERSITÉ DE SHERBROOKE	19	3.29
UNIVERSITY OF SASKATCHEWAN	20	3.28
QUEEN'S UNIVERSITY AT KINGSTON	21	3.27
UNIVERSITY OF WATERLOO	22	3.26
UNIVERSITY OF VICTORIA	23	3.25
DALHOUSE UNIVERSITY	24	3.24
CONCORDIA UNIVERSITY	25	3.23
UNIVERSITY OF GUELPH	26	3.20
THE UNIVERSITY OF REGINA	27	3.18
LAKEHEAD UNIVERSITY	28	3.16
LAURENTIAN UNIVERSITY OF SUDBURY	29	3.15
UNIVERSITÉ DE MONCTON	30	3.14
BRANDON UNIVERSITY	31	3.13
BISHOP'S UNIVERSITY	32	3.12
ROYAL MILITARY COLLEGE OF CANADA	33	3.11
TRENT UNIVERSITY	34	3.10
WILFRID LAURIER UNIVERSITY	35	3.09
ACADIA UNIVERSITY	36	3.08
BROCK UNIVERSITY	37	3.07
TECHNICAL UNIVERSITY OF NOVA SCOTIA	38	3.06
MOUNT ALLISON UNIVERSITY	39	3.05
MOUNT SAINT VINCENT UNIVERSITY	40	3.04
THE UNIVERSITY OF LETHBRIDGE	41	3.03
UNIVERSITY OF PRINCE ISLAND	42	3.02
UNIVERSITÉ DU QUEBEC (Montreal)	43	3.01
ATHZBASCA UNIVERSITY	44	2.99
SAINT MARY'S UNIVERSITY	45	2.97
ST. THOMAS UNIVERSITY	46	2.95
UNIVERSITÉ DUQUÉBEC À TROIS-RIVIÈRES	47	2.92
RYERSON POLYTECHNIC UNIVERSITY	48	2.90
UNIVERSITÉ DUQUÉBEC À CHICOUTIMI	49	2.85
UNIVERSITY OF ST. MICHAEL'S COLLEGE	50	2.84

A RATING OF CANADIAN COLLEGES AND UNIVERSITIES (Continued)
Leading Institutions

INSTITUTION	Rank	Score
TRINITY WESTERN UNIVERSITY	51	2.82
UNIVERSITÉ DE QUÉBEC À HULL	52	2.80
UNIVERSITÉ DU QUÉBEC À RIMOUSKI	53	2.77
NOVA SCOTIA AGRICULTURAL COLLEGE	54	2.73
UNIVERSITY COLLEGE OF CAPE BRETON	55	2.70
UNIVERSITÉ DU QUÉBEC EN ABITIBI-TÉMISCAMINQUE	56	2.69
ST. FRANCIS XAVIER UNIVERSITY	57	2.65
UNIVERSITÉ SAINTE-ANNE	58	2.60
UNIVERSITY OF KING'S COLLEGE	59	2.53
SAINT PAUL UNIVERSITY	60	2.47

The GOURMAN REPORT
PART IV

**A RATING OF PRELEGAL EDUCATION
IN THE UNITED STATES**

**A RATING OF PREMEDICAL EDUCATION
IN THE UNITED STATES**

A RATING OF PRELEGAL EDUCATION
Leading Institutions

Fifty institutions with scores in the 4.0-5.0 range, in rank order

INSTITUTION	Rank	Score	INSTITUTION	Rank	Score
HARVARD	1	4.93	INDIANA (Bloomington)	26	4.59
YALE	2	4.92	VANDERBILT	27	4.58
COLUMBIA (N.Y.)	3	4.91	WASHINGTON (Seattle)	28	4.56
MICHIGAN (Ann Arbor)	4	4.90	WASHINGTON (St. Louis)	29	4.54
CALIFORNIA, BERKELEY	5	4.89	IOWA (Iowa City)	30	4.53
CHICAGO	6	4.88	OHIO STATE (Columbus)	31	4.51
PRINCETON	7	4.86	PITTSBURGH (Pittsburgh)	32	4.50
CORNELL (N.Y.)	8	4.84	ROCHESTER (N.Y.)	33	4.48
STANFORD	9	4.83	TEXAS (Austin)	34	4.46
UCLA	10	4.80	GEORGE WASHINGTON	35	4.43
DUKE	11	4.79	RUTGERS (New Brunswick)	36	4.41
NOTRE DAME	12	4.78	SUNY (Buffalo)	37	4.38
PENNSYLVANIA	13	4.77	CALIFORNIA, DAVIS	38	4.36
NORTHWESTERN (Evanston)	14	4.76	U.S. AIR FORCE ACADEMY	39	4.34
M.I.T.	15	4.74	CALIFORNIA, SANTA BARBARA	40	4.32
ILLINOIS (Urbana)	16	4.73	MICHIGAN STATE	41	4.30
JOHNS HOPKINS	17	4.72	BRANDEIS	42	4.27
WISCONSIN (Madison)	18	4.70	CASE WESTERN RESERVE	43	4.25
DARTMOUTH	19	4.69	CALIFORNIA, RIVERSIDE	44	4.22
MINNESOTA (Minneapolis)	20	4.67	KANSAS	45	4.20
GEORGETOWN (D.C.)	21	4.65	UTAH (Salt Lake City)	46	4.18
BROWN	22	4.63	CLAREMONT McKENNA	47	4.17
N.Y.U.	23	4.62	TULANE	48	4.15
NORTH CAROLINA (Chapel Hill)	24	4.61	TUFTS	49	4.12
VIRGINIA (Charlottesville)	25	4.60	EMORY	50	4.11

A RATING OF PREMEDICAL EDUCATION
Leading Institutions

Fifty-eight institutions with scores in the 4.0-5.0 range, in rank order

INSTITUTION	Rank	Score	INSTITUTION	Rank	Score
HARVARD	1	4.93	WASHINGTON (Seattle)	30	4.46
JOHNS HOPKINS	2	4.92	NORTH CAROLINA (Chapel Hill)	31	4.43
YALE	3	4.91	IOWA (Iowa City)	32	4.42
CORNELL (N.Y.)	4	4.90	CALIFORNIA, DAVIS	33	4.40
CALIFORNIA, BERKELEY	5	4.88	VIRGINIA (Charlottesville)	34	4.38
STANFORD	6	4.86	TUFTS	35	4.37
ILLINOIS (Urbana)	7	4.84	U.S. AIR FORCE ACADEMY	36	4.36
COLUMBIA (N.Y.)	8	4.82	ROCHESTER (N.Y.)	37	4.33
U.C.L.A.	9	4.87	BRANDEIS	38	4.32
MICHIGAN (Ann Arbor)	10	4.80	CALIFORNIA, RIVERSIDE	39	4.30
CHICAGO	11	4.79	CASE WESTERN RESERVE	40	4.28
NOTRE DAME	12	4.78	TEXAS (Austin)	41	4.27
PRINCETON	13	4.76	CALIFORNIA, IRVINE	42	4.26
WISCONSIN (Madison)	14	4.73	EMORY	43	4.23
NORTHWESTERN (Evanston)	15	4.72	SUNY (Buffalo)	44	4.22
DUKE	16	4.70	PITTSBURGH (Pittsburgh)	45	4.21
BROWN	17	4.68	PENN STATE (University Park)	46	4.20
M.I.T.	18	4.66	MICHIGAN STATE	47	4.19
DARTMOUTH	19	4.64	TULANE	48	4.18
PENNSYLVANIA	20	4.62	BAYLOR	49	4.17
CAL TECH	21	4.61	UTAH (Salt Lake City)	50	4.16
N.Y.U.	22	4.60	OHIO STATE (Columbus)	51	4.15
WASHINGTON (St. Louis)	23	4.58	COLORADO (Boulder)	52	4.14
MINNESOTA (Minneapolis)	24	4.57	LOMA LINDA	53	4.13
INDIANA (Bloomington)	25	4.55	OREGON (Eugene)	54	4.12
VANDERBILT	26	4.53	BOSTON U.	55	4.11
CALIFORNIA, SAN DIEGO	27	4.52	KANSAS	56	4.09
RICE	28	4.50	CALIFORNIA, SANTA BARBARA	57	4.07
GEORGETOWN (D.C.)	29	4.48	MARQUETTE	58	4.06

The GOURMAN REPORT
PART V

A RATING OF UNIVERSITY ADMINISTRATIVE AREAS

Administration

Alumni Associations

Athletic-Academic Balance

Comparative Competition for Fellowships/Scholarships

Counseling Centers

Curriculum

Intercollegiate Athletic Departments

Libraries

Public Relations

Trustees/Regents
Public/Federal

Trustees/Regents
Private

A RATING OF ADMINISTRATION
Leading Institutions

Thirty-five institutions with scores in the 4.0-5.0 range, in rank order

INSTITUTION	Rank	Score	INSTITUTION	Rank	Score
HARVARD	1	4.86	PENNSYLVANIA	19	4.37
CHICAGO	2	4.82	PITTSBURGH (Pittsburgh)	20	4.35
PRINCETON	3	4.80	VANDERBILT	21	4.33
M.I.T.	4	4.75	CARNEGIE MELLON	22	4.31
MICHIGAN (Ann Arbor)	5	4.74	ROCHESTER (N.Y.)	23	4.30
CORNELL (N.Y.)	6	4.72	U.S. AIR FORCE ACADEMY	24	4.29
DARTMOUTH	7	4.69	BRANDEIS	25	4.27
CAL TECH	8	4.67	U.S. MILITARY ACADEMY	26	4.25
JOHNS HOPKINS	9	4.64	WILLIAMS (Massachusetts)	27	4.23
RICE	10	4.61	WASHINGTON (St. Louis)	28	4.22
BROWN	11	4.58	AMHERST	29	4.20
NOTRE DAME	12	4.57	WALK FOREST	30	4.18
DUKE	13	4.53	SWARTHMORE	31	4.14
NORTHWESTERN (Evanston)	14	4.49	HAVERFORD	32	4.13
YALE	15	4.47	TUFTS	33	4.11
COLUMBIA (N.Y.)	16	4.43	U.S. NAVAL ACADEMY	34	4.08
NORTH CAROLINA (Chapel Hill)	17	4.40	GEORGIA TECH	35	4.06
ILLINOIS (Urbana)	18	4.39			

A RATING OF ALUMNI ASSOCIATIONS
Leading Institutions

Fifty institutions with scores in the 4.0-5.0 range, in rank order

INSTITUTION	Rank	Score	INSTITUTION	Rank	Score
HARVARD	1	4.93	PURDUE (Lafayette)	26	4.36
PRINCETON	2	4.92	NEBRASKA (Lincoln)	27	4.34
YALE	3	4.91	TEXAS A&M (College Station)	28	4.31
MICHIGAN (Ann Arbor)	4	4.90	SOUTHERN CALIFORNIA	29	4.30
STANFORD	5	4.89	TULANE	30	4.29
NOTRE DAME	6	4.88	TEXAS (Austin)	31	4.27
DUKE	7	4.83	VANDERBILT	32	4.25
PENNSYLVANIA	8	4.81	OBERLIN	33	4.23
CORNELL (N.Y.)	9	4.79	PENN STATE (University Park)	34	4.22
M.I.T.	10	4.77	IOWA (Iowa City)	35	4.19
CHICAGO	11	4.72	CALIFORNIA, BERKELEY	36	4.18
DARTMOUTH	12	4.71	INDIANA (Bloomington)	37	4.17
NORTHWESTERN (Evanston)	13	4.69	PITTSBURGH (Pittsburgh)	38	4.16
UCLA	14	4.66	TENNESSEE (Knoxville)	39	4.15
MINNESOTA (Minneapolis)	15	4.62	BRANDEIS	40	4.13
WISCONSIN (Madison)	16	4.59	LOUISIANA STATE (Baton Rouge)	41	4.12
RICE	17	4.54	OKLAHOMA (Norman)	42	4.11
CAL TECH	18	4.52	MISSOURI (Columbia)	43	4.10
MICHIGAN STATE	19	4.51	WAKE FOREST	44	4.09
NORTH CAROLINA (Chapel Hill)	20	4.47	KANSAS	45	4.08
GEORGIA TECH	21	4.46	VIRGINIA (Charlottesville)	46	4.07
BROWN	22	4.42	JOHNS HOPKINS	47	4.06
ILLINOIS (Urbana)	23	4.40	AMHERST	48	4.05
COLUMBIA (N.Y.)	24	4.38	ROCHESTER (N.Y.)	49	4.03
OHIO STATE (Columbus)	25	4.37	WILLIAMS (Massachusetts)	50	4.02

A RATING OF ATHLETIC–ACADEMIC BALANCE

THE GOURMAN REPORT evaluated and ranked all Division I, II and III schools. For this report one hundred twenty-six schools with scores in the 1.00-4.95 range, in rank order were selected.

RATING CATEGORIES	Numerical Range
Good	4.70-4.95
Acceptable Plus	4.40-4.69
Acceptable	3.60-3.85
Marginal	2.00-2.98
Unsatisfactory	1.00-1.99

STATEMENT

The overemphasis and the abuse of intercollegiate athletics have plagued higher education for many decades. In spite of fulminations of faculty members and administrators, in spite of "sanity codes" and other attempted reforms, the evil persists.

THE GOURMAN REPORT adopted a comprehensive agenda and set priorities for the study of collegiate athletics. An institutional file for all colleges and universities participating in athletics was created. In addition THE GOURMAN REPORT has collected massive amounts of information and has a consistent database that permit unit cost comparison.

ACCREDITING STANDARDS

Academic Advising

Academic Standards

Administration

Admissions

Athletic Director and Office

Athletic Staff

Budget / Revenue / Expenses

Degree Program (Quality of)

Faculty Athletic Representation

Financial Aid (4 Year Institutions)

Graduation Rate

Image Perception

Percentage of Athletes Graduate/

Professional Schools
Post Graduate School Scholarships

Public Relations

SAT Scores

Scholarships (4 Year)

Sports Information

Transcripts (Summary)

Transfer Students (Jr./Community Colleges)

Transfer Students (4 Year Institutions)

A RATING OF ATHLETIC-ACADEMIC BALANCE (Continued)

SUMMARY OF ATHLETIC-ACADEMIC BALANCE IN RANK ORDER

INSTITUTION	Rank	Score
HARVARD	1	4.92
PRINCETON	2	4.91
YALE	3	4.90
CORNELL (N.Y.)	4	4.89
PENNSYLVANIA	5	4.88
BROWN	6	4.87
DARTMOUTH	7	4.86
COLUMBIA (N.Y.)	8	4.85
STANFORD	9	4.84
NOTRE DAME	10	4.83
DUKE	11	4.82
MICHIGAN (Ann Arbor)	12	4.81
NORTHWESTERN (Evanston)	13	4.80
NAVY	14	4.79
RICE	15	4.78
VIRGINIA (Charlottesville)	16	4.75
AIR FORCE	17	4.73
ARMY (West Point)	18	4.72
VANDERBILT	19	4.68
WISCONSIN (Madison)	20	3.90
RUTGERS (New Brunswick)	21	3.89
COLGATE	22	3.88
BOSTON COLLEGE	23	3.87
THE CITADEL	24	3.86
V.M.I.	25	3.85
GEORGIA TECH	26	3.84
MIAMI (Ohio)	27	3.83
BOSTON U.	28	3.82
WILLIAM & MARY	29	3.81
UCLA	30	3.80
CALIFORNIA, BERKELEY	31	3.79
IOWA (Iowa City)	32	3.76
WAKE FOREST	33	3.75
INDIANA (Bloomington)	34	3.74
OREGON (Eugene)	35	3.73
PACIFIC (California)	36	3.72
UTAH (Salt Lake City)	37	3.70
PITTSBURGH (Pittsburgh)	38	3.68
IDAHO (Moscow)	39	3.66
TULSA	40	3.65
B.Y.U.	41	3.62
PURDUE (West Lafayette)	42	2.85

A RATING OF ATHLETIC-ACADEMIC BALANCE (Continued)

SUMMARY OF ATHLETIC-ACADEMIC BALANCE IN RANK ORDER

INSTITUTION	Rank	Score
SYRACUSE	43	2.83
OREGON STATE	44	2.82
SMU	45	2.80
TEXAS CHRISTIAN	46	2.77
MISSOURI (Columbia)	47	2.74
PENN STATE (University Park)	48	2.73
NORTH CAROLINA (Chapel Hill)	49	2.70
COLORADO STATE	50	2.66
OHIO U. (Athens)	51	2.65
MINNESOTA (Minneapolis)	52	2.63
WYOMING	53	2.59
NORTH TEXAS, U. OF	54	2.55
TEMPLE (Philadelphia)	55	2.52
BAYLOR	56	2.48
NEVADA (Reno)	57	2.45
HAWAII (Monoa)	58	2.41
UTAH STATE	59	2.37
AKRON	60	2.35
WESTERN MICHIGAN	61	2.31
BOWLING GREEN	62	2.26
CENTRAL MICHIGAN	63	2.24
BALL STATE	64	2.20
CONNECTICUT (Storrs)	65	2.18
USC	66	1.90
TEXAS (Austin)	67	1.88
MARYLAND (College Park)	68	1.86
WASHINGTON STATE	69	1.85
ARIZONA (Tucson)	70	1.83
NEBRASKA (Lincoln)	71	1.80
FLORIDA (Gainesville)	72	1.78
CLEMSON	73	1.77
OKLAHOMA (Norman)	74	1.76
KANSAS	75	1.73
TEXAS A&M (College Station)	76	1.72
ARIZONA STATE	77	1.69
WASHINGTON (Seattle)	78	1.66
LOUISVILLE	79	1.64
ILLINOIS (Urbana)	80	1.62
KENTUCKY	81	1.61
OHIO STATE (Columbus)	82	1.60
GEORGIA (Athens)	83	1.59
MICHIGAN STATE	84	1.58

A RATING OF ATHLETIC-ACADEMIC BALANCE (Continued)

SUMMARY OF ATHLETIC-ACADEMIC BALANCE IN RANK ORDER

INSTITUTION	Rank	Score
LSU (Baton Rouge)	85	1.56
TULANE	86	1.55
ALABAMA (Tuscaloosa)	87	1.52
WEST VIRGINIA	88	1.49
SOUTH CAROLINA (Columbia)	89	1.48
AUBURN (Auburn)	90	1.46
CINCINNATI	91	1.44
TEXAS TECH	92	1.42
MEMPHIS, U. OF	93	1.41
IOWA STATE (Ames)	94	1.40
MISSISSIPPI, U. OF	95	1.39
TENNESSEE (Knoxville)	96	1.37
NORTH CAROLINA STATE (Raleigh)	97	1.36
MISSISSIPPI STATE	98	1.35
HOUSTON	99	1.34
KANSAS STATE	100	1.33
VIRGINIA TECH & STATE U.	101	1.30
ARKANSAS (Fayetteville)	102	1.29
NEW MEXICO, U. OF	103	1.28
COLORADO (Boulder)	104	1.27
OKLAHOMA STATE	105	1.26
SOUTHERN MISSISSIPPI	106	1.25
SOUTHWESTERN LOUISIANA, U. OF	107	1.24
LOUISIANA TECH	108	1.23
NORTHERN ILLINOIS	109	1.22
EASTERN MICHIGAN	110	1.21
NEW MEXICO STATE	111	1.20
KENT STATE	112	1.19
TOLEDO	113	1.18
EAST CAROLINA	114	1.17
TEXAS (El Paso)	115	1.16
ARKANSAS STATE	116	1.15
MASSACHUSETTS (Amherst)	117	1.14
CALIFORNIA STATE U. (San Diego State)	118	1.13
GEORGIA SOUTHERN	119	1.12
CALIFORNIA STATE U. (San Jose State)	120	1.10
CALIFORNIS STATE U. (Fresno State)	121	1.08
FLORIDA STATE	122	1.07
CALIFORNIA STATE U. (Fullerton)	123	1.06
NEVADA (Las Vegas)	124	1.05
MIAMI (Florida)	125	1.03
CALIFORNIA STATE U. (Northridge)	126	1.01

A RATING OF COMPARATIVE COMPETITION
FOR FELLOWSHIPS/SCHOLARSHIPS BY STUDENTS
Leading Institutions

Forty-three institutions with scores in the 4.0-5.0 range, in rank order

INSTITUTION	Rank	Score	INSTITUTION	Rank	Score
HARVARD	1	4.90	JOHNS HOPKINS	23	4.40
PRINCETON	2	4.89	MINNESOTA (Minneapolis)	24	4.37
YALE	3	4.87	NORTH CAROLINA (Chapel Hill)	25	4.33
MICHIGAN (Ann Arbor)	4	4.84	U.S. AIR FORCE ACADEMY	26	4.32
STANFORD	5	4.80	ILLINOIS (Urbana)	27	4.30
PENNSYLVANIA	6	4.78	IOWA (Iowa City)	28	4.26
CORNELL (N.Y.)	7	4.77	BRANDEIS	29	4.25
CHICAGO	8	4.75	TEXAS (Austin)	30	4.23
M.I.T.	9	4.74	OHIO STATE (Columbus)	31	4.21
WISCONSIN (Madison)	10	4.70	VANDERBILT	32	4.19
CALIFORNIA, BERKELEY	11	4.67	ROCHESTER (N.Y.)	33	4.17
UCLA	12	4.63	SWARTHMORE	34	4.16
COLUMBIA (N.Y.)	13	4.61	AMHERST	35	4.15
NOTRE DAME	14	4.58	N.Y.U.	36	4.14
DUKE	15	4.56	WASHINGTON (St. Louis)	37	4.12
DARTMOUTH	16	4.54	WILLIAMS (Massachusetts)	38	4.10
NORTHWESTERN (Evanston)	17	4.53	TULANE	39	4.09
CAL TECH	18	4.52	POMONA (California)	40	4.08
CALIFORNIA, SAN DIEGO	19	4.50	OBERLIN	41	4.06
BROWN	20	4.47	HAVERFORD	42	4.02
INDIANA (Bloomington)	21	4.45	RICE	43	4.01
MICHIGAN STATE	22	4.42			

A RATING OF COUNSELING CENTERS
Leading Institutions

Fifty institutions with scores in the 4.0-5.0 range, in rank order

INSTITUTION	Rank	Score	INSTITUTION	Rank	Score
CHICAGO	1	4.81	STANFORD	26	4.38
PURDUE (Lafayette)	2	4.79	DENVER	27	4.37
PENNSYLVANIA	3	4.75	CALIFORNIA, BERKELEY	28	4.36
BOSTON U.	4	4.74	CUNY (City)	29	4.35
MICHIGAN STATE	5	4.73	BROWN	30	4.33
WAYNE STATE (Michigan)	6	4.72	YALE	31	4.31
MINNESOTA (Minneapolis)	7	4.68	CATHOLIC U. (D.C.)	32	4.30
N.Y.U.	8	4.66	NORTH CAROLINA (Chapel Hill)	33	4.29
BRANDEIS	9	4.65	RICE	34	4.27
PRINCETON	10	4.63	TULANE	35	4.25
OHIO STATE (Columbus)	11	4.62	UCLA	36	4.23
ILLINOIS (Urbana)	12	4.61	CASE WESTERN RESERVE	37	4.22
KANSAS	13	4.59	RUTGERS (New Brunswick)	38	4.21
DUKE	14	4.57	VANDERBILT	39	4.20
ROCHESTER (N.Y.)	15	4.53	U.S. NAVAL ACADEMY	40	4.18
NORTHWESTERN (Illinois)	16	4.52	IOWA (Iowa City)	41	4.17
SUNY (Buffalo)	17	4.51	TUFTS	42	4.16
PENN STATE (University Park)	18	4.50	WASHINGTON (St. Louis)	43	4.15
INDIANA (Bloomington)	19	4.49	PITTSBURGH (Pittsburgh)	44	4.14
BAYLOR	20	4.48	JOHNS HOPKINS	45	4.11
DARTMOUTH	21	4.46	CARNEGIE-MELLON	46	4.09
MICHIGAN (Ann Arbor)	22	4.44	OBERLIN	47	4.08
CORNELL (N.Y.)	23	4.43	REED (Oregon)	48	4.06
WISCONSIN (Madison)	24	4.41	CALIFORNIA, RIVERSIDE	49	4.05
TEMPLE (Philadelphia)	25	4.40	CALIFORNIA, SANTA BARBARA	50	4.03

A RATING OF CURRICULUM
Leading Institutions

Fifty-two institutions with scores in the 4.0-5.0 range, in rank order

INSTITUTION	Rank	Score	INSTITUTION	Rank	Score
PRINCETON	1	4.92	CALIFORNIA, SAN DIEGO	27	4.33
HARVARD	2	4.91	TEXAS (Austin)	28	4.31
MICHIGAN (Ann Arbor)	3	4.90	IOWA (Iowa City)	29	4.30
YALE	4	4.88	OHIO STATE (Columbus)	30	4.29
STANFORD	5	4.84	RUTGERS (New Brunswick)	31	4.28
CALIFORNIA, BERKELEY	6	4.78	WASHINGTON (St. Louis)	32	4.27
CHICAGO	7	4.76	RICE	33	4.26
WISCONSIN (Madison)	8	4.74	PURDUE (Lafayette)	34	4.25
UCLA	9	4.72	PENN STATE (University Park)	35	4.24
PENNSYLVANIA	10	4.70	ROCHESTER (N.Y.)	36	4.23
JOHNS HOPKINS	11	4.68	CALIFORNIA, SANTA BARBARA	37	4.22
COLUMBIA (N.Y.)	12	4.65	VIRGINIA (Charlottesville)	38	4.21
MINNESOTA (Minneapolis)	13	4.62	CARNEGIE-MELLON	39	4.20
M.I.T.	14	4.61	TULANE	40	4.19
NORTHWESTERN (Evanston)	15	4.60	CASE WESTERN RESERVE	41	4.18
CORNELL (N.Y.)	16	4.57	PITTSBURGH (Pittsburgh)	42	4.17
DARTMOUTH	17	4.54	CALIFORNIA, DAVIS	43	4.14
NOTRE DAME	18	4.52	BRANDEIS	44	4.12
INDIANA (Bloomington)	19	4.50	TUFTS	45	4.11
DUKE	20	4.47	WAYNE STATE (Detroit)	46	4.10
BROWN	21	4.45	VANDERBILT	47	4.08
N.Y.U.	22	4.43	MICHIGAN STATE	48	4.07
ILLINOIS (Urbana)	23	4.41	UTAH (Salt Lake City)	49	4.05
SUNY (Buffalo)	24	4.39	CALIFORNIA, RIVERSIDE	50	4.04
NORTH CAROLINA (Chapel Hill)	25	4.37	KANSAS	51	4.03
WASHINGTON (Seattle)	26	4.35	U.S. AIR FORCE ACADEMY	52	4.01

A RATING OF SELECTIVE
INTERCOLLEGIATE ATHLETIC DEPARTMENTS

A RATING OF SELECTIVE INTERCOLLEGIATE ATHLETIC DEPARTMENTS

THE GOURMAN REPORT evaluated and ranked all Division I, II, and III schools. For this report one hundred twenty-seven schools with scores in the 1.00-1.99 range, in rank order were selected.

RATING CATEGORIES	Numerical Range
Good	4.40-4.95
Acceptable Plus	4.01-4.39
Acceptable	3.00-3.99
Marginal	2.00-2.99
Unsatisfactory	1.00-1.99

INSTITUTION	Gourman Ranking	Gourman Score
MICHIGAN (Ann Arbor)	1	4.85
STANFORD	2	4.84
NOTRE DAME	3	4.83
DUKE	4	4.81
PRINCETON	5	4.79
PENNSYLVANIA	6	4.76
RICE	7	4.72
HARVARD	8	4.70
DARTMOUTH	9	4.68
CORNELL (N.Y.)	10	4.63
U.S. AIR FORCE ACADEMY	11	4.61
YALE	12	4.58
U.S. MILITARY ACADEMY	13	4.55
NORTHWESTERN (Evanston)	14	4.53
U.S. NAVAL ACADEMY	15	4.50
VIRGINIA (Charlottesville)	16	4.46
BROWN	17	4.42
VANDERBILT	18	4.41
COLUMBIA (N.Y.)	19	4.40
WISCONSIN (Madison)	20	4.30
RUTGERS (New Brunswick)	21	4.24
COLGATE	22	4.21
BOSTON COLLEGE	23	4.16
GEORGIA TECH	24	4.14
THE CITADEL	25	4.12
V.M.I.	26	4.11
MIAMI (Ohio)	27	4.08
BOSTON U.	28	4.06
WILLIAM & MARY	29	4.02
WAKE FOREST	30	3.78
CALIFORNIA, BERKELEY	31	3.75
IOWA (Iowa City)	32	3.72
UCLA	33	3.68
INDIANA (Bloomington)	34	3.66
OREGON (Eugene)	35	3.62

A RATING OF SELECTIVE INTERCOLLEGIATE ATHLETIC DEPARTMENTS
(Continued)

INSTITUTION	Gourman Ranking	Gourman Score
PACIFIC (California)	36	3.60
UTAH (Salt Lake City)	37	3.57
PITTSBURGH (Pittsburgh)	38	3.54
IDAHO (Moscow)	39	3.52
TULSA	40	3.51
B.Y.U.	41	3.46
PURDUE (West Lafayette)	42	3.40
MISSOURI (Columbia)	43	3.28
OREGON STATE	44	3.24
S.M.U.	45	3.20
TEXAS CHRISTIAN	46	3.15
SYRACUSE	47	2.91
PENN STATE (University Park)	48	2.88
NORTH CAROLINA (Chapel Hill)	49	2.85
COLORADO STATE	50	2.79
OHIO U.	51	2.75
MINNESOTA (Minneapolis)	52	2.72
WYOMING	53	2.71
NORTH TEXAS, U. OF	54	2.68
TEMPLE (Philadelphia)	55	2.66
BAYLOR	56	2.60
NEVADA (Reno)	57	2.55
HAWAII (Manoa)	58	2.51
UTAH STATE	59	2.46
AKRON	60	2.43
WESTERN MICHIGAN	61	2.39
BOWLING GREEN	62	2.33
CENTRAL MICHIGAN	63	2.27
BALL STATE	64	2.25
CONNECTICUT (Storrs)	65	2.18
USC	66	1.87
TEXAS (Austin)	67	1.85
MARYLAND (College Park)	68	1.83
WASHINGTON STATE	69	1.82
ARIZONA (Tucson)	70	1.80
NEBRASKA (Lincoln)	71	1.79
FLORIDA (Gainesville)	72	1.78
CLEMSON	73	1.77
OKLAHOMA (Norman)	74	1.75
KANSAS	75	1.74
TEXAS A&M	76	1.70
ARIZONA STATE	77	1.68
WASHINGTON (Seattle)	78	1.65
LOUISVILLE	79	1.63
ILLINOIS (Urbana)	80	1.61
KENTUCKY	81	1.59

INSTITUTION	Gourman Ranking	Gourman Score
OHIO STATE (Columbus)	82	1.58
GEORGIA (Athens)	83	1.57
MICHIGAN STATE	84	1.56
L.S.U. (Baton Rouge)	85	1.55
TULANE	86	1.54
ALABAMA (Tuscaloosa)	87	1.53
WEST VIRGINIA	88	1.52
SOUTH CAROLINA (Columbia)	89	1.51
AUBURN (Auburn)	90	1.49
CINCINNATI	91	1.48
TEXAS TECH	92	1.47
MEMPHIS, U. OF	93	1.46
IOWA STATE (Ames)	94	1.44
MISSISSIPPI, U. OF	95	1.42
TENNESSEE (Knoxville)	96	1.41
NORTH CAROLINA STATE	97	1.40
MISSISSIPPI STATE	98	1.39
HOUSTON	99	1.38
KANSAS STATE	100	1.37
VIRGINIA TECH & STATE U.	101	1.36
ARKANSAS (Fayetteville)	102	1.35
NEW MEXICO, U. OF	103	1.34
COLORADO (Boulder)	104	1.33
OKLAHOMA STATE	105	1.32
SOUTHERN MISSISSIPPI	106	1.31
SOUTHWESTERN LOUISIANA, U. OF	107	1.30
LOUISIANA TECH	108	1.29
NORTHRN ILLINOIS	109	1.28
EASTERN MICHIGAN	110	1.27
NEW MEXICO STATE	111	1.26
KENT STATE	112	1.25
TOLEDO	113	1.24
EAST CAROLINA	114	1.22
TEXAS (El Paso)	115	1.20
ARKANSAS STATE	116	1.19
MASSACHUSETTS (Amherst)	117	1.17
CALIFORNIA STATE U. (San Diego State)	118	1.15
GEORGIA SOUTHERN	119	1.14
CALIFORNIA STATE U. (San Jose State)	120	1.12
CALIFORNIA STATE U. (Fresno State)	121	1.11
FLORIDA STATE	122	1.09
CALIFORNIA STATE U. (Fullerton)	123	1.07
NEVADA (Las Vegas)	124	1.06
MIAMI (FLORIDA)	125	1.04
MAINE (Orono)	126	1.03
CALIFORNIA STATE U. (Northridge)	127	1.02

A RATING OF LIBRARIES
Leading Institutions

Thirty-three institutions with scores in the 4.0-5.0 range, in rank order

INSTITUTION	Rank	Score	INSTITUTION	Rank	Score
HARVARD	1	4.94	PENNSYLVANIA	18	4.51
YALE	2	4.91	NOTRE DAME	19	4.50
ILLINOIS (Urbana)	3	4.89	DUKE	20	4.45
COLUMBIA (N.Y.)	4	4.85	N.Y.U.	21	4.42
CORNELL (N.Y.)	5	4.83	JOHNS HOPKINS	22	4.38
MICHIGAN (Ann Arbor)	6	4.81	VIRGINIA (Charlottesville)	23	4.37
CALIFORNIA, BERKELEY	7	4.77	WASHINGTON (Seattle)	24	4.36
WISCONSIN (Madison)	8	4.74	LOUISIANA STATE (Baton Rouge)	25	4.35
STANFORD	9	4.73	NORTH CAROLINA (Chapel Hill)	26	4.32
UCLA	10	4.70	MICHIGAN STATE	27	4.30
CHICAGO	11	4.67	SYRACUSE	28	4.26
MINNESOTA (Minneapolis)	12	4.64	RUTGERS (New Brunswick)	29	4.23
INDIANA (Bloomington)	13	4.62	IOWA (Iowa City)	30	4.22
OHIO STATE (Columbus)	14	4.60	BROWN	31	4.18
TEXAS (Austin)	15	4.58	U.S. AIR FORCE ACADEMY	32	4.15
PRINCETON	16	4.57	PITTSBURGH (Pittsburgh)	33	4.12
NORTHWESTERN (Evanston)	17	4.52			

A RATING OF PUBLIC RELATIONS
Leading Institutions

Thirty-nine institutions with scores in the 4.0-5.0 range, in rank order

INSTITUTION	Rank	Score	INSTITUTION	Rank	Score
HARVARD	1	4.87	ROCHESTER (N.Y.)	21	4.35
PRINCETON	2	4.86	COLUMBIA (N.Y.)	22	4.34
CAL TECH	3	4.85	NORTH CAROLINA (Chapel Hill)	23	4.31
NOTRE DAME	4	4.84	N.Y.U.	24	4.27
DUKE	5	4.79	TUFTS	25	4.25
NORTHWESTERN (Evanston)	6	4.75	GEORGETOWN (D.C.)	26	4.23
RICE	7	4.73	BROWN	27	4.22
CORNELL (N.Y.)	8	4.72	AMHERST	28	4.21
DARTMOUTH	9	4.68	SUNY (Buffalo)	29	4.19
M.I.T.	10	4.65	GEORGIA TECH	30	4.18
MICHIGAN (Ann Arbor)	11	4.63	WASHINGTON (St. Louis)	31	4.17
BRANDEIS	12	4.58	CARNEGIE MELLON	32	4.15
JOHNS HOPKINS	13	4.55	UTAH (Salt Lake City)	33	4.13
YALE	14	4.52	OBERLIN	34	4.11
U.S. NAVAL ACADEMY	15	4.51	U.S. AIR FORCE ACADEMY	35	4.10
PENNSYLVANIA	16	4.49	HAVERFORD	36	4.08
CHICAGO	17	4.45	SWARTHMORE	37	4.07
ILLINOIS (Urbana)	18	4.40	RENSSELAER (N.Y.)	38	4.06
VANDERBILT	19	4.38	EMORY	39	4.05
COLGATE	20	4.36			

TRUSTEES/REGENTS STATE AND FEDERALLY SUPPORTED COLLEGES AND UNIVERSITIES NOT ON THE APPROVED LIST OF THE GOURMAN REPORT

ALABAMA	Not Approved	MONTANA	Not Approved
ALASKA	Not Approved	NEBRASKA	Not Approved
ARIZONA	Not Approved	NEVADA	Not Approved
ARKANSAS	Not Approved	NEW HAMPSHIRE	Not Approved
CALIFORNIA	Not Approved	NEW JERSEY	Not Approved
COLORADO	Not Approved	NEW MEXICO	Not Approved
CONNECTICUT	Not Approved	NEW YORK	Not Approved
DISTRICT OF COLUMBIA	Not Approved	NORTH CAROLINA	Not Approved
DELAWARE	Not Approved	NORTH DAKOTA	Not Approved
FLORIDA	Not Approved	OHIO	Not Approved
GEORGIA	Not Approved	OKLAHOMA	Not Approved
HAWAII	Not Approved	OREGON	Not Approved
IDAHO	Not Approved	PENNSYLVANIA	Not Approved
ILLINOIS	Not Approved	RHODE ISLAND	Not Approved
INDIANA	Not Approved	SOUTH CAROLINA	Not Approved
IOWA	Not Approved	SOUTH DAKOTA	Not Approved
KANSAS	Not Approved	TENNESSEE	Not Approved
KENTUCKY	Not Approved	TEXAS	Not Approved
LOUISIANA	Not Approved	UTAH	Not Approved
MAINE	Not Approved	VERMONT	Not Approved
MARYLAND	Not Approved	VIRGINIA	Not Approved
MASSACHUSETTS	Not Approved	WASHINGTON	Not Approved
MICHIGAN	Not Approved	WEST VIRGINIA	Not Approved
MINNESOTA	Not Approved	WISCONSIN	Not Approved
MISSISSIPPI	Not Approved	WYOMING	Not Approved
MISSOURI	Not Approved		

NOTE:

THE GOURMAN REPORT evaluated Trustees/Regents of State and Federally supported Colleges/Universities in each state with reference to a multi-dimensional study. The Regents/Trustees did not meet the high standards of THE GOURMAN REPORT and therefore were not approved.

TRUSTEES/REGENTS OF THE FOLLOWING PRIVATE COLLEGES AND UNIVERSITIES ON THE APPROVED LIST OF THE GOURMAN REPORT

STATE	INSTITUTION
UTAH	
VIRGINIA	College of William and Mary
	Washington and Lee University
WASHINGTON	Gonzaga University
	Pacific Lutheran University
	Seattle University
	University of Puget Sound
	Whitman College
WEST VIRGINIA	
WISCONSIN	Beloit College
	Marquette University
	Ripon College
WYOMING	

NOTE:

THE GOURMAN REPORT evaluated Trustees/Regents of Private Colleges/Universities in each state with reference to a multi-dimensional study. Institutions approved from the list did meet the high standards of THE GOURMAN REPORT.

The GOURMAN REPORT
PART VI

**A COMPARATIVE RATING OF SELECTIVE UNIVERSITY
ADMINISTRATIONS / REGENTS / TRUSTEES**

- California State University

- University of California

- City University of New York (CUNY)

- State University of New York (SUNY)

- Rutgers–The State University of New Jersey

A COMPARATIVE RATING OF SELECTIVE UNIVERSITY ADMINISTRATIONS/REGENTS/TRUSTEES

RATING CATEGORIES	Numerical Range
Strong	4.41-4.99
Good	4.01-4.40
Adequate	3.01-3.99
Marginal	2.01-2.99
Unsatisfactory	0.01-1.99

THE CALIFORNIA STATE UNIVERSITY

Gourman Overall Administration Rating

Gourman Overall Trustee / Regent Rating: 1.45

Institution	Administration Leadership Management	Academic-Athletic Balance[1]	Curriculum[2] (Overall Disciplines)	Faculty[3] (All Disciplines)	Faculty Morale
Bakersfield	1.53	Division II Omitted	3.04	3.19	1.72
Chico	1.41	Division II Omitted	3.05	3.18	1.70
Dominguez Hills	1.45	Division II Omitted	3.17	3.25	1.68
Fresno	1.46	1.08	3.25	3.30	1.73
Fullerton	1.40	1.06	3.24	3.29	1.74
Hayward	1.44	Division II Omitted	3.05	3.14	1.39
Humboldt	1.47	Division II Omitted	3.07	3.13	1.66
Long Beach	1.48	1.37	3.31	3.32	1.80
Los Angeles	1.50	Division II Omitted	3.28	3.31	1.73
Northridge	0.60	1.01	3.08	3.21	1.10
Pomona	0.70	Division II Omitted	3.11	3.17	1.30
Sacramento	1.61	1.41	3.19	3.28	1.67
San Bernardino	1.39	Division II Omitted	3.16	3.27	1.65
San Diego	0.61	1.13	3.18	3.33	1.11
San Francisco	1.60	Division II Omitted	3.20	3.34	1.64
San Jose	1.62	1.10	3.22	3.35	1.71

A COMPARATIVE RATING OF SELECTIVE UNIVERSITY
ADMINISTRATIONS/REGENTS/TRUSTEES (Continued)

RATING CATEGORIES	Numerical Range
Strong	4.41-4.99
Good	4.01-4.40
Adequate	3.01-3.99
Marginal	2.01-2.99
Unsatisfactory	0.01-1.99

THE CALIFORNIA STATE UNIVERSITY

Gourman Overall Administration Rating

Gourman Overall Trustee / Regent Rating: 1.45

Institution	Administration Leadership Management	Academic-Athletic Balance[1]	Curriculum[2] (Overall Disciplines)	Faculty[3] (All Disciplines)	Faculty Morale
San Luis Obispo	3.15	1.61	3.48	3.50	1.98
San Marcos	2.02	No Athletics	3.01	3.03	1.97
Sonoma	1.43	Division II Omitted	3.14	3.16	1.68
Stanislaus	1.42	Division II Omitted	3.15	3.20	1.60

[1] BA/BS degrees in education not approved and excluded from THE GOURMAN REPORT

[2] Department of Education undergraduate curriculum not approved and excluded from THE GOURMAN REPORT

[3] Faculty members of the Department of Education not approved and excluded from THE GOURMAN REPORT

A COMPARATIVE RATING OF SELECTIVE UNIVERSITY ADMINISTRATIONS/REGENTS/TRUSTEES (Continued)

RATING CATEGORIES	Numerical Range
Strong	4.41-4.99
Good	4.01-4.40
Adequate	3.01-3.99
Marginal	2.01-2.99
Unsatisfactory	0.01-1.99

THE CALIFORNIA STATE UNIVERSITY

Institution	Faculty Salaries	Image of Institution	Public Relations	Standards (Academic)
Bakersfield	Marginal	None 0.01	None 0.01	3.12
Chico	Marginal	None 0.01	None 0.01	3.13
Dominguez Hills	Marginal	None 0.01	None 0.01	3.17
Fresno	Marginal	2.01	2.12	3.19
Fullerton	Marginal	2.04	2.14	3.21
Hayward	Marginal	None 0.01	None 0.01	3.10
Humboldt	Marginal	None 0.01	None 0.01	3.09
Long Beach	Marginal	2.10	1.80	3.20
Los Angeles	Marginal	None 0.01	None 0.01	3.16
Northridge	Marginal	None 0.01	None 0.01	1.99
Pomona	Marginal	None 0.01	None 0.01	3.14
Sacramento	Marginal	2.11	2.13	3.22
San Bernardino	Marginal	None 0.01	None 0.01	3.18

A COMPARATIVE RATING OF SELECTIVE UNIVERSITY ADMINISTRATIONS/REGENTS/TRUSTEES (Continued)

RATING CATEGORIES	Numerical Range
Strong	4.41-4.99
Good	4.01-4.40
Adequate	3.01-3.99
Marginal	2.01-2.99
Unsatisfactory	0.01-1.99

THE CALIFORNIA STATE UNIVERSITY

Institution	Faculty Salaries	Image of Institution	Public Relations	Standards (Academic)
San Diego	Marginal	2.19	1.71	3.28
San Francisco	Marginal	2.18	2.16	3.29
San Jose	Marginal	2.25	2.18	3.27
San Luis Obispo	Marginal	3.30	3.22	3.52
San Marcos	Marginal	None 0.01	None 0.01	3.01
Sonoma	Marginal	None 0.01	None 0.01	3.11
Stanislaus	Marginal	None 0.01	None 0.01	3.10

A COMPARATIVE RATING OF SELECTIVE UNIVERSITY
ADMINISTRATIONS/REGENTS/TRUSTEES (Continued)

RATING CATEGORIES	Numerical Range
Strong	4.41-4.99
Good	4.01-4.40
Adequate	3.01-3.99
Marginal	2.01-2.99
Unsatisfactory	0.01-1.99

THE UNIVERSITY OF CALIFORNIA

Gourman Overall Administration Rating

Gourman Overall Trustee / Regent Rating: 1.50

Institution	Administration Leadership Management	Academic-Athletic Balance[1]	Curriculum[2] (Overall Disciplines)	Faculty[3] (All Disciplines)	Faculty Morale
Berkeley	2.14	3.79	4.39	4.56	1.91
Davis	2.28	Division II Omitted	4.37	4.54	1.88
Irvine	1.55	3.04	4.20	4.30	1.86
Los Angeles (UCLA)	2.08	3.80	4.38	4.53	1.84
Riverside	2.20	Division II Omitted	4.29	4.32	1.87
San Diego	2.27	Division III Omitted	4.36	4.52	1.90
San Francisco	3.18	No Athletics	4.35	4.55	1.87
Santa Barbara	2.02	3.02	4.33	4.34	1.78
Santa Cruz	2.12	Division III Omitted	4.24	4.27	1.77

[1] BA/BS degrees in education not approved and excluded from THE GOURMAN REPORT

[2] Department of Education undergraduate curriculum not approved and excluded from THE GOURMAN REPORT

[3] Faculty members of the Department of Education not approved and excluded from THE GOURMAN REPORT

A COMPARATIVE RATING OF SELECTIVE UNIVERSITY ADMINISTRATIONS/REGENTS/TRUSTEES (Continued)

RATING CATEGORIES	Numerical Range
Strong	4.41-4.99
Good	4.01-4.40
Adequate	3.01-3.99
Marginal	2.01-2.99
Unsatisfactory	0.01-1.99

THE UNIVERSITY OF CALIFORNIA

Institution	Faculty Salaries	Image of Institution	Public Relations	Standards (Academic)
Berkeley	Adequate	4.12	4.15	4.64
Davis	Adequate	4.10	4.16	4.62
Irvine	Adequate	3.09	3.08	4.38
Los Angeles (UCLA)	Adequate	4.09	3.89	4.61
Riverside	Adequate	4.02	3.71	4.40
San Diego	Adequate	4.11	3.73	4.60
San Francisco	Adequate	4.14	3.76	4.63
Santa Barbara	Adequate	3.19	4.05	4.59
Santa Cruz	Adequate	3.18	3.60	4.58

RATING CATEGORIES	Numerical Range
Strong	4.41-4.99
Good	4.01-4.40
Adequate	3.01-3.99
Marginal	2.01-2.99
Unsatisfactory	0.01-1.99

CITY UNIVERSITY OF NEW YORK (CUNY)

Gourman Overall Administration Rating

Gourman Overall Trustee / Regent Rating: 1.61

Institution	Administration Leadership Management	Academic-Athletic Balance[1]	Curriculum[2] (Overall Disciplines)	Faculty[3] (All Disciplines)	Faculty Morale
Bernard M. Baruch College	2.15	Division III Omitted	4.01	4.12	1.64
Brooklyn College	2.14	Division III Omitted	3.38	3.46	1.62
City College	2.13	Division III Omitted	3.39	3.43	1.50
Herbert H. Lehman College	2.12	Division III Omitted	3.28	3.20	1.48
Hunter College	2.11	Division III Omitted	3.37	4.02	1.49
Queens College	2.07	Division III Omitted	3.36	3.45	1.47

[1] BA/BS degrees in education not approved and excluded from THE GOURMAN REPORT

[2] Department of Education undergraduate curriculum not approved and excluded from THE GOURMAN REPORT

[3] Faculty members of the Department of Education not approved and excluded from THE GOURMAN REPORT

A COMPARATIVE RATING OF SELECTIVE UNIVERSITY ADMINISTRATIONS/REGENTS/TRUSTEES (Continued)

RATING CATEGORIES	Numerical Range
Strong	4.41-4.99
Good	4.01-4.40
Adequate	3.01-3.99
Marginal	2.01-2.99
Unsatisfactory	0.01-1.99

CITY UNIVERSITY OF NEW YORK (CUNY)

Institution	Faculty Salaries	Image of Institution	Public Relations	Standards (Academic)
Bernard M. Baruch College	Marginal	3.70	3.12	3.20
Brooklyn College	Marginal	3.60	3.10	3.15
City College	Marginal	3.55	3.08	3.14
Herbert H. Lehman College	Marginal	3.50	3.06	3.13
Hunter College	Marginal	3.69	3.11	3.17
Queens College	Marginal	3.68	3.09	3.12

A COMPARATIVE RATING OF SELECTIVE UNIVERSITY
ADMINISTRATIONS/REGENTS/TRUSTEES (Continued)

RATING CATEGORIES	Numerical Range
Strong	4.41-4.99
Good	4.01-4.40
Adequate	3.01-3.99
Marginal	2.01-2.99
Unsatisfactory	0.01-1.99

STATE UNIVERSITY OF NEW YORK (SUNY)

Gourman Overall Administration Rating

Gourman Overall Trustee / Regent Rating: 1.64

Institution	Administration Leadership Management	Academic-Athletic Balance[1]	Curriculum[2] (Overall Disciplines)	Faculty[3] (All Disciplines)	Faculty Morale
Albany	2.10	Division III Omitted	3.95	3.98	1.85
Binghampton	2.14	Division III Omitted	3.97	3.99	1.84
Buffalo	2.16	1.81	4.28	4.34	1.92
Stony Brook	2.01	Division III Omitted	4.27	4.33	1.93

[1] BA/BS degrees in education not approved and excluded from THE GOURMAN REPORT

[2] Department of Education undergraduate curriculum not approved and excluded from THE GOURMAN REPORT

[3] Faculty members of the Department of Education not approved and excluded from THE GOURMAN REPORT

A COMPARATIVE RATING OF SELECTIVE UNIVERSITY
ADMINISTRATIONS/REGENTS/TRUSTEES (Continued)

RATING CATEGORIES	Numerical Range
Strong	4.41-4.99
Good	4.01-4.40
Adequate	3.01-3.99
Marginal	2.01-2.99
Unsatisfactory	0.01-1.99

STATE UNIVERSITY OF NEW YORK (SUNY)

Institution	Faculty Salaries	Image of Institution	Public Relations	Standards (Academic)
Albany	Adequate	None 0.01	None 0.01	4.35
Binghamton	Adequate	None 0.01	None 0.01	4.34
Buffalo	Adequate	3.40	3.05	4.38
Stony Brook	Adequate	3.45	3.07	4.39

A COMPARATIVE RATING OF SELECTIVE UNIVERSITY
ADMINISTRATIONS/REGENTS/TRUSTEES (Continued)

RATING CATEGORIES	Numerical Range
Strong	4.41-4.99
Good	4.01-4.40
Adequate	3.01-3.99
Marginal	2.01-2.99
Unsatisfactory	0.01-1.99

RUTGERS – THE STATE UNIVERSITY OF NEW JERSEY

Gourman Overall Administration Rating

Gourman Overall Trustee / Regent Rating: 1.58

Institution	Administration Leadership Management	Academic-Athletic Balance[1]	Curriculum[2] (Overall Disciplines)	Faculty[3] (All Disciplines)	Faculty Morale
Rutgers – Camden	2.07	Division III Omitted	3.60	3.63	1.79
Rutgers – Newark	2.06	Division III Omitted	3.62	3.64	1.78
Rutgers – New Brunswick	1.95	3.89	4.03	4.26	1.65

[1] BA/BS degrees in education not approved and excluded from
THE GOURMAN REPORT

[2] Department of Education undergraduate curriculum not approved and excluded from
THE GOURMAN REPORT

[3] Faculty members of the Department of Education not approved and excluded from
THE GOURMAN REPORT

A COMPARATIVE RATING OF SELECTIVE UNIVERSITY ADMINISTRATIONS/REGENTS/TRUSTEES (Continued)

RATING CATEGORIES	Numerical Range
Strong	4.41-4.99
Good	4.01-4.40
Adequate	3.01-3.99
Marginal	2.01-2.99
Unsatisfactory	0.01-1.99

RUTGERS – THE STATE UNIVERSITY OF NEW JERSEY

Institution	Faculty Salaries	Image of Institution	Public Relations	Standards (Academic)
Rutgers – Camden	Good	None 0.01	None 0.01	3.40
Rutgers – Newark	Good	None 0.01	None 0.01	3.42
Rutgers – New Brunswick	Good	4.32	3.50	4.35

The GOURMAN REPORT
PART VII

A RATING OF THE TOP 50 UNDERGRADUATE SCHOOLS IN THE UNITED STATES

A RATING OF QUALITY INSTITUTIONS
Leading Institutions

Fifty institutions with scores in the 4.41-4.99 range, in rank order

INSTITUTION	Rank	Score	INSTITUTION	Rank	Score
PRINCETON	1	4.95	WASHINGTON (Seattle)	26	4.70
HARVARD	2	4.94	INDIANA (Bloomington)	27	4.69
MICHIGAN (Ann Arbor)	3	4.93	NORTH CAROLINA (Chapel Hill)	28	4.68
YALE	4	4.92	WASHINGTON (St. Louis)	29	4.67
STANFORD	5	4.91	SUNY (Buffalo)	30	4.66
CORNELL (N.Y.)	6	4.90	TUFTS	31	4.65
CALIFORNIA, BERKELEY	7	4.89	VANDERBILT	32	4.64
CHICAGO	8	4.88	TEXAS (Austin)	33	4.63
WISCONSIN (Madison)	9	4.87	OHIO STATE (Columbus)	34	4.62
UCLA	10	4.86	VIRGINIA (Charlottesville)	35	4.61
M.I.T.	11	4.85	CALIFORNIA, IRVINE	36	4.60
CAL TECH	12	4.84	PENN STATE (University Park)	37	4.59
COLUMBIA (N.Y.)	13	4.83	N.Y.U.	38	4.58
NORTHWESTERN (Evanston)	14	4.82	CALIFORNIA, DAVIS	39	4.57
PENNSYLVANIA	15	4.81	ROCHESTER (N.Y.)	40	4.56
NOTRE DAME	16	4.80	IOWA (Iowa City)	41	4.55
DUKE	17	4.79	GEORGIA TECH	42	4.54
BROWN	18	4.78	MICHIGAN STATE	43	4.53
JOHNS HOPKINS	19	4.77	PURDUE (Lafayette)	44	4.52
DARTMOUTH	20	4.76	TULANE	45	4.50
ILLINOIS (Urbana)	21	4.75	RUTGERS (New Brunswick)	46	4.48
MINNESOTA (Minneapolis)	22	4.74	SUNY (Stony Brook)	47	4.46
RICE	23	4.73	CALIFORNIA, SANTA BARBARA	48	4.45
CARNEGIE-MELLON	24	4.72	BRANDEIS	49	4.44
CALIFORNIA, SAN DIEGO	25	4.71	U.S. AIR FORCE ACADEMY	50	4.43

The GOURMAN REPORT
PART VIII

A RATING OF INTERNATIONAL UNIVERSITIES

Curriculum

Faculty

Universities

A RATING OF QUALITY CURRICULUM
(Effectiveness of Program)
(Biological Sciences, Engineering, Humanities, Physical Sciences and Social Sciences)

INTERNATIONAL UNIVERSITIES
Leading Institutions

Forty-four institutions with scores in the 4.0-5.0 range, in rank order

INSTITUTION	COUNTRY	Rank	Score
PARIS (All Campuses)	France	1	4.94
OXFORD	United Kingdom	2	4.93
CAMBRIDGE	United Kingdom	3	4.92
HEIDELBERG	Federal Republic of Germany	4	4.91
LYON I, II, III	France	5	4.90
MUNICH	Federal Republic of Germany	6	4.89
MONTPELLIER I, II, III	France	7	4.88
VIENNA	Austria	8	4.84
EDINBURGH	United Kingdom (Scotland)	9	4.83
GENEVA	Switzerland	10	4.82
BRUSSELS	Belgium	11	4.80
GÖTTINGEN	Federal Republic of Germany	12	4.78
ZURICH	Switzerland	13	4.77
AIX-MARSEILLE I, II, III	France	14	4.76
McGILL	Canada	15	4.75
BORDEAUX I, II, III	France	16	4.73
NANCY I, II	France	17	4.71
TUEBINGEN	Federal Republic of Germany	18	4.69
ERLANGEN-NURNBERG	Federal Republic of Germany	19	4.68
TORONTO	Canada	20	4.67
GRENOBLE I, II, III	France	21	4.64
MARBURG	Federal Republic of Germany	22	4.63
LILLE I, II, III	France	23	4.57
COLOGNE	Federal Republic of Germany	24	4.56
DIJON	France	25	4.55
RENNES I, II	France	26	4.54
TOULOUSE I, II, III	France	27	4.53
LONDON	United Kingdom	28	4.52
CLERMONT-FERRAND	France	29	4.48
BONN	Federal Republic of Germany	30	4.47
FRANKFURT	Federal Republic of Germany	31	4.44
POITIERS	France	32	4.42
NICE	France	33	4.38
HEBREW	Israel	34	4.34
LOUVAIN	Belgium	35	4.19
STOCKHOLM	Sweden	36	4.18
COPENHAGEN	Denmark	37	4.15
MUNSTER	Federal Republic of Germany	38	4.14
WÜRZBURG	Federal Republic of Germany	39	4.13
MAINZ	Federal Republic of Germany	40	4.11
AMSTERDAM	Netherlands	41	4.10
ROUEN	France	42	4.08
BOLOGNA	Italy	43	4.07
MADRID	Spain	44	4.05

A RATING OF QUALITY FACULTY

INTERNATIONAL UNIVERSITIES
Leading Institutions

Forty-nine institutions with scores in the 4.0-5.0 range, in rank order

INSTITUTION	COUNTRY	Rank	Score
PARIS (All Campuses)	France	1	4.94
OXFORD	United Kingdom	2	4.93
CAMBRIDGE	United Kingdom	3	4.92
HEIDELBERG	Federal Republic of Germany	4	4.90
MUNICH	Federal Republic of Germany	5	4.89
MONTPELLIER I, II, III	France	6	4.88
LYON I, II, III	France	7	4.87
LILLE I, II, III	France	8	4.86
EDINBURGH	United Kingdom (Scotland)	9	4.85
VIENNA	Austria	10	4.81
GENEVA	Switzerland	11	4.80
GÖTTINGEN	Federal Republic of Germany	12	4.78
ZURICH	Switzerland	13	4.76
AIX-MARSEILLE I, II, III	France	14	4.75
BORDEAUX I, II, III	France	15	4.72
BRUSSELS	Belgium	16	4.71
DIJON	France	17	4.68
NANCY I, II	France	18	4.65
TUEBINGEN	Federal Republic of Germany	19	4.62
TORONTO	Canada	20	4.60
ERLANGEN-NURNBERG	Federal Republic of Germany	21	4.59
GRENOBLE I, II, III	France	22	4.58
MARBURG	Federal Republic of Germany	23	4.50
McGILL	Canada	24	4.48
RENNES I, II	France	25	4.46
TOULOUSE I, II, III	France	26	4.44
LONDON	United Kingdom	27	4.43
CLERMONT-FERRAND	France	28	4.39
COLOGNE	Federal Republic of Germany	29	4.34
BONN	Federal Republic of Germany	30	4.33
ROUEN	France	31	4.31
NICE	France	32	4.30
FRANKFURT	Federal Republic of Germany	33	4.28
HEBREW	Israel	34	4.22
STOCKHOLM	Sweden	35	4.18
LOUVAIN	Belgium	36	4.16
MUNSTER	Federal Republic of Germany	37	4.14
MAINZ	Federal Republic of Germany	38	4.13
WÜRZBURG	Federal Republic of Germany	39	4.12
AMSTERDAM	Netherlands	40	4.11
BESANCON	France	41	4.10
CAEN	France	42	4.09
TOKYO	Japan	43	4.08
BOLOGNA	Italy	44	4.07
NANTES	France	45	4.06
ORLEANS	France	46	4.05
COPENHAGEN	Denmark	47	4.04
POITIERS	France	48	4.03
MADRID	Spain	49	4.02

A RATING OF QUALITY INSTITUTIONS

INTERNATIONAL UNIVERSITIES
Leading Institutions

Forty-nine institutions with scores in the 4.0-5.0 range, in rank order

INSTITUTION	COUNTRY	Rank	Score
PARIS (All Campuses)	France	1	4.95
OXFORD	United Kingdom	2	4.93
CAMBRIDGE	United Kingdom	3	4.92
HEIDELBERG	Federal Republic of Germany	4	4.91
MONTPELLIER I, II, III	France	5	4.90
MUNICH	Federal Republic of Germany	6	4.89
LYON I, II, III	France	7	4.88
LILLE I, II, III	France	8	4.86
EDINBURGH	United Kingdom (Scotland)	9	4.85
VIENNA	Austria	10	4.84
AIX-MARSEILLE I, II, III	France	11	4.83
GÖTTINGEN	Federal Republic of Germany	12	4.82
GENEVA	Switzerland	13	4.81
ZURICH	Switzerland	14	4.80
BORDEAUX I, II, III	France	15	4.78
BRUSSELS	Belgium	16	4.77
DIJON	France	17	4.75
NANCY I, II	France	18	4.73
TORONTO	Canada	19	4.72
TUEBINGEN	Federal Republic of Germany	20	4.70
ERLANGEN-NURNBERG	Federal Republic of Germany	21	4.69
GRENOBLE I, II, III	France	22	4.68
McGILL	Canada	23	4.67
MARBURG	Federal Republic of Germany	24	4.64
RENNES I, II	France	25	4.62
TOULOUSE I, II, III	France	26	4.61
LONDON	United Kingdom	27	4.60
CLERMONT-FERRAND	France	28	4.59
BONN	Federal Republic of Germany	29	4.55
COLOGNE	Federal Republic of Germany	30	4.54
NICE	France	31	4.52
ROUEN	France	32	4.51
FRANKFURT	Federal Republic of Germany	33	4.49
HEBREW	Israel	34	4.42
LOUVAIN	Belgium	35	4.40
MUNSTER	Federal Republic of Germany	36	4.33
STOCKHOLM	Sweden	37	4.32
MAINZ	Federal Republic of Germany	38	4.30
WÜRZBURG	Federal Republic of Germany	39	4.28
BESANCON	France	40	4.26
AMSTERDAM	Netherlands	41	4.24
CAEN	France	42	4.22
TOKYO	Japan	43	4.21
NANTES	France	44	4.18
BOLOGNA	Italy	45	4.16
ORLEANS	France	46	4.15
COPENHAGEN	Denmark	47	4.09
POITIERS	France	48	4.07
MADRID	Spain	49	4.06

The GOURMAN REPORT
PART IX

**A RATING OF
AMERICAN UNDERGRADUATE INSTITUTIONS
ON THE APPROVED LIST OF
THE GOURMAN REPORT**

OVERALL ACADEMIC RATING OF AMERICAN INSTITUTIONS

RATING CATEGORIES	Numerical Range
Strong	4.41-4.99
Good	4.01-4.40
Acceptable Plus	3.51-3.99
Adequate	3.01-3.50
Marginal	2.01-2.99

STATE AND INSTITUTION

INSTITUTION	Gourman Overall Academic Rating
ALABAMA	
Alabama Agricultural and Mechanical University	3.07
Alabama State University	2.81
Auburn University	3.96
Auburn University at Montgomery	3.48
Birmingham-Southern College ..	3.38
Huntingdon College	3.04
Jacksonville State University ...	2.96
Judson College	2.69
Livingston University	3.02
Miles College	2.86
Oakwood College	2.64
Samford University	3.41
Spring Hill College	3.44
Stillman College	2.29
Talladega College	2.25
Troy State University	3.46
Troy State University at Dothan .	3.09
Troy State University in Montgomery	3.15
Tuskegee University	3.31
University of Alabama	3.97
University of Alabama in Birmingham	3.92
University of Alabama in Huntsville	3.60
University of Mobile	3.10
University of Montevallo	3.40
University of North Alabama	3.58
University of South Alabama ...	3.70
ALASKA	
Alaska Pacific University	2.87
University of Alaska/Anchorage .	3.50
University of Alaska/Fairbanks ..	3.45
University of Alaska/Southeast ..	3.06

INSTITUTION	Gourman Overall Academic Rating
ARIZONA	
Arizona State University	4.03
Arizona State University West ..	3.60
Grand Canyon University	3.03
Northern Arizona University	3.57
Prescott College	2.99
University of Arizona	4.08
ARKANSAS	
Arkansas College	2.99
Arkansas State University	3.10
Arkansas Tech University	3.08
Harding University	3.03
Henderson State University	3.06
Hendrix College	3.04
John Brown University	2.70
Ouachita Baptist University	3.15
Philander Smith College	2.42
Southern Arkansas University ..	3.02
University of Arkansas at Fayetteville	3.97
University of Arkansas at Little Rock	3.54
University of Arkansas at Monticello	3.15
University of Arkansas at Pine Bluff	3.20
University of Central Arkansas ..	3.19
University of the Ozarks	2.91
CALIFORNIA	
Azusa Pacific University	3.03
Biola University	3.02
California Baptist College	2.67
California Institute of Technology	4.84
California Lutheran University ..	3.05
California Polytechnic State University/San Luis Obispo ..	3.69
California Polytechnic State University/Pomona	3.55

OVERALL ACADEMIC RATING OF AMERICAN INSTITUTIONS

STATE AND INSTITUTION

INSTITUTION	Gourman Overall Academic Rating
CALIFORNIA (Continued)	
California State University/ Bakersfield	3.53
California State University/Chico	3.54
California State University/ Dominguez Hills	3.62
California State University/Fresno	3.63
California State University/Fullerton	3.61
California State University/Hayward	3.58
California State University/ Long Beach	3.56
California State University/ Los Angeles	3.59
California State University/ Northridge	3.60
California State University/ Sacramento	3.64
California State University/ San Bernardino	3.65
California State University/ San Marcos	3.27
California State University/ Stanislaus	3.29
Chapman College	3.05
Claremont McKenna College	4.00
College of Notre Dame	3.01
Dominican College of San Rafael	3.06
Golden Gate University	3.09
Harvey Mudd College	3.89
Holy Names College	2.90
Humboldt State University	3.57
Loma Linda University	3.61
Loyola Marymount University	3.52
Mills College	3.16
Mount St. Mary's College	3.04
Occidental College	3.50
Pepperdine University	3.26
Pitzer College	3.40
Point Loma Nazarene College	2.73
Pomona College	4.01
Saint Mary's College of California	3.49
San Diego State University	3.66
San Francisco State University	3.67
San Jose State University	3.68
Santa Clara University	3.64

INSTITUTION	Gourman Overall Academic Rating
CALIFORNIA (Continued)	
Scripps College	3.27
Sonoma State University	3.30
Southern California College	2.81
Stanford University	4.91
United States International University	3.11
University of California, Berkeley	4.89
University of California/Davis	4.57
University of California/Irvine	4.60
University of California/Los Angeles	4.86
University of California/Riverside	4.33
University of California/San Diego	4.71
University of California/ Santa Barbara	4.45
University of California/Santa Cruz	4.11
University of La Verne	3.13
University of the Pacific	3.81
University of Redlands	3.40
University of San Diego	3.12
University of San Francisco	3.47
University of Southern California	3.95
Westmont College	2.86
Whittier College	3.00
COLORADO	
Adams State College	3.15
Colorado College	3.18
Colorado School of Mines	4.20
Colorado State University	3.58
Fort Lewis College	3.22
Mesa State College	3.02
Metropolitan State College	3.12
Regis University	3.06
United States Air Force Academy	4.43
University of Colorado at Boulder	3.99
University of Colorado at Colorado Springs	3.30
University of Colorado at Denver	3.54
University of Denver	3.90
University of Northern Colorado	3.30
University of Southern Colorado	3.26
Western State College of Colorado	3.12

OVERALL ACADEMIC RATING OF AMERICAN INSTITUTIONS

RATING CATEGORIES	Numerical Range
Strong	4.41-4.99
Good	4.01-4.40
Acceptable Plus	3.51-3.99
Adequate	3.01-3.50
Marginal	2.01-2.99

STATE AND INSTITUTION

INSTITUTION	Gourman Overall Academic Rating
CONNECTICUT	
Albertus Magnus College	2.88
Central Connecticut State University	3.14
Connecticut College	3.11
Eastern Connecticut State University	3.12
Fairfield University	3.04
Quinnipiac College	3.20
Sacred Heart University	3.03
Saint Joseph College	2.96
Southern Connecticut State University	3.16
Trinity College	3.62
United States Coast Guard Academy	3.41
University of Bridgeport	3.48
University of Connecticut	3.94
University of Connecticut at Avery Point	3.02
University of Connecticut at Hartford	3.05
University of Connecticut at Stamford	3.13
University of Connecticut at Waterbury	3.01
University of Hartford	3.56
University of New Haven	3.21
Wesleyan University	3.63
Western Connecticut State University	3.33
Yale University	4.92
DELAWARE	
Delaware State College	2.83
University of Delaware	3.95
DISTRICT OF COLUMBIA	
The American University	3.87
Catholic University of America ..	3.97

INSTITUTION	Gourman Overall Academic Rating
DISTRICT OF COLUMBIA (Continued)	
Gallaudet College	3.14
Georgetown University	4.15
The George Washington University	3.96
Howard University	3.78
Mount Vernon College	2.88
Trinity College	3.02
University of the District of Columbia	3.04
FLORIDA	
Barry University	3.03
Bethune-Cookman College	2.67
Eckerd College	3.22
Edward Waters College	2.86
Flagler College	2.73
Florida Agricultural and Mechanical University	3.19
Florida Atlantic University	3.26
Florida Institute of Technology ..	3.14
Florida International University ..	3.21
Florida Memorial College	2.70
Florida Southern College	2.93
Florida State University	3.91
Jacksonville University	3.26
Nova Southeastern University ..	3.15
Palm Beach Atlantic College ...	2.85
Rollins College	3.20
Saint Leo College	2.87
Saint Thomas University	2.95
Stetson University	3.17
University of Central Florida	3.36
University of Florida	3.98
University of Miami	3.76
University of North Florida	3.20
University of South Florida	3.37
University of South Florida – New College	3.12
University of Tampa	3.18
University of West Florida	3.16

OVERALL ACADEMIC RATING OF AMERICAN INSTITUTIONS

STATE AND INSTITUTION

INSTITUTION	Gourman Overall Academic Rating
GEORGIA	
Agnes Scott College	3.08
Albany State College	3.01
Armstrong State College	3.02
Augusta College	2.93
Berry College	2.90
Brenau University	3.00
Clark Atlanta University	2.96
Columbus College	2.89
Emory University	4.36
Fort Valley State College	2.82
Georgia College	2.85
Georgia Institute of Technology	4.54
Georgia Southern University	3.09
Georgia Southwestern College	2.88
Georgia State University	3.35
Kennesaw State College	2.86
LaGrange College	2.92
Mercer University	3.15
Mercer University, Cecil B. Day Campus	3.03
Morehouse College	3.04
Morris Brown College	2.73
North Georgia College	2.83
Oglethorpe University	3.14
Paine College	2.57
Piedmont College	2.58
Savannah State College	2.79
Shorter College	2.98
Spelman College	2.62
University of Georgia	3.97
Valdosta State University	3.06
Wesleyan College	2.87
West Georgia College	2.99
GUAM	
University of Guam	2.87
HAWAII	
Brigham Young University/ Hawaii Campus	2.70
Chaminade University of Honolulu	2.78
Hawaii Pacific University	2.66
University of Hawaii – West Oahu	3.01
University of Hawaii at Hilo	3.02
University of Hawaii at Manoa	3.84

INSTITUTION	Gourman Overall Academic Rating
IDAHO	
Albertson College	3.10
Boise State University	3.18
Idaho State University	3.21
Lewis-Clark State College	3.02
Northwest Nazarene College	2.95
University of Idaho	3.90
ILLINOIS	
Augustana College	3.11
Aurora University	3.05
Barat College	3.06
Blackburn College	2.94
Bradley University	3.39
Chicago State University	3.16
College of St. Francis	2.84
Concordia University	2.93
De Paul University	3.68
Eastern Illinois University	3.67
Elmhurst College	3.01
Eureka College	2.96
Greenville College	2.88
Illinois College	2.76
Illinois Institute of Technology	3.30
Illinois State University	3.45
Illinois Wesleyan University	3.07
Judson College	2.66
Knox College	3.10
Lake Forest College	3.09
Lewis University	2.90
Loyola University–Chicago	3.84
MacMurray College	2.79
McKendree College	2.73
Millikin University	2.92
Monmouth College	3.04
Mundelein College	3.00
North Central College	2.93
Northeastern Illinois University	3.14
Northern Illinois University	3.40
Northwestern University	4.82
Olivet Nazarene University	2.85
Principia College	2.83
Quincy University	2.90
Rockford College	3.12
Roosevelt University	3.16
Rosary College	3.03

OVERALL ACADEMIC RATING OF AMERICAN INSTITUTIONS

RATING CATEGORIES	Numerical Range
Strong	4.41-4.99
Good	4.01-4.40
Acceptable Plus	3.51-3.99
Adequate	3.01-3.50
Marginal	2.01-2.99

STATE AND INSTITUTION

INSTITUTION	Gourman Overall Academic Rating
ILLINOIS (Continued)	
Saint Xavier University	2.70
Sangamon State University	3.07
Southern Illinois University at Carbondale	3.80
Southern Illinois University at Edwardsville	3.30
The University of Chicago	4.88
University of Illinois at Chicago ..	3.82
University of Illinois at Urbana-Champaign	4.75
Western Illinois University	3.38
Wheaton College	3.13
INDIANA	
Anderson University	3.08
Ball State University	3.46
Bethel College	3.05
Butler University	3.39
Calumet College of St. Joseph ..	2.88
Depauw University	3.49
Earlham College	3.42
Franklin College of Indiana	3.09
Goshen College	3.04
Grace College	2.86
Hanover College	3.06
Huntington College	2.87
Indiana Institute of Technology ..	2.95
Indiana State University	3.20
Indiana University/Bloomington .	4.69
Indiana University East	3.07
Indiana University Kokomo	3.03
Indiana University Northwest ...	3.11
Indiana University–Purdue University at Fort Wayne	3.47
Indiana University–Purdue University Indianapolis	3.51

INSTITUTION	Gourman Overall Academic Rating
INDIANA (Continued)	
Indiana University South Bend ..	3.28
Indiana University Southeast ...	3.16
Manchester College	3.10
Marian College	2.92
Oakland City College	2.68
Purdue University	4.52
Purdue University Calmuet	3.30
Purdue University North Central .	3.13
Rose-Hulman Institute of Technology	3.35
Saint Francis College	2.77
Saint Joseph's College	3.14
Saint Mary-of-the-Woods College	3.02
Saint Mary's College	3.21
Taylor University	2.96
Tri-State University	3.15
University of Evansville	3.22
University of Indianapolis	3.17
University of Notre Dame	4.80
Valparaiso University	3.46
Wabash College	3.29
IOWA	
Briar Cliff College	3.04
Buena Vista College	3.05
Central College	2.89
Clarke College	3.06
Coe College	3.03
Cornell College	3.17
Dordt College	2.90
Drake University	3.42
Graceland College	2.96
Grand View College	2.83
Grinnell College	3.30
Iowa State University	4.30
Iowa Wesleyan College	3.08
Loras College	3.09

STATE AND INSTITUTION

INSTITUTION	Gourman Overall Academic Rating
IOWA (Continued)	
Luther College	3.10
Morningside College	3.06
Mount Mercy College	2.78
Northwestern College	2.85
St. Ambrose University	3.12
Simpson College	3.14
Teikyo Marycrest University	2.80
Teikyo Westmar University	2.86
University of Dubuque	3.20
University of Iowa	4.55
University of Northern Iowa	3.28
Upper Iowa University	3.00
Wartburg College	2.93
William Penn College	2.91
KANSAS	
Baker University	3.10
Benedictine College	2.90
Bethany College	2.91
Bethel College	2.80
Emporia State University	3.25
Fort Hays State University	3.15
Friends University	3.10
Kansas Newman College	2.73
Kansas State University	3.93
Kansas Wesleyan University	3.04
McPherson College	3.02
Mid-America Nazarene College	2.88
Ottawa University	3.06
Pittsburg State University	3.08
Saint Mary College	2.66
Southwestern College	2.84
Sterling College	2.98
Tabor College	3.07
University of Kansas	4.34
Washburn University of Topeka	3.32
Wichita State University	3.29
KENTUCKY	
Asbury College	2.80
Bellarmine College	2.98
Berea College	3.05
Brescia College	2.79
Campbellsville College	2.94
Centre College	3.06

INSTITUTION	Gourman Overall Academic Rating
KENTUCKY (Continued)	
Cumberland College	2.88
Eastern Kentucky University	3.22
Georgetown College	2.97
Kentucky State University	3.09
Kentucky Wesleyan College	2.74
Morehead State University	3.16
Murray State University	3.17
Northern Kentucky University	3.13
Pikeville College	2.70
Spalding University	2.95
Thomas More College	2.92
Transylvania University	2.98
Union College	2.72
University of Kentucky	3.90
University of Louisville	3.62
Western Kentucky University	3.44
LOUISIANA	
Centenary College of Louisiana	3.15
Dillard University	3.01
Grambling State University	2.96
Louisiana College	2.97
Louisiana State University and Agricultural & Mechanical College	3.98
Louisiana State University in Shreveport	3.31
Louisiana Tech University	3.23
Loyola University/New Orleans	3.27
McNeese State University	3.16
Nicholls State University	3.20
Northeast Louisiana University	3.17
Northwestern State University of Louisiana	3.13
Our Lady of Holy Cross College	2.75
Southeastern Louisiana University	3.11
Southern University & A&M College	3.05
Southern University at New Orleans	2.70
Tulane University	4.50
University of New Orleans	3.31
University of Southwestern Louisiana	3.22
Xavier University of Louisiana	3.02
MAINE	
Bates College	3.28
Bowdoin College	3.30

OVERALL ACADEMIC RATING OF AMERICAN INSTITUTIONS

RATING CATEGORIES	Numerical Range
Strong	4.41-4.99
Good	4.01-4.40
Acceptable Plus	3.51-3.99
Adequate	3.01-3.50
Marginal	2.01-2.99

STATE AND INSTITUTION

INSTITUTION	Gourman Overall Academic Rating
MAINE (Continued)	
Colby College	3.15
Saint Joseph's College	2.80
University of Maine	3.90
University of Maine at Augusta ..	2.80
University of Maine at Farmington	3.16
University of Maine at Fort Kent .	3.14
University of Maine at Machias ..	3.13
University of Maine at Presque Isle	3.19
University of New England	3.04
University of Southern Maine ...	3.06
MARYLAND	
Bowie State University	2.80
College of Notre Dame of Maryland	3.01
Columbia Union College	2.63
Coppin State College	2.85
Frostburg State University	3.13
Goucher College	3.10
Hood College	2.97
Johns Hopkins University	4.77
Loyola College	3.11
Morgan State University	2.90
Mount St. Mary's College	2.93
St. John's College	3.15
St. Mary's College of Maryland ..	2.84
Salisbury State University	3.18
Towson State University	3.17
United States Naval Academy ..	4.36
University of Baltimore	3.12
University of Maryland Baltimore County	3.14
University of Maryland College Park	4.01
University of Maryland Eastern Shore	3.03
University of Maryland University College	3.20

INSTITUTION	Gourman Overall Academic Rating
MARYLAND (Continued)	
Washington College	3.02
Western Maryland College	3.09
MASSACHUSETTS	
American International College .	3.15
Amherst College	4.14
Anna Maria College	2.87
Assumption College	2.85
Atlantic Union College	2.82
Boston College	3.88
Boston University	4.03
Bradford College	2.75
Brandeis University	4.44
Bridgewater State College	3.23
Clark University	3.85
College of the Holy Cross	3.68
Curry College	2.77
Eastern Nazarene College	2.78
Elms College	2.81
Emerson College	2.86
Emmanuel College	2.85
Fitchburg State College	3.17
Framingham State College	3.18
Gordon College	2.79
Hampshire College	2.75
Harvard University–Harvard and Radcliffe Colleges	4.94
Massachusetts Institute of Technology	4.85
Merrimack College	3.02
Mount Holyoke College	3.89
North Adams State College	3.04
Northeastern University	3.44
Pine Manor College	2.71
Regis College	2.90
Salem State College	3.11
Simmons College	3.20

STATE AND INSTITUTION

INSTITUTION	Gourman Overall Academic Rating
MASSACHUSETTS (Continued)	
Simon's Rock of Bard College ..	2.80
Smith College	3.90
Springfield College	3.12
Stonehill College	3.00
Suffolk University	3.40
Tufts University	4.65
University of Massachusetts Amherst	3.91
University of Massachusetts Boston	3.26
University of Massachusetts Dartmouth	3.18
University of Massachusetts Lowell	3.39
Wellesley College	3.60
Western New England College ..	3.06
Westfield State College	3.07
Wheaton College	3.03
Williams College	3.91
Worcester Polytechnic Institute .	3.41
Worcester State College	3.28
MICHIGAN	
Adrian College	2.90
Albion College	2.91
Alma College	3.01
Andrews University	2.82
Aquinas College	2.76
Calvin College	3.03
Central Michigan University	3.27
Concordia College	2.75
Eastern Michigan University	3.26
Ferris State University	3.35
GMI Engineering and Management Institute	3.41
Grand Valley State University ...	3.05
Hillsdale College	2.94
Hope College	2.77
Kalamazoo College	3.10
Lake Superior State University ..	3.07
Lawrence Technological University	3.15
Madonna University	2.75
Marygrove College	2.70
Michigan State University	4.53
Michigan Technological University	3.56

INSTITUTION	Gourman Overall Academic Rating
MICHIGAN (Continued)	
Northern Michigan University ...	3.13
Oakland University	3.80
Olivet College	2.96
Saginaw Valley State University .	3.04
Saint Mary's College	2.69
Siena Heights College	2.99
Spring Arbor College	2.95
University of Detroit Mercy	3.80
University of Michigan/Ann Arbor	4.93
University of Michigan/Dearborn	3.66
University of Michigan/Flint	3.60
Wayne State University	4.11
Western Michigan University ...	3.54
MINNESOTA	
Augsburg College	2.95
Bemidji State University	3.11
Bethel College	2.80
Carleton College	3.33
College of St. Benedict	2.90
College of St. Catherine	3.04
College of St. Scholastica	2.90
Concordia College/Moorhead ...	2.77
Concordia College/St. Paul	2.74
Gustavus Adolphus College	3.10
Hamline University	3.28
Macalester College	3.31
Mankato State University	3.14
Moorhead State University	3.16
Northwestern College	2.69
St. Cloud State University	3.17
Saint John's University	3.18
Saint Mary's College of Minnesota	2.88
St. Olaf College	3.03
Southwest State University	3.08
University of Minnesota/Crookston	3.07
University of Minnesota/Duluth ..	3.66
University of Minnesota/Morris ..	3.59
University of Minnesota/Twin Cities	4.74
University of St. Thomas	3.22
Winona State University	3.29
MISSISSIPPI	
Alcorn State University	2.85
Belhaven College	2.80

OVERALL ACADEMIC RATING OF AMERICAN INSTITUTIONS

RATING CATEGORIES	Numerical Range
Strong	4.41-4.99
Good	4.01-4.40
Acceptable Plus	3.51-3.99
Adequate	3.01-3.50
Marginal	2.01-2.99

STATE AND INSTITUTION

INSTITUTION	Gourman Overall Academic Rating	INSTITUTION	Gourman Overall Academic Rating
MISSISSIPPI (Continued)		**MISSOURI (Continued)**	
Blue Mountain College	2.62	Southeast Missouri State University	3.15
Delta State University	2.84	Southwest Baptist University ...	2.84
Jackson State University	2.94	Southwest Missouri State Universiy	3.23
Millsaps College	3.09	Stephens College	3.16
Mississippi College	2.96	University of Missouri/Columbia .	4.38
Mississippi State University	3.66	University of Missouri/Kansas City	3.70
Mississippi University for Women	3.01	University of Missouri/Rolla	3.61
Mississippi Valley State University	2.86	University of Missouri/St. Louis .	3.60
Rust College	2.60	Washington University	4.67
Tougaloo College	2.58	Webster University	3.06
University of Mississippi	3.78	Westminster College	2.96
University of Southern Mississippi	3.31	William Jewell College	2.82
William Carey College	2.98	William Woods University	2.81
MISSOURI		**MONTANA**	
Avila College	2.81	Carroll College	3.01
Central Methodist College	2.72	College of Great Falls	3.02
Central Missouri State University	3.06	Eastern Montana College	3.05
Columbia College	2.73	Montana College of Mineral Science	
Culver-Stockton College	2.95	and Technology	3.38
Drury College	2.94	Montana State University	3.50
Evangel College	2.83	Northern Montana College	3.03
Fontbonne College	2.86	Rocky Mountain College	3.00
Lincoln University	2.75	University of Montana	3.65
Lindenwood College	2.92	Western Montana College	
Maryville University of Saint Louis	2.75	of the University of Montana .	2.97
Missouri Baptist College	2.78		
Missouri Southern State College	3.05	**NEBRASKA**	
Missouri Valley College	2.79	Bellevue College	2.83
Missouri Western State College .	3.07	Chadron State College	3.08
Northeast Missouri State University	3.10	College of Saint Mary	2.75
Northwest Missouri State University	3.21	Concordia College	2.87
Park College	2.85	Creighton University	3.76
Rockhurst College	3.04	Dana College	2.87
Saint Louis University	3.88	Doane College	2.85
School of the Ozarks	2.91		

STATE AND INSTITUTION

INSTITUTION	Gourman Overall Academic Rating
NEBRASKA (Continued)	
Hastings College	3.04
Midland Lutheran College	2.80
Nebraska Wesleyan University	3.02
Peru State College	3.05
Union College	2.88
University of Nebraska at Lincoln	3.95
University of Nebraska at Kearney	3.14
University of Nebraska at Omaha	3.43
Wayne State College	3.06
NEVADA	
University of Nevada/Las Vegas	3.20
University of Nevada/Reno	3.40
NEW HAMPSHIRE	
Colby-Sawyer College	2.87
Dartmouth College	4.76
Franklin Pierce College	3.03
Keene State College	3.18
New England College	3.04
Notre Dame College	2.85
Plymouth State College of the University System of New Hampshire	3.20
Rivier College	2.96
St. Anselm College	3.07
University of New Hampshire	3.80
University of New Hampshire at Manchester	3.10
NEW JERSEY	
Bloomfield College	2.86
Caldwell College	2.91
Centenary College	2.82
College of Saint Elizabeth	2.76
Drew University	3.31
Fairleigh Dickinson University, Florham-Madison Campus	3.34
Fairleigh Dickinson University, Teaneck-Hackensack Campus	3.27
Felician College	2.81
Georgian Court College	2.88
Jersey City State College	3.16
Kean College of New Jersey	3.20
Monmouth College	3.12
Monclair State College	3.14

INSTITUTION	Gourman Overall Academic Rating
NEW JERSEY (Continued)	
New Jersey Institute of Technology	3.18
Princeton University	4.95
Ramapo College of New Jersey	3.04
The Richard Stockton College of New Jersey	3.17
Rider College	3.05
Rowan College of New Jersey	3.22
Rutgers University/Camden	3.23
Rutgers University/Newark	3.24
Rutgers University/New Brunswick	4.48
Saint Peter's College	3.06
Seton Hall University	3.15
Stevens Institute of Technology	3.80
Thomas A. Edison State College	3.11
Trenton State College	3.25
Upsala College	3.10
William Paterson College of New Jersey	3.17
NEW MEXICO	
College of Santa Fe	2.95
College of the Southwest	2.76
Eastern New Mexico University	3.13
New Mexico Highlands University	3.02
New Mexico Institute of Mining and Technology	3.30
New Mexico State University	3.44
St. John's College	3.01
University of New Mexico	3.78
Western New Mexico University	3.15
NEW YORK	
Adelphi University	3.10
Alfred University	3.52
Bard College	3.11
Barnard College	3.57
Canisius College	3.08
City University of New York/ Baruch College	3.40
City University of New York/ Brooklyn College	3.41
City University of New York/ City College	3.42
City University of New York/ College of Staten Island	3.09

OVERALL ACADEMIC RATING OF AMERICAN INSTITUTIONS

RATING CATEGORIES	Numerical Range
Strong	4.41-4.99
Good	4.01-4.40
Acceptable Plus	3.51-3.99
Adequate	3.01-3.50
Marginal	2.01-2.99

STATE AND INSTITUTION

INSTITUTION	Gourman Overall Academic Rating
NEW YORK (Continued)	
City University of New York/ Herbert H. Lehman College . .	3.39
City University of New York/ Hunter College	3.38
City University of New York/ John Jay College of Criminal Justice	3.47
City University of New York/ Medgar Evers College	3.03
City University of New York/ Queens College	3.44
City University of New York/ York College	3.12
Clarkson University	3.60
Colgate University	4.11
College of Mount Saint Vincent .	2.91
College of New Rochelle	2.90
College of Saint Rose	2.87
Columbia University	4.83
Concordia College	2.74
Cooper Union	3.70
Cornell University	4.90
Daemen College	2.79
Dominican College of Blauvelt . .	2.75
Dowling College	2.81
D'Youville College	2.71
Elmira College	2.86
Eugene Lang College – New School for Social Research . .	3.07
Fordham University	4.02
Hamilton College	3.45
Hartwick College	3.09
Hobart College	3.23
Hofstra University	3.50
Houghton College	2.93
Iona College	2.87

INSTITUTION	Gourman Overall Academic Rating
NEW YORK (Continued)	
Ithaca College	3.04
Keuka College	2.63
King's College	2.76
Le Moyne College	2.94
Long Island University/ Brooklyn Campus	3.18
Long Island University/ C.W. Post Campus	3.27
Long Island University/ Southhamton Campus	2.88
Manhattan College	3.19
Manhattanville College	3.03
Marist College	2.80
Marymount College Tarrytown . .	2.94
Marymount Manhattan College .	2.76
Medaille College	2.69
Mercy College	2.86
Molloy College	2.68
Mount Saint Mary College	2.66
Nazareth College of Rochester .	2.92
New York Institute of Technology	3.00
New York University	4.58
Niagara University	3.09
Nyack College	2.78
Pace University	3.06
Pace University at Pleasantville/ Briarcliff	3.01
Polytechnic University (Brooklyn)	3.91
Polytechnic University, (Farmdale)	3.22
Pratt Institute	3.79
Rensselaer Polytechnic Institute	4.38
Roberts Wesleyan College	2.77
Rochester Institute of Technology	3.12
Russell Sage College	3.17
St. Bonaventure University	2.90
St. Francis College	2.62

STATE AND INSTITUTION

INSTITUTION	Gourman Overall Academic Rating
NEW YORK (Continued)	
St. John Fisher College	2.94
St. John's University	3.20
St. Joseph's College, New York	2.97
St. Joseph's College Sulfolk Campus	2.93
St. Lawrence University	3.51
St. Thomas Aquinas College	2.64
Sarah Lawrence College	3.52
Siena College	2.65
Skidmore College	3.60
State University of New York at Albany	4.01
State University of New York at Binghamton	4.03
State University of New York at Buffalo	4.66
State University of New York at Stony Brook	4.46
State University of New York/ College at Brockport	3.26
State University of New York/ College at Buffalo	3.38
State University of New York/ College at Cortland	3.35
State University of New York/ College at Fredonia	3.30
State University of New York/ College at Geneseo	3.33
State University of New York/ College at New Paltz	3.37
State University of New York/ College at Old Westbury	3.28
State University of New York/ College at Oneonta	3.34
State University of New York/ College at Oswego	3.36
State University of New York/ College at Plattsburgh	3.29
State University of New York/ College at Potsdam	3.27
State University of New York at Purchase	2.97
State University of New York/ College of Environmental Science and Forestry, Syracuse	3.90

INSTITUTION	Gourman Overall Academic Rating
NEW YORK (Continued)	
State University of New York/ Maritime College	3.31
Syracuse University	3.82
Touro College	3.26
Union College	3.69
United States Merchant Marine Academy	3.15
United States Military Academy	4.02
University of Rochester	4.56
Utica College of Syracuse University	3.16
Vassar College	3.56
Wagner College	2.84
Webb Institute of Naval Architecture	3.56
Wells College	3.54
William Smith College	3.05
Yeshiva University and Stern College for Women	3.92
NORTH CAROLINA	
Appalachian State University	3.08
Atlantic Christian College	2.71
Barber-Scotia College	2.78
Belmont Abbey College	2.85
Bennett College	2.81
Campbell University	3.14
Catawba College	3.06
Davidson College	3.33
Duke University	4.79
East Carolina University	3.20
Elizabeth City State University	2.82
Elon College	3.04
Fayetteville State University	2.74
Gardner-Webb University	2.87
Greensboro College	2.83
Guilford College	2.97
High Point University	2.86
Johnson C. Smith University	2.67
Lenoir-Rhyne College	2.99
Livingstone College	2.61
Mars Hill College	3.00
Meredith College	2.90
Methodist College	2.84
North Carolina Agricultural and Technical State University	3.12

RATING CATEGORIES	Numerical Range
Strong	4.41-4.99
Good	4.01-4.40
Acceptable Plus	3.51-3.99
Adequate	3.01-3.50
Marginal	2.01-2.99

STATE AND INSTITUTION

INSTITUTION	Gourman Overall Academic Rating	INSTITUTION	Gourman Overall Academic Rating
NORTH CAROLINA (Continued)		**OHIO**	
North Carolina Central University	3.11	Antioch College	3.30
North Carolina State University .	3.72	Ashland University	2.97
North Carolina Wesleyan College	2.76	Baldwin-Wallace College	3.04
Pembroke State University	3.07	Bluffton College	2.89
Pfeiffer College	2.86	Bowling Green State University .	3.45
Queens College	2.96	Capital University	3.19
St. Andrews Presbyterian College	2.88	Case Western Reserve University	4.39
Saint Augustine College	2.60	Cedarville College	2.88
Salem College	2.75	Central State University	2.83
Shaw University	2.64	Cleveland State University	3.20
University of North Carolina at Asheville	3.19	College of Mount Saint Joseph ..	3.02
		The College of Wooster	3.09
University of North Carolina at Chapel Hill	4.68	The Defiance College	2.95
		Denison University	3.13
University of North Carolina at Charlotte	3.61	Franciscan University of Steubenville	2.84
		Franklin University	2.91
University of North Carolina at Greensboro	3.51	Heidelberg College	2.96
		Hiram College	2.90
University of North Carolina at Wilmington	3.50	John Carroll University	3.08
Wake Forest University	3.84	Kent State University	3.27
Warren Wilson College	2.72	Kenyon College	3.33
Western Carolina University	3.24	Lake Erie College	2.87
Wingate College	2.70	Malone College	2.86
Winston-Salem State University .	2.73	Marietta College	3.05
		Miami University	3.47
		Mount Union College	2.81
NORTH DAKOTA		Mount Vernon Nazarene College	2.78
Dickinson State University	3.06	Muskingum College	2.92
Jamestown College	2.94	Notre Dame College of Ohio ...	2.85
Mayville State University	3.03	Oberlin College	3.67
Minot State University	3.10	Ohio Dominican College	2.82
North Dakota State University ..	3.50	Ohio Northern University	3.21
University of Mary	2.76	Ohio State University	4.62
University of North Dakota	3.61	Ohio State – Lima	3.14
Valley City State University	3.05	Ohio State – Mansfield	3.15

STATE AND INSTITUTION

INSTITUTION	Gourman Overall Academic Rating
OHIO (Continued)	
Ohio State – Marion	3.16
Ohio State – Newark	3.17
Ohio University	3.60
Ohio University – Chillecothe	2.93
Ohio University – Eastern	2.99
Ohio University – Lancaster	3.01
Ohio University – Southern	3.03
Ohio University – Zainesville	3.11
Ohio Wesleyan University	3.29
Otterbein College	2.98
University of Akron	3.28
University of Cincinnati	3.58
University of Dayton	3.22
The University of Findlay	2.94
University of Rio Grande	2.74
University of Toledo	3.23
Urbana University	2.65
Ursuline College	2.75
Walsh College	3.18
Wilberforce University	2.79
Wilmington College	2.66
Wittenberg University	3.00
Wright State University	3.35
Xavier University	3.06
Youngstown State University	3.07
OKLAHOMA	
Bartlesville Wesleyan College	2.67
Cameron University	2.69
Central State University	2.97
East Central University	2.98
Langston University	2.65
Northeastern State University	3.06
Northwestern Oklahoma State University	3.11
Oklahoma Baptist University	3.01
Oklahoma Christian University of Science and Arts	3.02
Oklahoma City University	3.16
Oklahoma Panhandle State University	3.03
Oklahoma State University	3.59
Oral Roberts University	3.04
Phillips University	3.22

INSTITUTION	Gourman Overall Academic Rating
OKLAHOMA (Continued)	
Southwestern Oklahoma State University	3.12
University of Oklahoma	3.81
University of Science and Arts of Oklahoma	2.96
University of Tulsa	3.63
OREGON	
Concordia College	2.72
Eastern Oregon State College	3.06
George Fox College	2.74
Lewis and Clark College	3.14
Linfield College	3.08
Marylhurst College	2.90
Oregon State University	3.90
Pacific University	3.12
Portland State University	3.34
Reed College	3.32
Southern Oregon State College	3.07
University of Oregon	3.91
University of Portland	3.15
Warner Pacific College	3.02
Western Oregon State College	3.04
Williamette University	3.33
PENNSYLVANIA	
Albright College	3.06
Allegheny College	3.05
Allentown College of St. Francis de Sales	2.66
Alvernia College	2.65
Beaver College	2.73
Bloomsburg University of Pennsylvania	3.24
Bryn Mawr College	4.02
Bucknell University	3.30
Cabrini College	2.56
California University of Pennsylvania	3.29
Carlow College	2.79
Carnegie-Mellon University	4.72
Cedar Crest College	2.82
Chatham College	2.98
Chestnut Hill College	2.93
Cheyney University of Pennsylvania	3.27

OVERALL ACADEMIC RATING OF AMERICAN INSTITUTIONS

RATING CATEGORIES	Numerical Range
Strong	4.41-4.99
Good	4.01-4.40
Acceptable Plus	3.51-3.99
Adequate	3.01-3.50
Marginal	2.01-2.99

STATE AND INSTITUTION

INSTITUTION	Gourman Overall Academic Rating
PENNSYLVANIA (Continued)	
College Misericordia	2.75
Delaware Valley College	2.89
Dickinson College	3.18
Drexel University	3.65
Duquesne University	3.32
East Stroudsburg University of Pennsylvania	3.28
Eastern College	2.72
Edinboro University of Pennsylvania	3.26
Elizabethtown College	2.47
Franklin and Marshall College	3.04
Gannon University	2.96
Geneva College	2.80
Gettysburg College	2.99
Grove City College	2.84
Gwynedd-Mercy College	2.81
Haverford College	3.90
Holy Family College	2.62
Immaculata College	2.69
Indiana University of Pennsylvania	3.20
Juniata College	2.94
King's College	2.61
Kutztown University of Pennsylvania	3.10
Lafayette College	3.49
La Roche College	2.60
La Salle University	3.09
Lebanon Valley College	2.85
Lehigh University	3.94
Lincoln University	2.59
Lock Haven University of Pennsylvania	3.25
Lycoming College	2.49
Mansfield University of Pennsylvania	3.13
Marywood College	2.46
Mercyhurst College	2.53
Messiah College	2.52

INSTITUTION	Gourman Overall Academic Rating
PENNSYLVANIA (Continued)	
Millersville University of Pennsylvania	3.14
Moravian College	2.86
Muhlenberg College	3.00
Neumann College	2.57
Pennsylvania State University/ Erie Behrend Colleg	2.97
Pennsylvania State University University Park Campus	4.59
Philadelphia College of Pharmacy and Science	3.12
Philadelphia College of Textiles and Science	3.26
Point Park College	2.58
Rosemont College	2.90
Saint Francis College	2.54
Saint Joseph's University	2.85
Saint Vincent College	2.55
Seton Hall College	2.77
Shippensburg University of Pennsylvania	3.11
Slippery Rock University of Pennsylvania	3.03
Spring Garden College	2.48
Susquehanna University	3.15
Swarthmore College	3.91
Temple University	3.66
Thiel College	2.70
University of Pennsylvania	4.81
University of Pittsburgh	4.36
University of Pittsburgh at Bradford	3.17
University of Pittsburgh at Greensburg	3.08
University of Pittsburgh at Johnstown	3.19
University of Scranton	3.02

STATE AND INSTITUTION

INSTITUTION	Gourman Overall Academic Rating
PENNSYLVANIA (Continued)	
Ursinus College	3.07
Villa Maria College	2.53
Villanova University	3.46
Washington and Jefferson College	3.23
Westminster College	2.69
Westchester University of Pennsylvania	3.21
Widener University	3.16
Wilkes College	2.88
Wilson College	2.87
York College of Pennsylvania	3.05
RHODE ISLAND	
Brown University	4.78
Providence College	3.08
Rhode Island College	3.15
Roger Williams College	3.06
Salve Regina University	3.03
University of Rhode Island	3.67
SOUTH CAROLINA	
Benedict College	2.50
Central Wesleyan College	2.41
Charleston Southern University	
The Citadel	3.30
Claflin College	2.40
Clemson University	3.46
Coker College	2.37
College of Charleston	3.02
Columbia College	2.86
Converse College	2.88
Erskine College	2.93
Francis Marion University	3.01
Furman University	3.17
Lander College	2.67
Limestone College	2.42
Newberry College	2.84
Presbyterian College	3.05
South Carolina State University	2.70
University of South Carolina	3.68
University of South Carolina at Aiken	3.09
University of South Carolina at Coastal Carolina College	3.04
University of South Carolina at Spartanburg	3.07

INSTITUTION	Gourman Overall Academic Rating
SOUTH CAROLINA (Continued)	
Voorhees College	2.54
Winthrop College	2.97
Wofford College	3.08
SOUTH DAKOTA	
Augustana College	3.15
Black Hills State University	3.02
Dakota State University	2.91
Dakota Wesleyan University	2.81
Huron University	2.74
Mount Marty College	2.72
Northern State University	3.03
Sioux Falls College	2.87
South Dakota School of Mines and Technology	3.79
South Dakota State University	3.27
University of South Dakota	3.76
TENNESSEE	
Austin Peay State University	2.86
Belmont University	2.71
Bethel College	2.75
Carson-Newman College	2.85
Christian Brothers University	3.00
David Lipscomb University	3.03
East Tennessee State University	3.07
Fisk University	3.02
Freed-Hardman University	2.73
King College	2.70
Knoxville College	2.69
Lambuth University	2.68
Lane College	2.61
Lee College	2.67
LeMoyne-Owen College	2.60
Lincoln Memorial University	2.77
Maryville College	2.64
Middle Tennessee State University	3.13
Milligan College	2.76
Rhodes College	3.23
Southern College of Seventh-Day Adventists	2.85
Tennessee State University	3.04
Tennessee Technological University	3.06
Tennessee Wesleyan College	2.59

OVERALL ACADEMIC RATING OF AMERICAN INSTITUTIONS

RATING CATEGORIES	Numerical Range
Strong	4.41-4.99
Good	4.01-4.40
Acceptable Plus	3.51-3.99
Adequate	3.01-3.50
Marginal	2.01-2.99

STATE AND INSTITUTION

INSTITUTION	Gourman Overall Academic Rating
TENNESSEE (Continued)	
Trevecca Nazarene College	2.60
Tusculum College	2.61
Union University	2.66
The University of Memphis	3.61
University of the South	3.07
University of Tennessee at Chattanooga	3.17
University of Tennessee at Martin	3.10
University of Tennessee, Knoxville	3.88
Vanderbilt University	4.64
TEXAS	
Abilene Christian University	3.05
Angelo State University	3.02
Austin College	2.80
Baylor University	2.69
Dallas Baptist University	2.61
East Texas Baptist University . . .	2.72
East Texas State University	3.07
East Texas State University at Texarkana	2.94
Hardin-Simmons University	3.21
Houston Baptist University	2.85
Howard Payne University	2.82
Huston-Tillotson College	2.58
Incarnate Word College	2.56
Jarvis Christian College	2.54
Lamar University	3.06
Le Tourneau University	2.79
Lubbock Christian University . . .	2.42
McMurry University	2.75
Midwestern State University	2.96
Our Lady of the Lake University of San Antonio	2.63
Paul Quinn College	2.58
Prairie View A&M University	2.97

INSTITUTION	Gourman Overall Academic Rating
TEXAS (Continued)	
Rice University	4.73
St. Edward's University	2.83
St. Mary's University of San Antonio	3.10
Sam Houston State University . .	3.13
Southern Methodist University . .	3.79
Southwestern Adventist College .	2.40
Southwestern University	2.68
Southwest Texas State University	3.09
Stephen F. Austin State University	3.19
Sul Ross State University	3.11
Tarleton State University	3.17
Texas A&M International University	2.84
Texas A&M University	3.99
Texas A&M University – Corpus Christi	3.16
Texas A&M University – Kingsville	3.00
Texas A&M University at Galveston	3.12
Texas Christian University	3.63
Texas College	2.42
Texas Lutheran College	2.59
Texas Southern University	3.20
Texas Tech University	3.58
Texas Wesleyan University	2.64
Texas Woman's University	3.23
Trinity University	2.88
University of Central Texas	2.98
University of Dallas	3.09
University of Houston	3.68
University of Houston-Clear Lake	3.15
University of Houston-Downtown .	3.08
University of Houston-Victoria . .	3.01
University of Mary Hardin-Baylor	2.67
University of North Texas	3.24
University of St. Thomas	2.65

STATE AND INSTITUTION

INSTITUTION	Gourman Overall Academic Rating
TEXAS (Continued)	
University of Texas at Arlington	3.26
University of Texas at Austin	4.14
The University of Texas at Brownsville	2.90
University of Texas at Dallas	3.31
University of Texas at El Paso	3.27
University of Texas-Pan American	2.91
University of Texas at San Antonio	3.30
University of Texas at Tyler	3.18
University of Texas of The Permian Basin	2.91
Wayland-Baptist University	2.74
West Texas A&M University	3.14
Wiley College	2.48
UTAH	
Brigham Young University	3.62
Southern Utah University	3.07
University of Utah	3.80
Utah State University	3.60
Weber State University	3.09
Westminster College of Salt Lake City	3.01
VERMONT	
Bennington College	3.09
Castleton State College	3.04
Goddard College	2.60
Green Mountain College	2.51
Johnson State College	2.87
Lyndon State College	2.90
Marlboro College	2.70
Middlebury College	3.15
Norwich University	3.19
Saint Michael's College	2.96
Southern Vermont College	2.63
Trinity College of Vermont	2.72
University of Vermont	3.61
VIRGIN ISLANDS	
University of the Virgin Islands	2.71
VIRGINIA	
Averett College	2.63
Bluefield College	2.53
Bridgewater College	2.52

INSTITUTION	Gourman Overall Academic Rating
VIRGINIA (Continued)	
Christopher Newport University	2.84
Clinch Valley College of the University of Virginia	3.06
College of William and Mary	3.89
Eastern Mennonite College	2.92
Emory and Henry College	3.03
Ferrum College	2.54
George Mason University	3.22
Hampden-Sydney College	3.11
Hampton University	2.76
Hollins College	2.93
James Madison University	3.32
Liberty University	2.90
Longwood College	2.86
Lynchburg College	2.88
Mary Baldwin College	2.64
Mary Washington College	2.90
Marymount University	2.77
Norfolk State University	2.72
Old Dominion University	3.36
Radford University	3.09
Randolph-Macon College	3.05
Randolph-Macon Woman's College	3.03
Roanoke College	2.96
Saint Paul's College	2.48
Shenandoah University	2.57
Sweet Briar College	3.07
University of Richmond	3.12
University of Virginia	4.61
Virginia Commonwealth University	3.39
Virginia Intermont College	2.61
Virginia Military Institute	3.21
Virginia Polytechnic Institute and State University	3.68
Virginia State University	2.50
Virginia Union University	2.49
Virginia Wesleyan College	2.58
Washington and Lee University	3.77
WASHINGTON	
Central Washington University	3.12
Eastern Washington University	3.16
Evergreen State College	3.06
Gonzaga University	3.51
Pacific Lutheran University	3.10

OVERALL ACADEMIC RATING OF AMERICAN INSTITUTIONS

RATING CATEGORIES	Numerical Range
Strong	4.41-4.99
Good	4.01-4.40
Acceptable Plus	3.51-3.99
Adequate	3.01-3.50
Marginal	2.01-2.99

STATE AND INSTITUTION

INSTITUTION	Gourman Overall Academic Rating
WASHINGTON (Continued)	
Saint Martin's College	3.05
Seattle Pacific University	3.09
Seattle University	3.62
University of Puget Sound	3.14
University of Washington	4.70
Walla Walla College	2.97
Washington State University ...	3.80
Western Washington University .	3.17
Whitman College	3.29
Whitworth College	2.86
WEST VIRGINIA	
Alderson-Broaddus College	2.73
Bethany College	2.76
Bluefield State College	2.68
Concord College	2.67
Davis and Elkins College	3.11
Fairmont State College	2.75
Glenville State College	2.74
Marshall University	3.20
Salem–Teikyo University	2.79
Shepherd College	2.77
University of Charleston	2.81
West Liberty State College	2.80
West Virginia State College	2.62
West Virginia University	3.62
West Virginia Wesleyan College	2.70
Wheeling Jesuit College	2.94
WISCONSIN	
Alverno College	3.03
Beloit College	3.06
Cardinal Stritch College	2.74

INSTITUTION	Gourman Overall Academic Rating
WISCONSIN (Continued)	
Carroll College	2.77
Carthage College	2.78
Concordia University Wisconsin .	2.73
Edgewood College	2.72
Lakeland College	2.71
Lawrence University	3.77
Marian College of Fond du Lac .	2.70
Marquette University	3.89
Mount Mary College	2.68
Mount Senario College	2.66
Northland College	2.65
Ripon College	3.08
St. Norbert College	3.04
Silver Lake College	2.62
University of Wisconsin/Eau Claire	3.31
University of Wisconsin/Green Bay	3.29
University of Wisconsin/La Crosse	3.27
University of Wisconsin/Madison	4.87
University of Wisconsin/Milwaukee	3.79
University of Wisconsin/Oshkosh	3.26
University of Wisconsin/Parkside	3.25
University of Wisconsin/Platteville	3.23
University of Wisconsin/River Falls	3.21
University of Wisconsin/Stevens Point	3.28
University of Wisconsin/Stout ...	3.30
University of Wisconsin/Superior	3.19
University of Wisconsin/ Whitewater	3.17
Viterbo College	2.69
WYOMING	
University of Wyoming	3.69

The GOURMAN REPORT
PART X

**A RATING OF
UNDERGRADUATE SCHOOLS
IN BUSINESS ADMINISTRATION
ON THE APPROVED LIST
OF THE GOURMAN REPORT**

A RATING OF SCHOOLS IN BUSINESS ADMINISTRATION

RATING CATEGORIES	Numerical Range
Strong	4.61-4.99
Very Good	4.01-4.59
Good	3.61-3.99
Acceptable Plus	3.01-3.59
Adequate	2.01-2.99

INSTITUTIONS IN ALPHABETICAL ORDER

INSTITUTION	Gourman Overall Academic Rating	Score
UNIVERSITY OF AKRON Akron, Ohio	143	3.04
UNIVERSITY OF ALABAMA University, Alabama	60	3.95
UNIVERSITY OF ALABAMA IN BIRMINGHAM Birmingham, Alabama	79	3.71
APPALACHIAN STATE UNIVERSITY Boone, North Carolina	225	2.09
UNIVERSITY OF ARIZONA Tucson, Arizona	33	4.42
ARIZONA STATE UNIVERSITY Tempe, Arizona	44	4.25
UNIVERSITY OF ARKANSAS Fayetteville, Arkansas	71	3.79
UNIVERSITY OF ARKANSAS AT LITTLE ROCK Little Rock, Arkansas	144	3.03
ARKANSAS STATE UNIVERSITY State University, Arkansas	228	2.05
AUBURN UNIVERSITY Auburn University, Alabama	122	3.25
BABSON COLLEGE Babson Park, Massachusetts	170	2.75
BALL STATE UNIVERSITY Muncie, Indiana	214	2.24
UNIVERSITY OF BALTIMORE Baltimore, Maryland	148	2.97

A RATING OF SCHOOLS IN BUSINESS ADMINISTRATION (Continued)

INSTITUTIONS IN ALPHABETICAL ORDER

INSTITUTION	Gourman Overall Academic Rating	Score
BARUCH COLLEGE – THE CITY UNIVERSITY OF NEW YORK New York, New York	16	4.70
BAYLOR UNIVERSITY Waco, Texas	80	3.70
BOISE STATE UNIVERSITY Boise, Idaho	198	2.45
BOSTON COLLEGE Chestnut Hill, Massachusetts	69	3.82
BOSTON UNIVERSITY Boston, Massachusetts	48	4.18
BOWLING GREEN STATE UNIVERSITY Bowling Green, Ohio	149	2.96
BRADLEY UNIVERSITY Peoria, Illinois	126	3.21
UNIVERSITY OF BRIDGEPORT Bridgeport, Connecticut	145	3.02
BRIGHAM YOUNG UNIVERSITY Provo, Utah	97	3.51
UNIVERSITY OF CALIFORNIA Berkeley, California	5	4.86
CALIFORNIA POLYTECHNIC STATE UNIVERSITY, SAN LUIS OBISPO San Luis Obispo, California	176	2.69
CALIFORNIA STATE UNIVERSITY, BAKERSFIELD Bakersfield, California	200	2.43
CALIFORNIA STATE UNIVERSITY, CHICO Chico, California	183	2.62
CALIFORNIA STATE UNIVERSITY, FRESNO Fresno, California	162	2.83
CALIFORNIA STATE UNIVERSITY, FULLERTON Fullerton, California	150	2.95
CALIFORNIA STATE UNIVERSITY, HAYWARD Hayward, California	197	2.46

RATING CATEGORIES	Numerical Range
Strong	4.61-4.99
Very Good	4.01-4.59
Good	3.61-3.99
Acceptable Plus	3.01-3.59
Adequate	2.01-2.99

INSTITUTIONS IN ALPHABETICAL ORDER

INSTITUTION	Gourman Overall Academic Rating	Score
CALIFORNIA STATE UNIVERSITY, LONG BEACH Long Beach, California	161	2.84
CALIFORNIA STATE UNIVERSITY, LOS ANGELES Los Angeles, California	139	3.08
CALIFORNIA STATE UNIVERSITY, NORTHRIDGE Northridge, California	96	3.53
CALIFORNIA STATE UNIVERSITY, SACRAMENTO Sacramento, California	168	2.77
CANISIUS COLLEGE Buffalo, New York	151	2.94
CARNEGIE-MELLON UNIVERSITY Pittsburgh, Pennsylvania	8	4.81
CASE WESTERN RESERVE UNIVERSITY Cleveland, Ohio	19	4.65
UNIVERSITY OF CENTRAL ARKANSAS Conway, Arkansas	227	2.06
UNIVERSITY OF CENTRAL FLORIDA Orlando, Florida	177	2.68
CENTRAL MICHIGAN UNIVERSITY Mt. Pleasant, Michigan	190	2.55
UNIVERSITY OF CINCINNATI Cincinnati, Ohio	66	3.86
CLARK UNIVERSITY Worcester, Massachusetts	104	3.43
CLARKSON UNIVERSITY Potsdam, New York	107	3.40

INSTITUTIONS IN ALPHABETICAL ORDER

INSTITUTION	Gourman Overall Academic Rating	Score
CLEMSON UNIVERSITY Clemson, South Carolina	103	3.44
CLEVELAND STATE UNIVERSITY Cleveland, Ohio	140	3.07
UNIVERSITY OF COLORADO Boulder, Colorado	45	4.23
UNIVERSITY OF COLORADO AT DENVER Denver, Colorado	105	3.42
COLORADO STATE UNIVERSITY Fort Collins, Colorado	127	3.20
UNIVERSITY OF CONNECTICUT Storrs, Connecticut	81	3.69
CREIGHTON UNIVERSITY Omaha, Nebraska	119	3.26
UNIVERSITY OF DAYTON Dayton, Ohio	158	2.87
UNIVERSITY OF DELAWARE Newark, Delaware	74	3.76
UNIVERSITY OF DENVER Denver, Colorado	49	4.16
DePAUL UNIVERSITY Chicago, Illinois	63	3.90
UNIVERSITY OF DETROIT MERCY Detroit, Michigan	99	3.48
DRAKE UNIVERSITY Des Moines, Iowa	125	3.22
DREXEL UNIVERSITY Philadelphia, Pennsylvania	53	4.08
DUQUESNE UNIVERSITY Pittsburgh, Pennsylvania	152	2.93
EAST CAROLINA UNIVERSITY Greenville, North Carolina	108	3.39

A RATING OF SCHOOLS IN BUSINESS ADMINISTRATION (Continued)

RATING CATEGORIES	Numerical Range
Strong	4.61-4.99
Very Good	4.01-4.59
Good	3.61-3.99
Acceptable Plus	3.01-3.59
Adequate	2.01-2.99

INSTITUTIONS IN ALPHABETICAL ORDER

INSTITUTION	Gourman Overall Academic Rating	Score
EAST TEXAS STATE UNIVERSITY Commerce, Texas	217	2.19
EASTERN MICHIGAN UNIVERSITY Ypsilanti, Michigan	147	2.98
EASTERN WASHINGTON UNIVERSITY Cheney, Washington	199	2.44
EMORY UNIVERSITY Atlanta, Georgia	31	4.45
UNIVERSITY OF FLORIDA Gainesville, Florida	30	4.46
FLORIDA ATLANTIC UNIVERSITY Boca Raton, Florida	153	2.92
FLORIDA INTERNATIONAL UNIVERSITY Miami, Florida	163	2.82
FLORIDA STATE UNIVERSITY Tallahassee, Florida	75	3.75
FORDHAM UNIVERSITY New York, New York	65	3.87
FORT LEWIS COLLEGE Durango, Colorado	223	2.12
GEORGE WASHINGTON UNIVERSITY Washington, D.C.	29	4.48
GEORGETOWN UNIVERSITY Washington, D.C.	64	3.88
UNIVERSITY OF GEORGIA Athens, Georgia	50	4.13

A RATING OF SCHOOLS IN BUSINESS ADMINISTRATION (Continued)

INSTITUTIONS IN ALPHABETICAL ORDER

INSTITUTION	Gourman Overall Academic Rating	Score
GEORGIA INSTITUTE OF TECHNOLOGY Atlanta, Georgia	52	4.10
GEORGIA SOUTHERN UNIVERSITY Statesboro, Georgia	201	2.42
GEORGIA STATE UNIVERSITY Atlanta, Georgia	42	4.28
UNIVERSITY OF HAWAII Manoa, Hawaii	109	3.38
HOFSTRA UNIVERSITY Hempstead, New York	110	3.37
UNIVERSITY OF HOUSTON Houston, Texas	25	4.56
UNIVERSITY OF HOUSTON AT CLEAR LAKE CITY Houston, Texas	164	2.81
HOWARD UNIVERSITY Washington, D.C.	165	2.80
IDAHO STATE UNIVERSITY Pocatello, Idaho	192	2.53
UNIVERSITY OF ILLINOIS AT CHICAGO Chicago, Illinois	54	4.06
UNIVERSITY OF ILLINOIS AT URBANA-CHAMPAIGN Champaign, Illinois	9	4.80
ILLINOIS STATE UNIVERSITY Normal, Illinois	141	3.06
INDIANA STATE UNIVERSITY AT TERRE HAUTE Terre Haute, Indiana	189	2.56
INDIANA UNIVERSITY Bloomington, Indiana	3	4.90
INDIANA UNIVERSITY-NORTHWEST Gary, Indiana	221	2.15
UNIVERSITY OF IOWA Iowa City, Iowa	34	4.40

RATING CATEGORIES	Numerical Range
Strong	4.61-4.99
Very Good	4.01-4.59
Good	3.61-3.99
Acceptable Plus	3.01-3.59
Adequate	2.01-2.99

INSTITUTIONS IN ALPHABETICAL ORDER

INSTITUTION	Gourman Overall Academic Rating	Score
JAMES MADISON UNIVERSITY Harrisonburg, Virginia	154	2.91
UNIVERSITY OF KANSAS Lawrence, Kansas	46	4.21
KANSAS STATE UNIVERSITY Manhattan, Kansas	128	3.19
KENT STATE UNIVERSITY Kent, Ohio	68	3.84
UNIVERSITY OF KENTUCKY Lexington, Kentucky	94	3.55
LAMAR UNIVERSITY Beaumont, Texas	206	2.35
LEHIGH UNIVERSITY Bethlehem, Pennsylvania	28	4.50
LOUISIANA STATE UNIVERSITY Baton Rouge, Louisiana	32	4.44
LOUISIANA TECH UNIVERSITY Ruston, Louisiana	204	2.37
UNIVERSITY OF LOUISVILLE Louisville, Kentucky	111	3.36
LOYOLA MARYMOUNT UNIVERSITY Los Angeles, California	203	2.38
LOYOLA UNIVERSITY CHICAGO Chicago, Illinois	82	3.68
LOYOLA UNIVERSITY New Orleans, Louisiana	166	2.79

INSTITUTIONS IN ALPHABETICAL ORDER

INSTITUTION	Gourman Overall Academic Rating	Score
UNIVERSITY OF MAINE AT ORONO Orono, Maine	112	3.35
MARQUETTE UNIVERSITY Milwaukee, Wisconsin	83	3.67
UNIVERSITY OF MARYLAND College Park, Maryland	37	4.36
UNIVERSITY OF MASSACHUSETTS-AMHERST Amherst, Massachusetts	38	4.34
MASSACHUSETTS INSTITUTE OF TECHNOLOGY Cambridge, Massachusetts	2	4.92
THE UNIVERSITY OF MEMPHIS Memphis, Tennessee	93	3.56
UNIVERSITY OF MIAMI Coral Gables, Florida	61	3.94
MIAMI UNIVERSITY Oxford, Ohio	84	3.66
THE UNIVERSITY OF MICHIGAN Ann Arbor, Michigan	4	4.88
THE UNIVERSITY OF MICHIGAN-FLINT Flint, Michigan	169	2.76
MICHIGAN STATE UNIVERSITY East Lansing, Michigan	17	4.68
MIDDLE TENNESSEE STATE UNIVERSITY Murfreesboro, Tennessee	178	2.67
UNIVERSITY OF MINNESOTA Minneapolis, Minnesota	14	4.72
UNIVERSITY OF MISSISSIPPI University, Mississippi	88	3.61
MISSISSIPPI STATE UNIVERSITY Mississippi State, Mississippi	102	3.45
UNIVERSITY OF MISSOURI-COLUMBIA Columbia, Missouri	41	4.29

RATING CATEGORIES	Numerical Range
Strong	4.61-4.99
Very Good	4.01-4.59
Good	3.61-3.99
Acceptable Plus	3.01-3.59
Adequate	2.01-2.99

INSTITUTIONS IN ALPHABETICAL ORDER

INSTITUTION	Gourman Overall Academic Rating	Score
UNIVERSITY OF MISSOURI-KANSAS CITY Kansas City, Missouri	115	3.32
UNIVERSITY OF MISSOURI-ST. LOUIS St. Louis, Missouri	100	3.47
UNIVERSITY OF MONTANA Missoula, Montana	136	3.11
MONTANA STATE UNIVERSITY Bozeman, Montana	179	2.66
MURRAY STATE UNIVERSITY Murray, Kentucky	218	2.18
UNIVERSITY OF NEBRASKA-LINCOLN Lincoln, Nebraska	43	4.27
UNIVERSITY OF NEBRASKA AT OMAHA Omaha, Nebraska	167	2.78
UNIVERSITY OF NEVADA, RENO Reno, Nevada	205	2.36
UNIVERSITY OF NEW MEXICO Albuquerque, New Mexico	101	3.46
NEW MEXICO STATE UNIVERSITY Las Cruces, New Mexico	188	2.57
UNIVERSITY OF NEW ORLEANS New Orleans, Louisiana	142	3.05
NEW YORK UNIVERSITY New York, New York	7	4.83
NICHOLIS STATE UNIVERSITY Thibodaux, Louisiana	195	2.49

INSTITUTIONS IN ALPHABETICAL ORDER

INSTITUTION	Gourman Overall Academic Rating	Score
THE UNIVERSITY OF NORTH CAROLINA AT CHAPEL HILL Chapel Hill, North Carolina	12	4.76
UNIVERSITY OF NORTH CAROLINA AT CHARLOTTE Charlotte, North Carolina	114	3.33
UNIVERSITY OF NORTH CAROLINA AT GREENSBORO Greensboro, North Carolina	137	3.10
NORTH CAROLINA A&T STATE UNIVERSITY Greensboro, North Carolina	224	2.10
UNIVERSITY OF NORTH DAKOTA Grand Forks, North Dakota	172	2.73
UNIVERSITY OF NORTH FLORIDA Jacksonville, Florida	116	3.31
UNIVERSITY OF NORTH TEXAS Denton, Texas	85	3.65
NORTHEAST LOUISIANA UNIVERSITY Monroe, Louisiana	216	2.21
NORTHEASTERN UNIVERSITY Boston, Massachusetts	146	3.01
NORTHERN ARIZONA UNIVERSITY Flagstaff, Arizona	207	2.34
NORTHERN ILLINOIS UNIVERSITY DeKalb, Illinois	118	3.29
UNIVERSITY OF NOTRE DAME Notre Dame, Indiana	23	4.60
THE OHIO STATE UNIVERSITY Columbus, Ohio	26	4.55
OHIO UNIVERSITY Athens, Ohio	92	3.57
UNIVERSITY OF OKLAHOMA Norman, Oklahoma	56	4.03
OKLAHOMA STATE UNIVERSITY Stillwater, Oklahoma	213	2.25

A RATING OF SCHOOLS IN BUSINESS ADMINISTRATION (Continued)

RATING CATEGORIES	Numerical Range
Strong	4.61-4.99
Very Good	4.01-4.59
Good	3.61-3.99
Acceptable Plus	3.01-3.59
Adequate	2.01-2.99

INSTITUTIONS IN ALPHABETICAL ORDER

INSTITUTION	Gourman Overall Academic Rating	Score
OLD DOMINION UNIVERSITY Norfolk, Virginia	117	3.30
UNIVERSITY OF OREGON Eugene, Oregon	36	4.37
OREGON STATE UNIVERSITY Corvallis, Oregon	89	3.60
UNIVERSITY OF THE PACIFIC Stockton, California	173	2.72
PACIFIC LUTHERAN UNIVERSITY Tacoma, Washington	210	2.29
UNIVERSITY OF PENNSYLVANIA Philadelphia, Pennsylvania	1	4.93
THE PENNSYLVANIA STATE UNIVERSITY University Park, Pennsylvania	22	4.61
UNIVERSITY OF PORTLAND Portland, Oregon	208	2.32
PORTLAND STATE UNIVERSITY Portland, Oregon	184	2.61
PURDUE UNIVERSITY West Lafayette, Indiana	11	4.77
RENSSELAER POLYTECHNIC INSTITUTE Troy, New York	51	4.12
UNIVERSITY OF RHODE ISLAND Kingston, Rhode Island	130	3.17
UNIVERSITY OF RICHMOND University of Richmond, Virginia	185	2.60

A RATING OF SCHOOLS IN BUSINESS ADMINISTRATION (Continued)

INSTITUTIONS IN ALPHABETICAL ORDER

INSTITUTION	Gourman Overall Academic Rating	Score
RUTGERS–THE STATE UNIVERSITY OF NEW JERSEY Newark, New Jersey	73	3.77
SAINT CLOUD STATE UNIVERSITY Saint Cloud, Minnesota	211	2.28
ST. JOHN'S UNIVERSITY Jamaica, New York	106	3.41
ST. LOUIS UNIVERSITY St. Louis, Missouri	62	3.93
UNIVERSITY OF SAN DIEGO San Diego, California	180	2.65
SAN DIEGO STATE UNIVERSITY San Diego, California	95	3.54
UNIVERSITY OF SAN FRANCISCO San Francisco, California	98	3.49
SAN FRANCISCO STATE UNIVERSITY San Francisco, California	113	3.34
SAN JOSE STATE UNIVERSITY San Jose, California	171	2.74
SANTA CLARA UNIVERSITY Santa Clara, California	77	3.73
SEATTLE UNIVERSITY Seattle, Washington	132	3.15
SETON HALL UNIVERSITY South Orange, New Jersey	138	3.09
SHIPPENSBURG UNIVERSITY Shippensburg, Pennsylvania	226	2.07
UNIVERSITY OF SOUTH ALABAMA Mobile, Alabama	174	2.71
UNIVERSITY OF SOUTH CAROLINA Columbia, South Carolina	40	4.30
UNIVERSITY OF SOUTH DAKOTA Vermillion, South Dakota	159	2.86

RATING CATEGORIES	Numerical Range
Strong	4.61-4.99
Very Good	4.01-4.59
Good	3.61-3.99
Acceptable Plus	3.01-3.59
Adequate	2.01-2.99

INSTITUTIONS IN ALPHABETICAL ORDER

INSTITUTION	Gourman Overall Academic Rating	Score
UNIVERSITY OF SOUTH FLORIDA Tampa, Florida	131	3.16
UNIVERSITY OF SOUTHERN CALIFORNIA Los Angeles, California	20	4.64
SOUTHERN ILLINOIS UNIVERSITY AT CARBONDALE Carbondale, Illinois	76	3.74
SOUTHERN ILLINOIS UNIVERSITY AT EDWARDSVILLE Edwardsville, Illinois	155	2.90
SOUTHERN METHODIST UNIVERSITY Dallas, Texas	27	4.53
UNIVERSITY OF SOUTHERN MISSISSIPPI Hattiesburg, Mississippi	160	2.85
STATE UNIVERSITY OF NEW YORK AT ALBANY Albany, New York	78	3.72
STATE UNIVERSITY OF NEW YORK AT BUFFALO Buffalo, New York	24	4.58
STEPHEN F. AUSTIN STATE UNIVERSITY Nacogdoches, Texas	194	2.51
SYRACUSE UNIVERSITY Syracuse, New York	39	4.32
TEMPLE UNIVERSITY Philadelphia, Pennsylvania	57	4.00
UNIVERSITY OF TENNESSEE AT CHATTANOOGA Chattanooga, Tennessee	181	2.64
UNIVERSITY OF TENNESSEE, KNOXVILLE Knoxville, Tennessee	58	3.98

INSTITUTIONS IN ALPHABETICAL ORDER

INSTITUTION	Gourman Overall Academic Rating	Score
TENNESSEE TECHNOLOGICAL UNIVERSITY Cookeville, Tennessee	196	2.48
THE UNIVERSITY OF TEXAS AT ARLINGTON Arlington, Texas	70	3.80
UNIVERSITY OF TEXAS AT AUSTIN Austin, Texas	6	4.85
UNIVERSITY OF TEXAS – PAN AMERICAN Edinburg, Texas	219	2.17
THE UNIVERSITY OF TEXAS AT SAN ANTONIO San Antonio, Texas	156	2.89
TEXAS A&M UNIVERSITY College Station, Texas	10	4.78
TEXAS CHRISTIAN UNIVERSITY Fort Worth, Texas	120	3.27
TEXAS TECH UNIVERSITY Lubbock, Texas	67	3.85
UNIVERSITY OF TOLEDO Toledo, Ohio	133	3.14
TULANE UNIVERSITY New Orleans, Louisiana	47	4.20
UNIVERSITY OF TULSA Tulsa, Oklahoma	86	3.64
UNIVERSITY OF UTAH Salt Lake City, Utah	35	4.38
UTAH STATE UNIVERSITY Logan, Utah	134	3.13
VALDOSTA STATE UNIVERSITY Valdosta, Georgia	215	2.22
UNIVERSITY OF VERMONT Burlington, Vermont	121	3.26
VILLANOVA UNIVERSITY Villanova, Pennsylvania	72	3.78

A RATING OF SCHOOLS IN BUSINESS ADMINISTRATION (Continued)

RATING CATEGORIES	Numerical Range
Strong	4.61-4.99
Very Good	4.01-4.59
Good	3.61-3.99
Acceptable Plus	3.01-3.59
Adequate	2.01-2.99

INSTITUTIONS IN ALPHABETICAL ORDER

INSTITUTION	Gourman Overall Academic Rating	Score
UNIVERSITY OF VIRGINIA Charlottesville, Virginia	15	4.71
VIRGINIA COMMONWEALTH UNIVERSITY Richmond, Virginia	129	3.18
VIRGINIA POLYTECHNIC INSTITUTE AND STATE UNIVERSITY Blacksburg, Virginia	55	4.04
WAKE FOREST UNIVERSITY Winston-Salem, North Carolina	90	3.59
UNIVERSITY OF WASHINGTON Seattle, Washington	13	4.74
WASHINGTON UNIVERSITY St. Louis, Missouri	18	4.67
WASHINGTON AND LEE UNIVERSITY Lexington, Virginia	187	2.58
WASHINGTON STATE UNIVERSITY Pullman, Washington	91	3.58
WAYNE STATE UNIVERSITY Detroit, Michigan	87	3.62
WEST GEORGIA COLLEGE Carrollton, Georgia	212	2.26
WEST VIRGINIA UNIVERSITY Morgantown, West Virginia	135	3.12
WESTERN CAROLINA UNIVERSITY Cullowhee, North Carolina	182	2.63
WESTERN ILLINOIS UNIVERSITY Macomb, Illinois	124	3.23

INSTITUTIONS IN ALPHABETICAL ORDER

INSTITUTION	Gourman Overall Academic Rating	Score
WESTERN KENTUCKY UNIVERSITY Bowling Green, Kentucky	191	2.54
WESTERN MICHIGAN UNIVERSITY Kalamazoo, Michigan	123	3.24
WICHITA STATE UNIVERSITY Wichita, Kansas	186	2.59
COLLEGE OF WILLIAM AND MARY Williamsburg, Virginia	175	2.70
WINTHROP UNIVERSITY Rock Hill, South Carolina	222	2.14
UNIVERSITY OF WISCONSIN – LA CROSSE La Crosse, Wisconsin	220	2.16
UNIVERSITY OF WISCONSIN – MADISON Madison, Wisconsin	21	4.62
UNIVERSITY OF WISCONSIN – MILWAUKEE Milwaukee, Wisconsin	59	3.96
UNIVERSITY OF WISCONSIN – OSHKOSH Oshkosh, Wisconsin	209	2.31
UNIVERSITY OF WISCONSIN – WHITEWATER Whitewater, Wisconsin	202	2.39
WRIGHT STATE UNIVERSITY Dayton, Ohio	193	2.52
UNIVERSITY OF WYOMING Laramie, Wyoming	157	2.88

The GOURMAN REPORT
PART XI

**A RATING OF
UNDERGRADUATE SCHOOLS
IN ENGINEERING
ON THE APPROVED LIST
OF THE GOURMAN REPORT**

A RATING OF SCHOOLS IN ENGINEERING

RATING CATEGORIES	Numerical Range
Very Strong	4.51-4.99
Strong	4.01-4.49
Good	3.61-3.99
Acceptable Plus	3.01-3.59
Adequate	2.00-2.99

INSTITUTIONS IN ALPHABETICAL ORDER

INSTITUTION	Gourman Overall Academic Rating	Gourman Overall Score
UNIVERSITY OF AKRON Akron, Ohio	129	3.47
UNIVERSITY OF ALABAMA University, Alabama	90	3.88
UNIVERSITY OF ALABAMA IN BIRMINGHAM Birmingham, Alabama	141	3.35
UNIVERSITY OF ALABAMA IN HUNTSVILLE Huntsville, Alabama	161	3.15
UNIVERSITY OF ALASKA, FAIRBANKS Fairbanks, Alaska	156	3.20
NEW YORK STATE COLLEGE OF CERAMICS Alfred, New York	See Part I for Program Rating	See Part I for Program Score
ARIZONA STATE UNIVERSITY Tempe, Arizona	83	3.96
UNIVERSITY OF ARIZONA Tucson, Arizona	37	4.46
UNIVERSITY OF ARKANSAS Fayetteville, Arkansas	138	3.38
AUBURN UNIVERSITY Auburn, Alabama	80	4.00
BOSTON UNIVERSITY Boston Massachusetts	74	4.06
BRADLEY UNIVERSITY Peoria, Illinois	169	3.05
UNIVERSITY OF BRIDGEPORT Bridgeport, Connecticut	230	2.25

INSTITUTIONS IN ALPHABETICAL ORDER

INSTITUTION	Gourman Overall Academic Rating	Score
BRIGHAM YOUNG UNIVERSITY Provo, Utah	139	3.37
BROWN UNIVERSITY Providence, Rhode Island	23	4.66
BUCKNELL UNIVERSITY Lewisburg, Pennsylvania	163	3.13
CALIFORNIA INSTITUTE OF TECHNOLOGY Pasadena, California	3	4.89
CALIFORNIA STATE POLYTECHNIC UNIVERSITY, SAN LUIS OBISPO San Luis Obispo, California	113	3.64
CALIFORNIA STATE POLYTECHNIC UNIVERSITY, POMONA Pomona, California	166	3.10
CALIFORNIA STATE UNIVERSITY, CHICO Chico, California	209	2.50
CALIFORNIA STATE UNIVERSITY, FRESNO Fresno, California	162	3.14
CALIFORNIA STATE UNIVERSITY, FULLERTON Fullerton, California	159	3.17
CALIFORNIA STATE UNIVERSITY, LONG BEACH Long Beach, California	135	3.41
CALIFORNIA STATE UNIVERSITY, LOS ANGELES Los Angeles, California	154	3.22
CALIFORNIA STATE UNIVERSITY, NORTHRIDGE Northridge, California	137	3.39
CALIFORNIA STATE UNIVERSITY, SACRAMENTO Sacramento, California	202	2.62
UNIVERSITY OF CALIFORNIA, BERKELEY Berkeley, California	2	4.90
UNIVERSITY OF CALIFORNIA, DAVIS Davis, California	45	4.36

RATING CATEGORIES	Numerical Range
Very Strong	4.51-4.99
Strong	4.01-4.49
Good	3.61-3.99
Acceptable Plus	3.01-3.59
Adequate	2.00-2.99

INSTITUTIONS IN ALPHABETICAL ORDER

INSTITUTION	Gourman Overall Academic Rating	Gourman Overall Score
UNIVERSITY OF CALIFORNIA, IRVINE Irvine, California	125	3.51
UNIVERSITY OF CALIFORNIA, LOS ANGELES (UCLA) Los Angeles, California	29	4.58
UNIVERSITY OF CALIFORNIA, SAN DIEGO La Jolla, California	73	4.07
UNIVERSITY OF CALIFORNIA, SANTA BARBARA Santa Barbara, California	72	4.08
CARNEGIE-MELLON UNIVERSITY Pittsburgh, Pennsylvania	12	4.78
CASE WESTERN RESERVE UNIVERSITY Cleveland, Ohio	25	4.62
CATHOLIC UNIVERSITY OF AMERICA Washington, D.C.	121	3.55
UNIVERSITY OF CENTRAL FLORIDA Orlando, Florida	153	3.23
CHRISTIAN BROTHERS UNIVERSITY Memphis, Tennessee	246	2.09
UNIVERSITY OF CINCINNATI Cincinnati, Ohio	60	4.20
THE CITADEL Charleston, South Carolina	185	2.80
CLARKSON UNIVERSITY Potsdam, New York	66	4.14
CLEMSON UNIVERSITY Clemson, South Carolinaᐃ	104	3.73

INSTITUTIONS IN ALPHABETICAL ORDER

INSTITUTION	Gourman Overall Academic Rating	Score
CLEVELAND STATE UNIVERSITY Cleveland, Ohio	181	2.85
COLORADO SCHOOL OF MINES Golden, Colorado	14	4.76
COLORADO STATE UNIVERSITY Fort Collins, Colorado	62	4.18
UNIVERSITY OF COLORADO AT BOULDER Boulder, Colorado	50	4.31
UNIVERSITY OF COLORADO AT DENVER Denver, Colorado	173	2.95
COLUMBIA UNIVERSITY New York, New York	20	4.70
UNIVERSITY OF CONNECTICUT Storrs, Connecticut	117	3.59
THE COOPER UNION New York, New York	130	3.46
CORNELL UNIVERSITY Ithaca, New York	5	4.85
DARTMOUTH COLLEGE Hanover, New Hampshire	65	4.15
UNIVERSITY OF DAYTON Dayton, Ohio	151	3.25
UNIVERSITY OF DELAWARE Newark, Delaware	69	4.11
UNIVERSITY OF DETROIT MERCY Detroit, Michigan	147	3.29
UNIVERSITY OF THE DISTRICT OF COLUMBIA Washington, D.C.	254	2.01
DREXEL UNIVERSITY Philadelphia, Pennsylvania	86	3.92
DUKE UNIVERSITY Durham, North Carolina	44	4.37

RATING CATEGORIES	Numerical Range
Very Strong	4.51-4.99
Strong	4.01-4.49
Good	3.61-3.99
Acceptable Plus	3.01-3.59
Adequate	2.00-2.99

INSTITUTIONS IN ALPHABETICAL ORDER

INSTITUTION	Gourman Overall Academic Rating	Gourman Overall Score
UNIVERSITY OF EVANSVILLE Evansville, Indiana	223	2.35
FLORIDA ATLANTIC UNIVERSITY Boca Raton, Florida	140	3.36
FLORIDA A&M UNIVERSITY / FLORIDA STATE UNIVERSITY (FAMU/FSU) Tallahassee, Florida	126	3.50
FLORIDA INSTITUTE OF TECHNOLOGY Melbourne, Florida	157	3.19
FLORIDA INTERNATIONAL UNIVERSITY Miami, Florida	217	2.41
UNIVERSITY OF FLORIDA Gainesville, Florida	41	4.40
GANNON UNIVERSITY Erie, Pennsylvania	244	2.11
GEORGE MASON UNIVERSITY Fairfax, Virginia	242	2.13
GEORGE WASHINGTON UNIVERSITY Washington, D.C.	95	3.83
GEORGIA INSTITUTE OF TECHNOLOGY Atlanta, Georgia	18	4.72
UNIVERSITY OF GEORGIA Athens, Georgia	See Part I for Program Rating	See Part I for Program Score
GMI ENGINEERING AND MANAGEMENT INSTITUTE Flint, Michigan	170	3.04

INSTITUTIONS IN ALPHABETICAL ORDER

INSTITUTION	Gourman Overall Academic Rating	Score
GONZAGA UNIVERSITY Spokane, Washington	176	2.91
UNIVERSITY OF HARTFORD Hartford, Connecticut	216	2.42
HARVARD UNIVERSITY Cambridge, Massachusetts	6	4.84
HARVEY MUDD COLLEGE Claremont, California	46	4.35
UNIVERSITY OF HAWAII AT MANOA Honolulu, Hawaii	93	3.85
HOFSTRA UNIVERSITY Hempstead, New York	221	2.35
UNIVERSITY OF HOUSTON Houston, Texas	56	4.24
HOWARD UNIVERSITY Washington, D.C.	204	2.56
UNIVERSITY OF IDAHO Moscow, Idaho	97	3.81
ILLINOIS INSTITUTE OF TECHNOLOGY Chicago, Illinois	81	3.93
UNIVERSITY OF ILLINOIS AT CHICAGO Chicago, Illinois	84	3.95
UNIVERSITY OF ILLINOIS AT URBANA-CHAMPAIGN Urbana, Illinois	7	4.83
INDIANA UNIVERSITY–PURDUE UNIVERSITY INDIANAPOLIS Indianapolis, Indiana	227	2.31
IOWA STATE UNIVERSITY Ames, Iowa	24	4.64
UNIVERSITY OF IOWA Iowa City, Iowa	54	4.26
JOHNS HOPKINS UNIVERSITY Baltimore, Maryland	31	4.55

RATING CATEGORIES	Numerical Range
Very Strong	4.51-4.99
Strong	4.01-4.49
Good	3.61-3.99
Acceptable Plus	3.01-3.59
Adequate	2.00-2.99

INSTITUTIONS IN ALPHABETICAL ORDER

INSTITUTION	Gourman Overall Academic Rating	Gourman Overall Score
KANSAS STATE UNIVERSITY Manhattan, Kansas	71	4.09
UNIVERSITY OF KANSAS Lawrence, Kansas	53	4.27
UNIVERSITY OF KENTUCKY Lexington, Kentucky	96	3.82
LAFAYETTE COLLEGE Easton, Pennsylvania	131	3.45
LAMAR UNIVERSITY Beaumont, Texas	219	2.39
LAWRENCE INSTITUTE OF TECHNOLOGY Southfield, Michigan	115	3.62
LEHIGH UNIVERSITY Bethlehem, Pennsylvania	40	4.41
LOUISIANA STATE UNIVERSITY Baton Rouge, Louisiana	78	4.02
LOUISIANA TECH UNIVERSITY Ruston, Louisiana	112	3.65
LOYOLA MARYMOUNT UNIVERSITY Los Angeles, California	229	2.26
UNIVERSITY OF MAINE AT ORONO Orono, Maine	124	3.52
MANHATTAN COLLEGE Bronx, New York	175	2.93
MARIETTA COLLEGE Marietta, Ohio	See Part I for Program Rating	See Part I for Program Score

INSTITUTIONS IN ALPHABETICAL ORDER

INSTITUTION	Gourman Overall Academic Rating	Score
MARQUETTE UNIVERSITY Milwaukee, Wisconsin	100	3.78
UNIVERSITY OF MARYLAND College Park, Maryland	35	4.48
MASSACHUSETTS INSTITUTE OF TECHNOLOGY Cambridge, Massachusetts	1	4.91
UNIVERSITY OF MASSACHUSETTS AT AMHERST Amherst, Massachusetts	55	4.25
UNIVERSITY OF MASSACHUSETTS DARTMOUTH North Dartmouth, Massachusetts	199	2.65
UNIVERSITY OF MASSACHUSETTS LOWELL Lowell, Massachusetts	132	3.44
UNIVERSITY OF MEMPHIS Memphis, Tennessee	180	2.86
MERRIMACK COLLEGE North Andover, Massachusetts	245	2.10
UNIVERSITY OF MIAMI Coral Gables, Florida	94	3.84
MICHIGAN STATE UNIVERSITY East Lansing, Michigan	49	4.32
MICHIGAN TECHNOLOGICAL UNIVERSITY Houghton, Michigan	103	3.74
UNIVERSITY OF MICHIGAN Ann Arbor, Michigan	9	4.81
UNIVERSITY OF MICHIGAN – DEARBORN Dearborn, Michigan	211	2.47
MILWAUKEE SCHOOL OF ENGINEERING Milwaukee, Wisconsin	191	2.74
UNIVERSITY OF MINNESOTA Minneapolis, Minnesota	10	4.80
MISSISSIPPI STATE UNIVERSITY Mississippi State, Mississippi	107	3.70

INSTITUTIONS IN ALPHABETICAL ORDER

INSTITUTION	Gourman Overall Academic Rating	Score
UNIVERSITY OF MISSISSIPPI University, Mississippi	160	3.16
UNIVERSITY OF MISSOURI – COLUMBIA Columbia, Missouri	64	4.16
UNIVERSITY OF MISSOURI – ROLLA Rolla, Missouri	43	4.38
MONTANA COLLEGE OF MINERAL SCIENCE AND TECHNOLOGY Butte, Montana	105	3.72
MONTANA STATE UNIVERSITY Bozeman, Montana	146	3.30
UNIVERSITY OF NEBRASKA – LINCOLN Lincoln, Nebraska	120	3.56
UNIVERSITY OF NEVADA – LAS VEGAS Las Vegas, Nevada	193	2.72
UNIVERSITY OF NEVADA – RENO Reno, Nevada	102	3.75
UNIVERSITY OF NEW HAMPSHIRE Durham, New Hampshire	177	2.90
UNIVERSITY OF NEW HAVEN West Haven, Connecticut	201	2.63
NEW JERSEY INSTITUTE OF TECHNOLOGY Newark, New Jersey	115	3.62
NEW MEXICO INSTITUTE OF MINING AND TECHNOLOGY Socorro, New Mexico	92	3.86
NEW MEXICO STATE UNIVERSITY Las Cruces, New Mexico	119	3.57
UNIVERSITY OF NEW MEXICO Albuquerque, New Mexico	98	3.80
UNIVERSITY OF NEW ORLEANS New Orleans, Louisiana	236	2.19
STATE UNIVERSITY OF NEW YORK AT BINGHAMTON Binghamton, New York	206	2.54

RATING CATEGORIES	Numerical Range
Very Strong	4.51-4.99
Strong	4.01-4.49
Good	3.61-3.99
Acceptable Plus	3.01-3.59
Adequate	2.00-2.99

INSTITUTIONS IN ALPHABETICAL ORDER

INSTITUTION	Gourman Overall Academic Rating	Gourman Overall Score
STATE UNIVERSITY OF NEW YORK AT BUFFALO Buffalo, New York	52	4.28
STATE UNIVERSITY OF NEW YORK AT STONY BROOK Stony Brook, New York	106	3.71
NEW YORK INSTITUTE OF TECHNOLOGY Old Westbury, New York	196	2.68
STATE UNIVERSITY OF NEW YORK MARITIME COLLEGE Bronx, New York	See Part I for Program Rating	See Part I for Program Score
CITY COLLEGE OF THE CITY UNIVERSITY OF NEW YORK New York, New York	70	4.10
NORTH CAROLINA AGRICULTURAL AND TECHNICAL STATE UNIVERSITY Greensboro, North Carolina	182	2.84
UNIVERSITY OF NORTH CAROLINA AT CHARLOTTE Charlotte, North Carolina	174	2.94
NORTH CAROLINA STATE UNIVERSITY AT RALEIGH Raleigh, North Carolina	51	4.30
NORTH DAKOTA STATE UNIVERSITY Fargo, North Dakota	142	3.34
UNIVERSITY OF NORTH DAKOTA Grand Forks, North Dakota	167	3.09
NORTHEASTERN UNIVERSITY Boston, Massachusetts	158	3.18
NORTHERN ARIZONA UNIVERSITY Flagstaff, Arizona	215	2.43

INSTITUTIONS IN ALPHABETICAL ORDER

INSTITUTION	Gourman Overall Academic Rating	Score
NORTHWESTERN UNIVERSITY Evanston, Illinois	13	4.77
NORWICH UNIVERSITY Northfield, Vermont	183	2.83
UNIVERSITY OF NOTRE DAME Notre Dame, Indiana	32	4.53
OAKLAND UNIVERSITY Rochester, Michigan	123	3.53
OHIO NORTHERN UNIVERSITY Ada, Ohio	218	2.40
OHIO STATE UNIVERSITY Columbus, Ohio	17	4.73
OHIO UNIVERSITY Athens, Ohio	144	3.32
OKLAHOMA STATE UNIVERSITY Stillwater, Oklahoma	76	4.04
UNIVERSITY OF OKLAHOMA Norman, Oklahoma	58	4.22
OLD DOMINION UNIVERSITY Norfolk, Virginia	192	2.73
OREGON STATE UNIVERSITY Corvallis, Oregon	75	4.05
UNIVERSITY OF THE PACIFIC Stockton, California	190	2.75
PARKS COLLEGE OF ST. LOUIS UNIVERSITY Cahokia, Illinois	210	2.49
PENNSYLVANIA STATE UNIVERSITY University Park, Pennsylvania	26	4.61
UNIVERSITY OF PENNSYLVANIA Philadelphia, Pennsylvania	19	4.71
UNIVERSITY OF PITTSBURGH Pittsburgh, Pennsylvania	36	4.47

A RATING OF SCHOOLS IN ENGINEERING (Continued)

RATING CATEGORIES	Numerical Range
Very Strong	4.51-4.99
Strong	4.01-4.49
Good	3.61-3.99
Acceptable Plus	3.01-3.59
Adequate	2.00-2.99

INSTITUTIONS IN ALPHABETICAL ORDER

INSTITUTION	Gourman Overall Academic Rating	Gourman Overall Score
POLYTECHNIC UNIVERSITY OF NEW YORK Brooklyn, New York	61	4.19
PORTLAND STATE UNIVERSITY Portland, Oregon	207	2.52
UNIVERSITY OF PORTLAND Portland, Oregon	228	2.30
PRAIRIE VIEW A&M UNIVERSITY Prairie View, Texas	233	2.22
PRINCETON UNIVERSITY Princeton, New Jersey	8	4.82
UNIVERSITY OF PUERTO RICO, MAYAGUEZ CAMPUS Mayaguez, Puerto Rico	226	2.32
PURDUE UNIVERSITY West Lafayette, Indiana	15	4.75
PURDUE UNIVERSITY CALUMET Hammond, Indiana	235	2.20
RENSSELAER POLYTECHNIC INSTITUTE Troy, New York	22	4.68
UNIVERSITY OF RHODE ISLAND Kingston, Rhode Island	116	3.61
RICE UNIVERSITY Houston, Texas	21	4.69
ROCHESTER INSTITUTE OF TECHNOLOGY Rochester, New York	164	3.12
UNIVERSITY OF ROCHESTER Rochester, New York	57	4.23

INSTITUTIONS IN ALPHABETICAL ORDER

INSTITUTION	Gourman Overall Academic Rating	Score
ROSE-HULMAN INSTITUTE OF TECHNOLOGY Terre Haute, Indiana	133	3.43
THE STATE UNIVERSITY OF NEW JERSEY, RUTGERS New Brunswick, New Jersey	85	3.92
ST. MARTIN'S COLLEGE Olympia, Washington	241	2.14
ST. MARY'S UNIVERSITY San Antonio, Texas	238	2.17
SAN DIEGO STATE UNIVERSITY San Diego, California	165	3.11
SAN FRANCISCO STATE UNIVERSITY San Francisco, California	184	2.81
SAN JOSE STATE UNIVERSITY San Jose, California	149	3.27
UNIVERSITY OF SANTA CLARA Santa Clara, California	118	3.58
SEATTLE UNIVERSITY Seattle, Washington	198	2.66
UNIVERSITY OF SOUTH ALABAMA Mobile, Alabama	197	2.67
UNIVERSITY OF SOUTH CAROLINA Columbia, South Carolina	152	3.24
SOUTH DAKOTA SCHOOL OF MINES AND TECHNOLOGY Rapid City, South Dakota	108	3.69
SOUTH DAKOTA STATE UNIVERSITY Brookings, South Dakota	143	3.33
UNIVERSITY OF SOUTH FLORIDA Tampa, Florida	178	2.89
UNIVERSITY OF SOUTHERN CALIFORNIA Los Angeles, California	38	4.44
SOUTHERN ILLINOIS UNIVERSITY – CARBONDALE Carbondale, Illinois	134	3.42

RATING CATEGORIES	Numerical Range
Very Strong	4.51-4.99
Strong	4.01-4.49
Good	3.61-3.99
Acceptable Plus	3.01-3.59
Adequate	2.00-2.99

INSTITUTIONS IN ALPHABETICAL ORDER

INSTITUTION	Gourman Overall Academic Rating	Gourman Overall Score
SOUTHERN ILLINOIS UNIVERSITY – EDWARDSVILLE Edwardsville, Illinois	234	2.21
SOUTHERN METHODIST UNIVERSITY Dallas, Texas	110	3.67
SOUTHERN UNIVERSITY AND AGRICULTURAL AND MECHANICAL COLLEGE Baton Rouge, Louisiana	231	2.24
UNIVERSITY OF SOUTHWESTERN LOUISIANA Lafayette, Louisiana	169	3.07
STANFORD UNIVERSITY Stanford, California	4	4.88
STEVENS INSTITUTE OF TECHNOLOGY Hoboken, New Jersey	30	4.57
SYRACUSE UNIVERSITY Syracuse, New York	59	4.20
TEMPLE UNIVERSITY Philadelphia, Pennsylvania	127	3.49
TENNESSEE STATE UNIVERSITY Nashville, Tennessee	200	2.64
TENNESSEE TECHNOLOGICAL UNIVERSITY Cookeville, Tennessee	194	2.71
UNIVERSITY OF TENNESSEE AT KNOXVILLE Knoxville, Tennessee	67	4.13
TEXAS A&M UNIVERSITY – KINGSVILLE Kingsville, Texas	171	3.03
TEXAS A&M UNIVERSITY College Station, Texas	27	4.60

A RATING OF SCHOOLS IN ENGINEERING (Continued)

INSTITUTIONS IN ALPHABETICAL ORDER

INSTITUTION	Gourman Overall Academic Rating	Score
TEXAS A&M UNIVERSITY AT GALVESTON Galveston, Texas	See Part I for Program Rating	See Part I for Program Score
TEXAS TECH UNIVERSITY Lubbock, Texas	77	4.03
UNIVERSITY OF TEXAS AT ARLINGTON Arlington, Texas	148	3.28
UNIVERSITY OF TEXAS AT AUSTIN Austin, Texas	11	4.79
UNIVERSITY OF TEXAS AT EL PASO El Paso, Texas	136	3.40
UNIVERSITY OF TEXAS AT SAN ANTONIO San Antonio, Texas	189	2.76
UNIVERSITY OF TOLEDO Toledo, Ohio	155	3.21
TRI-STATE UNIVERSITY Angola, Indiana	212	2.46
TUFTS UNIVERSITY Medford, Massachusetts	91	3.87
TULANE UNIVERSITY New Orleans, Louisiana	82	3.97
UNIVERSITY OF TULSA Tulsa, Oklahoma	88	3.90
TUSKEGEE UNIVERSITY Tuskegee, Alabama	225	2.33
UNION COLLEGE Schenectady, New York	187	2.78
UNITED STATES AIR FORCE ACADEMY USAF Academy, Colorado	39	4.43
UNITED STATES COAST GUARD ACADEMY New London, Connecticut	See Part I for Program Rating	See Part I for Program Score

RATING CATEGORIES	Numerical Range
Very Strong	4.51-4.99
Strong	4.01-4.49
Good	3.61-3.99
Acceptable Plus	3.01-3.59
Adequate	2.00-2.99

INSTITUTIONS IN ALPHABETICAL ORDER

INSTITUTION	Gourman Overall Academic Rating	Gourman Overall Score
UNITED STATES MERCHANT MARINE ACADEMY Kings Point, New York	See Part I for Program Rating	See Part I for Program Score
UNITED STATES MILITARY ACADEMY West Point, New York	89	3.89
UNITED STATES NAVAL ACADEMY Annapolis, Maryland	42	4.39
UTAH STATE UNIVERSITY Logan, Utah	79	4.01
UNIVERSITY OF UTAH Salt Lake City, Utah	63	4.17
VALPARAISO UNIVERSITY Valparaiso, Indiana	179	2.87
VANDERBILT UNIVERSITY Nashville, Tennessee	99	3.79
UNIVERSITY OF VERMONT Burlington, Vermont	170	3.04
VILLANOVA UNIVERSITY Villanova, Pennsylvania	168	3.08
VIRGINIA MILITARY INSTITUTE Lexington, Virginia	188	2.77
VIRGINIA POLYTECHNIC INSTITUTE AND STATE UNIVERSITY Blacksburg, Virginia	47	4.34
UNIVERSITY OF VIRGINIA Charlottesville, Virginia	48	4.33
WASHINGTON STATE UNIVERSITY Pullman, Washington	101	3.76

A RATING OF SCHOOLS IN ENGINEERING (Continued)

INSTITUTION	Gourman Overall Academic Rating	Score
WASHINGTON UNIVERSITY St. Louis, Missouri	28	4.59
UNIVERSITY OF WASHINGTON Seattle, Washington	34	4.50
WAYNE STATE UNIVERSITY Detroit, Michigan	68	4.12
WEBB INSTITUTE OF NAVAL ARCHITECTURE Glen Cove, New York	See Part I for Program Rating	See Part I for Program Score
WEST VIRGINIA INSTITUTE OF TECHNOLOGY Montgomery, West Virginia	213	2.45
WEST VIRGINIA UNIVERSITY Morgantown, West Virginia	87	3.91
WESTERN MICHIGAN UNIVERSITY Kalamazoo, Michigan	195	2.70
WESTERN NEW ENGLAND COLLEGE Springfield, Massachusetts	243	2.12
WICHITA STATE UNIVERSITY Wichita, Kansas	145	3.31
WIDENER UNIVERSITY Chester, Pennsylvania	224	2.34
UNIVERSITY OF WISCONSIN – MADISON Madison, Wisconsin	16	4.74
UNIVERSITY OF WISCONSIN – MILWAUKEE Milwaukee, Wisconsin	111	3.66
UNIVERSITY OF WISCONSIN – PLATTEVILLE Platteville, Wisconsin	172	3.01
WORCHESTER POLYTECHNIC INSTITUTE Worchester, Massachusetts	128	3.48
WRIGHT STATE UNIVERSITY Dayton, Ohio	122	3.54
UNIVERSITY OF WYOMING Laramie, Wyoming	109	3.68

A RATING OF SCHOOLS IN ENGINEERING (Continued)

RATING CATEGORIES	Numerical Range
Very Strong	4.51-4.99
Strong	4.01-4.49
Good	3.61-3.99
Acceptable Plus	3.01-3.59
Adequate	2.00-2.99

INSTITUTIONS IN ALPHABETICAL ORDER

INSTITUTION	Gourman Overall Academic Rating	Gourman Overall Score
YALE UNIVERSITY New Haven, Connecticut	33	4.51
YOUNGSTOWN STATE UNIVERSITY Youngstown, Ohio	205	2.55

The GOURMAN REPORT
PART XII

CRIMINAL JUSTICE AND FORENSIC SCIENCE
NOT ON THE APPROVED LIST
OF THE GOURMAN REPORT

CRIMINAL JUSTICE
Not On The Approved List of The Gourman Report

IN ALPHABETICAL ORDER

INSTITUTION	STATE	INSTITUTION	STATE
Abilene Christian University	TX	Central Michigan University	MI
Alabama State University	AL	Central Missouri State University	MO
Albany State College	GA	Central State University	OK
Alfred University	NY	Central Washington University	WA
American International College	MA	Chadron State College	NE
Anna Maria College	MA	Chaminade University of Honolulu	HI
Appalachian State University	NC	Chapman College	CA
Arizona State University	AZ	Chicago State University	IL
Arkansas State University	AR	Christopher Newport College	VA
Armstrong State College	GA	Coppin State College	MD
Athens State College	AL	Culver-Stockton College	MO
Auburn University (Auburn)	AL		
Aurora University	IL	Dallas Baptist University	TX
		The Defiance College	OH
Baldwin-Wallace College	OH	Delaware State College	DE
Ball State University	IN	Drake University	IA
Barry University	FL	Duquesne University	PA
Bemidji State University	MN		
Bethune-Cookman College	FL	East Carolina University	NC
Bluefield State College	WV	East Central University	OK
Boise State University	ID	Eastern Michigan University	MI
Bowling Green State University	OH	Eastern Washington University	WA
Bradley University	IL	East Tennessee State University	TN
Bridgewater State College	MA	East Texas State University	
		(Commerce)	TX
California Lutheran University	CA	Edinboro University of Pennsylvania	PA
California State University		Elizabeth City State University	NC
(Bakersfield)	CA		
California State University		Fairmont State College	WV
(Chico)	CA	Fayetteville State University	NC
California State University		Ferris State University	MI
(Dominguez Hills)	CA	Florida Agricultural and Mechanical	
California State University		University	FL
(Fresno)	CA	Florida Atlantic University	FL
California State University		Florida International University	FL
(Fullerton)	CA	Florida Southern College	FL
California State University		Florida State University	FL
(Hayward)	CA	Fordham University	NY
California State University		Fort Valley State College	GA
(Long Beach)	CA	Frostburg State University	MD
California State University			
(Los Angeles)	CA	George Washington University	DC
California State University		Georgia College	GA
(Sacramento)	CA	Georgia Southern University	GA
California State University		Georgia State University	GA
(San Bernardino)	CA	Golden Gate University	CA
Cameron University	OK	Gonzaga University	WA
Capital University	OH	Governors State University	IL
Castleton State College	VT	Grambling State University	LA

IN ALPHABETICAL ORDER

INSTITUTION	STATE	INSTITUTION	STATE
Grand Canyon University	AZ	McMurry University	TX
Grand Valley State University	MI	McNeese State University	LA
		Memphis, University of	TN
Hampton University	VA	Mercer University (Macon)	GA
Hardin-Simmons University	TX	Mercyhurst College	PA
		Mesa State College	CO
Illinois State University	IL	Metropolitan State College of Denver	CO
Indiana State University (Terre Haute)	IN	Michigan State University	MI
Indiana University (South Bend)	IN	Middle Tennessee State University	TN
Indiana University (Bloomington)	IN	Midwestern State University	TX
Indiana University (Northwest)	IN	Minot State University	ND
Indiana University of Pennsylvania	PA	Missouri Southern State College	MO
Indiana University–Purdue University		Missouri Western State College	MO
(Fort Wayne)	IN	Monmouth College	NJ
Indiana University–Purdue University		Montana State University	MT
(Indianapolis)	IN	Moorhead State University	MN
Iona College	NY	Murray State University	KY
Jersey City State College	NJ	New Mexico State University	NM
		New York Institute of Technology	NY
Kansas State University	KS	Niagara University	NY
Kean College of New Jersey	NJ	North Carolina Central University	NC
Kent State University	OH	North Carolina State University	NC
Kentucky State University	KY	Northeastern Illinois University	IL
Kutztown University of Pennsylvania	PA	Northeastern State University	OK
		Northeastern University	MA
Lake Superior State University	MI	Northeast Louisiana University	LA
Lamar University	TX	Northeast Missouri State University	MO
La Salle University	PA	Northern Arizona University	AZ
Lewis-Clark State College	ID	Northern Illinois University	IL
Lewis University	IL	Northern Michigan University	MI
Liberty University	VA		
Lock Haven University of Pennsylvania	PA	Ohio Northern University	OH
Loma Linda University	CA	Ohio State University (Columbus)	OH
Long Island University (Brooklyn)	NY	Ohio University (Athens)	OH
Long Island University (C.W. Post)	NY	Ohio University (Chillicothe)	OH
Louisiana College	LA	Ohio University (Lancaster)	OH
Louisiana State University		Oklahoma Baptist University	OK
(Baton Rouge)	LA	Oklahoma City University	OK
Louisiana State University		Old Dominion University	VA
(Shreveport)	LA		
Loyola University (Chicago)	IL	Pace University (Pleasantville/Briarcliff)	NY
Loyola University (New Orleans)	LA	Pacific Lutheran University	WA
		Pembroke State University	NC
Mansfield University of Pennsylvania	PA	Penn State University at Harrisburg–	
Marquette University	WI	The Capital College	PA
Marshall University	WV	Pittsburg State University	KS
Marywood College	PA	Portland State University	

IN ALPHABETICAL ORDER

INSTITUTION	STATE	INSTITUTION	STATE
Purdue University (West Lafayette)	IN	State University of New York College (Oswego)	NY
Purdue University (Calumet)	IN	State University of New York College (Plattsburgh)	NY
Radford University	VA		
Rochester Institute of Technology	NY	Stephen F. Austin State University	TX
Roosevelt University	IL	The Richard Stockton College of New Jersey	NJ
Rutgers (Livingston College) New Brunswick	NJ	Suffolk University	MA
Rutgers (University College) Newark	NJ	Tarleton State University	TX
Rutgers (University College) New Brunswick	NJ	Temple University (Philadelphia)	PA
		Tennessee State University	TN
		Texas Christian University	TX
Saginaw Valley State University	MI	Texas Woman's University	TX
St. Cloud State University	MN	Thomas A. Edison State College	NJ
St. Edward's University	TX	Trenton State College	NJ
St. John's University	NY	Troy State University (Troy)	AL
Saint Joseph's University	PA	Troy State University (Dothan)	AL
Saint Louis University	MO	Troy State University (Montgomery)	AL
St. Mary's University of San Antonio	TX		
Salem State College	MA	University of Alabama (Tuscaloosa)	AL
Salve Regina University	RI	University of Alabama (Birmingham)	AL
Sam Houston State University	TX	University of Alaska (Anchorage)	AK
San Diego State University	CA	University of Alaska (Fairbanks)	AK
Sangamon State University	IL	University of Arizona	AZ
San Jose State University	CA	University of Arkansas (Fayetteville)	AR
Savannah State College	GA	University of Arkansas (Little Rock)	AR
Seattle University	WA	University of Arkansas (Pine Bluff)	AR
Seton Hall University	NJ	University of Baltimore	MD
Shippensburg University of Pennsylvania	PA	University of California (Santa Barbara)	CA
		University of Central Florida	FL
Sonoma State University	CA	University of Central Texas	TX
Southeastern Louisiana University	LA	University of Cincinnati	OH
Southeastern Oklahoma State University	OK	University of Dayton	OH
		University of Delaware (Newark)	DE
Southeast Missouri State University	MO	University of Detroit	MI
Southern Illinois University (Carbondale)	IL	University of Dubuque	IA
		University of Florida	FL
Southern Methodist University	TX	University of Georgia	GA
Southern Oregon State College	OR	University of Hartford	CT
Southwestern Oklahoma State University	OK	University of Idaho	ID
		University of Illinois (Chicago)	IL
Southwest Texas State University	TX	University of Maryland (College Park)	MD
State University of New York (Albany)	NY	University of Maryland (Eastern Shore)	MD
		University of Maryland (University College)	MD
State University of New York College (Brockport)	NY	University of Massachusetts (Boston)	MA
State University of New York College (Buffalo)	NY	University of Massachusetts (Lowell)	MA
		University of Miami	FL

IN ALPHABETICAL ORDER

INSTITUTION	STATE	INSTITUTION	STATE
University of Michigan (Flint)	MI	University of Texas (Tyler)	TX
University of Mississippi	MS	University of Texas (Pan American)	TX
University of Missouri (Kansas City)	MO	University of the District of Columbia	DC
University of Missouri (St. Louis)	MO	University of the Pacific	CA
University of Nebraska Kearney	NE	University of Toledo	OH
University of Nebraska Lincoln	NE	University of Washington (Seattle)	WA
University of Nebraska Omaha	NE	University of West Florida	FL
University of Nevada (Las Vegas)	NV	University of Wisconsin	
University of Nevada (Reno)	NV	(Eau Claire)	WI
University of New Mexico	NM	University of Wisconsin	
University of North Alabama	AL	(Milwaukee)	WI
University of North Carolina		University of Wisconsin	
(Ashville)	NC	(Oshkosh)	WI
University of North Carolina		University of Wisconsin	
(Chapel Hill)	NC	(Parkside)	WI
University of North Carolina		University of Wisconsin	
(Charlotte)	NC	(Platteville)	WI
University of North Carolina		University of Wisconsin	
(Wilmington)	NC	(Superior)	WI
University of North Dakota	ND	University of Wyoming	WY
University of Northern Colorado	CO		
University of Northern Iowa	IA	Valdosta State University	GA
University of North Florida	FL	Valparaiso University	IN
University of North Texas	TX	Villanova University	PA
University of Pittsburgh (Pittsburgh)	PA	Virginia Commonwealth University	VA
University of Pittsburgh (Greensburg)	PA		
University of Portland	OR	Washburn University of Topeka	KS
University of Richmond	VA	Washington State University	WA
University of Scranton	PA	Wayne State University	MI
University of South Alabama	AL	Weber State University	UT
University of South Carolina		West Chester University of	
(Columbia)	SC	Pennsylvania	PA
University of South Carolina		Western Carolina University	NC
(Spartanburg)	SC	Western Michigan University	MI
University of South Dakota	SD	Western New Mexico University	NM
University of Southern Colorado	CO	Western Oregon State College	OR
University of Southern Maine	ME	Westfield State College	MA
University of Southern Mississippi	MS	West Georgia College	GA
University of South Florida	FL	West Texas State University	TX
University of Southwestern Louisiana	LA	West Virginia State College	WV
University of Tampa	FL	Wichita State University	KS
University of Tennessee		Winona State University	MN
(Chattanooga)	TN	Wright State University	OH
University of Tennessee			
(Martin)	TN	Xavier University	OH
University of Texas (Arlington)	TX		
University of Texas (El Paso)	TX	Youngstown State University	OH
University of Texas (San Antonio)	TX		

FORENSIC SCIENCE UNDERGRADUATE PROGRAMS
Not On The Approved List of The Gourman Report

IN ALPHABETICAL ORDER

INSTITUTION	STATE	INSTITUTION	STATE
Albany State College Albany	GA	Weber State University Ogden	UT
California State University-Sacramento Sacramento	CA	West Chester University West Chester	PA
Eastern Kentucky University Richmond	KY	York College of Pennsylvania York	PA
The George Washington University Washington, DC		University of Alabama at Birmingham Birmingham	AL
Jacksonville State University Jacksonville	AL	The University of Central Florida Orlando	FL
John Jay College of Criminal Justice[1] New York	NY	University of Central Oklahoma Edmond	OK
Metropolitan State College Denver	CO	University of Mississippi University	MS
Michigan State University East Lansing	MI	University of New Haven[2] West Haven	CT
Ohio University Athens	OH	The University of Southern Mississippi Hattiesburg	MS
St. John's University Jamaica	NY		

Notes:

[1]Approved by THE GOURMAN REPORT
[2]Approved by THE GOURMAN REPORT

The GOURMAN REPORT
PART XIII

**EDUCATION
NOT ON THE APPROVED LIST
OF THE GOURMAN REPORT**

**EDUCATION DEGREES/MAJORS (at any level)
Not on the Approved List of THE GOURMAN REPORT**

**ELEMENTARY EDUCATION
Not on the Approved List of THE GOURMAN REPORT**

**SECONDARY EDUCATION
Not on the Approved List of THE GOURMAN REPORT**

**TEACHER EDUCATION
Not on the Approved List of THE GOURMAN REPORT**

**UNDERGRADUATE DEPARTMENT OF EDUCATION
COLLEGES/UNIVERSITIES
Not on the Approved List of THE GOURMAN REPORT**

**POSTSECONDARY EDUCATION COMMISSION
Not on the Approved List of THE GOURMAN REPORT**

**STATE DEPARTMENT OF EDUCATION
Not on the Approved List of THE GOURMAN REPORT**

EDUCATION DEGREES/MAJORS (AT ANY LEVEL)
Not On The Approved List of The Gourman Report

IN ALPHABETICAL ORDER

STATE		STATE	
ALABAMA	Not Approved	MONTANA	Not Approved
ALASKA	Not Approved	NEBRASKA	Not Approved
ARIZONA	Not Approved	NEVADA	Not Approved
ARKANSAS	Not Approved	NEW HAMPSHIRE	Not Approved
CALIFORNIA	Not Approved	NEW JERSEY	Not Approved
COLORADO	Not Approved	NEW MEXICO	Not Approved
CONNECTICUT	Not Approved	NEW YORK	Not Approved
DELAWARE	Not Approved	NORTH CAROLINA	Not Approved
DISTRICT OF COLUMBIA	Not Approved	NORTH DAKOTA	Not Approved
FLORIDA	Not Approved	OHIO	Not Approved
GEORGIA	Not Approved	OKLAHOMA	Not Approved
HAWAII	Not Approved	OREGON	Not Approved
IDAHO	Not Approved	PENNSYLVANIA	Not Approved
ILLINOIS	Not Approved	RHODE ISLAND	Not Approved
INDIANA	Not Approved	SOUTH CAROLINA	Not Approved
IOWA	Not Approved	SOUTH DAKOTA	Not Approved
KANSAS	Not Approved	TENNESSEE	Not Approved
KENTUCKY	Not Approved	TEXAS	Not Approved
LOUISIANA	Not Approved	UTAH	Not Approved
MAINE	Not Approved	VERMONT	Not Approved
MARYLAND	Not Approved	VIRGINIA	Not Approved
MASSACHUSETTS	Not Approved	WASHINGTON	Not Approved
MICHIGAN	Not Approved	WEST VIRGINIA	Not Approved
MINNESOTA	Not Approved	WISCONSIN	Not Approved
MISSISSIPPI	Not Approved	WYOMING	Not Approved
MISSOURI	Not Approved		

NOTE:

THE GOURMAN REPORT does not approve of Education Degrees/Majors Public and Private Colleges/Universities in each state. Meaningless courses of no substance down grades the major. The major should be abolished by all institutions.

ELEMENTARY EDUCATION
Not On The Approved List of The Gourman Report

IN ALPHABETICAL ORDER

STATE		STATE	
ALABAMA	Not Approved	MONTANA	Not Approved
ALASKA	Not Approved	NEBRASKA	Not Approved
ARIZONA	Not Approved	NEVADA	Not Approved
ARKANSAS	Not Approved	NEW HAMPSHIRE	Not Approved
CALIFORNIA	Not Approved	NEW JERSEY	Not Approved
COLORADO	Not Approved	NEW MEXICO	Not Approved
CONNECTICUT	Not Approved	NEW YORK	Not Approved
DELAWARE	Not Approved	NORTH CAROLINA	Not Approved
DISTRICT OF COLUMBIA	Not Approved	NORTH DAKOTA	Not Approved
FLORIDA	Not Approved	OHIO	Not Approved
GEORGIA	Not Approved	OKLAHOMA	Not Approved
HAWAII	Not Approved	OREGON	Not Approved
IDAHO	Not Approved	PENNSYLVANIA	Not Approved
ILLINOIS	Not Approved	RHODE ISLAND	Not Approved
INDIANA	Not Approved	SOUTH CAROLINA	Not Approved
IOWA	Not Approved	SOUTH DAKOTA	Not Approved
KANSAS	Not Approved	TENNESSEE	Not Approved
KENTUCKY	Not Approved	TEXAS	Not Approved
LOUISIANA	Not Approved	UTAH	Not Approved
MAINE	Not Approved	VERMONT	Not Approved
MARYLAND	Not Approved	VIRGINIA	Not Approved
MASSACHUSETTS	Not Approved	WASHINGTON	Not Approved
MICHIGAN	Not Approved	WEST VIRGINIA	Not Approved
MINNESOTA	Not Approved	WISCONSIN	Not Approved
MISSISSIPPI	Not Approved	WYOMING	Not Approved
MISSOURI	Not Approved		

NOTE:

Preparation for Elementary Education in both Public and Private Colleges/Universities in each state not on the approved list of THE GOURMAN REPORT.

SECONDARY EDUCATION
Not On The Approved List of The Gourman Report

IN ALPHABETICAL ORDER

STATE		STATE	
ALABAMA	Not Approved	MONTANA	Not Approved
ALASKA	Not Approved	NEBRASKA	Not Approved
ARIZONA	Not Approved	NEVADA	Not Approved
ARKANSAS	Not Approved	NEW HAMPSHIRE	Not Approved
CALIFORNIA	Not Approved	NEW JERSEY	Not Approved
COLORADO	Not Approved	NEW MEXICO	Not Approved
CONNECTICUT	Not Approved	NEW YORK	Not Approved
DELAWARE	Not Approved	NORTH CAROLINA	Not Approved
DISTRICT OF COLUMBIA	Not Approved	NORTH DAKOTA	Not Approved
FLORIDA	Not Approved	OHIO	Not Approved
GEORGIA	Not Approved	OKLAHOMA	Not Approved
HAWAII	Not Approved	OREGON	Not Approved
IDAHO	Not Approved	PENNSYLVANIA	Not Approved
ILLINOIS	Not Approved	RHODE ISLAND	Not Approved
INDIANA	Not Approved	SOUTH CAROLINA	Not Approved
IOWA	Not Approved	SOUTH DAKOTA	Not Approved
KANSAS	Not Approved	TENNESSEE	Not Approved
KENTUCKY	Not Approved	TEXAS	Not Approved
LOUISIANA	Not Approved	UTAH	Not Approved
MAINE	Not Approved	VERMONT	Not Approved
MARYLAND	Not Approved	VIRGINIA	Not Approved
MASSACHUSETTS	Not Approved	WASHINGTON	Not Approved
MICHIGAN	Not Approved	WEST VIRGINIA	Not Approved
MINNESOTA	Not Approved	WISCONSIN	Not Approved
MISSISSIPPI	Not Approved	WYOMING	Not Approved
MISSOURI	Not Approved		

NOTE:

Preparation for Secondary Education in both Public and Private Colleges/Universities in each state not on the approved list of THE GOURMAN REPORT.

IN ALPHABETICAL ORDER

STATE		STATE	
ALABAMA	Not Approved	MONTANA	Not Approved
ALASKA	Not Approved	NEBRASKA	Not Approved
ARIZONA	Not Approved	NEVADA	Not Approved
ARKANSAS	Not Approved	NEW HAMPSHIRE	Not Approved
CALIFORNIA	Not Approved	NEW JERSEY	Not Approved
COLORADO	Not Approved	NEW MEXICO	Not Approved
CONNECTICUT	Not Approved	NEW YORK	Not Approved
DELAWARE	Not Approved	NORTH CAROLINA	Not Approved
DISTRICT OF COLUMBIA	Not Approved	NORTH DAKOTA	Not Approved
FLORIDA	Not Approved	OHIO	Not Approved
GEORGIA	Not Approved	OKLAHOMA	Not Approved
HAWAII	Not Approved	OREGON	Not Approved
IDAHO	Not Approved	PENNSYLVANIA	Not Approved
ILLINOIS	Not Approved	RHODE ISLAND	Not Approved
INDIANA	Not Approved	SOUTH CAROLINA	Not Approved
IOWA	Not Approved	SOUTH DAKOTA	Not Approved
KANSAS	Not Approved	TENNESSEE	Not Approved
KENTUCKY	Not Approved	TEXAS	Not Approved
LOUISIANA	Not Approved	UTAH	Not Approved
MAINE	Not Approved	VERMONT	Not Approved
MARYLAND	Not Approved	VIRGINIA	Not Approved
MASSACHUSETTS	Not Approved	WASHINGTON	Not Approved
MICHIGAN	Not Approved	WEST VIRGINIA	Not Approved
MINNESOTA	Not Approved	WISCONSIN	Not Approved
MISSISSIPPI	Not Approved	WYOMING	Not Approved
MISSOURI	Not Approved		

NOTE:

Teacher Education preparation in both Public and Private Colleges/Universities in each state not on the approved list of THE GOURMAN REPORT.

UNDERGRADUATE DEPARTMENT OF EDUCATION COLLEGES/ UNIVERSITIES Not On The Approved List of The Gourman Report

IN ALPHABETICAL ORDER

STATE		STATE	
ALABAMA	Not Approved	MONTANA	Not Approved
ALASKA	Not Approved	NEBRASKA	Not Approved
ARIZONA	Not Approved	NEVADA	Not Approved
ARKANSAS	Not Approved	NEW HAMPSHIRE	Not Approved
CALIFORNIA	Not Approved	NEW JERSEY	Not Approved
COLORADO	Not Approved	NEW MEXICO	Not Approved
CONNECTICUT	Not Approved	NEW YORK	Not Approved
DELAWARE	Not Approved	NORTH CAROLINA	Not Approved
DISTRICT OF COLUMBIA	Not Approved	NORTH DAKOTA	Not Approved
FLORIDA	Not Approved	OHIO	Not Approved
GEORGIA	Not Approved	OKLAHOMA	Not Approved
HAWAII	Not Approved	OREGON	Not Approved
IDAHO	Not Approved	PENNSYLVANIA	Not Approved
ILLINOIS	Not Approved	RHODE ISLAND	Not Approved
INDIANA	Not Approved	SOUTH CAROLINA	Not Approved
IOWA	Not Approved	SOUTH DAKOTA	Not Approved
KANSAS	Not Approved	TENNESSEE	Not Approved
KENTUCKY	Not Approved	TEXAS	Not Approved
LOUISIANA	Not Approved	UTAH	Not Approved
MAINE	Not Approved	VERMONT	Not Approved
MARYLAND	Not Approved	VIRGINIA	Not Approved
MASSACHUSETTS	Not Approved	WASHINGTON	Not Approved
MICHIGAN	Not Approved	WEST VIRGINIA	Not Approved
MINNESOTA	Not Approved	WISCONSIN	Not Approved
MISSISSIPPI	Not Approved	WYOMING	Not Approved
MISSOURI	Not Approved		

NOTE:

THE GOURMAN REPORT does not approve of the Undergraduate Department of Education Public and Private Colleges/Universities in each state. The Department of Education should be abolished by each institution.

POSTSECONDARY EDUCATION COMMISSION
Not On The Approved List of The Gourman Report

IN ALPHABETICAL ORDER

STATE		STATE	
ALABAMA	Not Approved	MONTANA	Not Approved
ALASKA	Not Approved	NEBRASKA	Not Approved
ARIZONA	Not Approved	NEVADA	Not Approved
ARKANSAS	Not Approved	NEW HAMPSHIRE	Not Approved
CALIFORNIA	Not Approved	NEW JERSEY	Not Approved
COLORADO	Not Approved	NEW MEXICO	Not Approved
CONNECTICUT	Not Approved	NEW YORK	Not Approved
DELAWARE	Not Approved	NORTH CAROLINA	Not Approved
DISTRICT OF COLUMBIA	Not Approved	NORTH DAKOTA	Not Approved
FLORIDA	Not Approved	OHIO	Not Approved
GEORGIA	Not Approved	OKLAHOMA	Not Approved
HAWAII	Not Approved	OREGON	Not Approved
IDAHO	Not Approved	PENNSYLVANIA	Not Approved
ILLINOIS	Not Approved	RHODE ISLAND	Not Approved
INDIANA	Not Approved	SOUTH CAROLINA	Not Approved
IOWA	Not Approved	SOUTH DAKOTA	Not Approved
KANSAS	Not Approved	TENNESSEE	Not Approved
KENTUCKY	Not Approved	TEXAS	Not Approved
LOUISIANA	Not Approved	UTAH	Not Approved
MAINE	Not Approved	VERMONT	Not Approved
MARYLAND	Not Approved	VIRGINIA	Not Approved
MASSACHUSETTS	Not Approved	WASHINGTON	Not Approved
MICHIGAN	Not Approved	WEST VIRGINIA	Not Approved
MINNESOTA	Not Approved	WISCONSIN	Not Approved
MISSISSIPPI	Not Approved	WYOMING	Not Approved
MISSOURI	Not Approved		

NOTE:

THE GOURMAN REPORT does not approve of the Postsecondary Commission or any Commission in each state. Their recommendations on higher education does not meet the standard of complex issues of education with reference to colleges and universities. There is a definite omission of leadership which affect good judgment on action taken by the Commission.

STATE DEPARTMENT OF EDUCATION
Not On The Approved List of The Gourman Report

IN ALPHABETICAL ORDER

STATE		STATE	
ALABAMA	Not Approved	MONTANA	Not Approved
ALASKA	Not Approved	NEBRASKA	Not Approved
ARIZONA	Not Approved	NEVADA	Not Approved
ARKANSAS	Not Approved	NEW HAMPSHIRE	Not Approved
CALIFORNIA	Not Approved	NEW JERSEY	Not Approved
COLORADO	Not Approved	NEW MEXICO	Not Approved
CONNECTICUT	Not Approved	NEW YORK	Not Approved
DELAWARE	Not Approved	NORTH CAROLINA	Not Approved
DISTRICT OF COLUMBIA	Not Approved	NORTH DAKOTA	Not Approved
FLORIDA	Not Approved	OHIO	Not Approved
GEORGIA	Not Approved	OKLAHOMA	Not Approved
HAWAII	Not Approved	OREGON	Not Approved
IDAHO	Not Approved	PENNSYLVANIA	Not Approved
ILLINOIS	Not Approved	RHODE ISLAND	Not Approved
INDIANA	Not Approved	SOUTH CAROLINA	Not Approved
IOWA	Not Approved	SOUTH DAKOTA	Not Approved
KANSAS	Not Approved	TENNESSEE	Not Approved
KENTUCKY	Not Approved	TEXAS	Not Approved
LOUISIANA	Not Approved	UTAH	Not Approved
MAINE	Not Approved	VERMONT	Not Approved
MARYLAND	Not Approved	VIRGINIA	Not Approved
MASSACHUSETTS	Not Approved	WASHINGTON	Not Approved
MICHIGAN	Not Approved	WEST VIRGINIA	Not Approved
MINNESOTA	Not Approved	WISCONSIN	Not Approved
MISSISSIPPI	Not Approved	WYOMING	Not Approved
MISSOURI	Not Approved		

NOTE:

THE GOURMAN REPORT does not approve of the State Department of Education in each state with reference to their requirements for teacher certification.

The GOURMAN REPORT
PART XIV

APPENDIXES

Appendix A
List of Tables

Appendix B
International Institutions of Higher Learning

APPENDIX A
A List of Tables

TABLE 1
A Rating of 140 Undergraduate Programs in the United States

FIELD OF STUDY	Selected Number of Institutions Granting Degree	Total Number of Programs (Curriculum) Evaluated	Total Number of Areas of Study Evaluated	Total Number of Faculty Areas Evaluated	Institutions Listed In Part I
Accounting	631	631	25,810	1,114	41
Aerospace Engineering	46	46	3,612	999	43
Agricultural Business	110	110	826	103	9
Agricultural Economics	70	70	640	97	21
Agricultural Engineering	45	45	2,419	990	38
Agriculture	120	120	8,688	2,111	46
Agronomy	121	121	6,815	1,915	45
American Studies	80	80	1,910	561	33
Animal Science	64	64	2,380	433	35
Anthropology	102	102	1,521	738	50
Applied Mathematics	51	51	1,936	541	16
Arabic	17	17	496	98	9
Architectural Engineering	10	10	430	66	8
Architecture	94	94	1,495	380	39
Art	490	490	8,800	3,001	42
Art History	60	60	4,085	630	41
Asian/Oriental Studies	27	27	1,330	412	13
Astronomy	40	40	1,951	655	25
Astrophysics	25	25	1,162	784	10
Atmospheric Sciences	22	22	751	220	8
Bacteriology/Microbiology	219	219	4,670	1,014	37
Behavioral Sciences	50	50	994	114	9
Biochemistry	312	312	2,699	900	32
Bioengineering/Biomedical Engineering	42	42	2,830	940	16
Biology	630	630	13,224	2,401	61
Biophysics	60	60	1,866	739	13
Botany	173	173	2,985	819	31
Business Administration	730	730	34,720	3,010	45
Cell Biology	40	40	1,100	458	19
Ceramic Art/Design	48	48	1,120	647	14
Ceramic Engineering	15	15	418	83	10
Chemical Engineering	120	120	2,215	843	54
Chemistry	555	555	15,221	2,170	53
Child Psychology	164	164	1,014	467	17
Chinese	50	50	961	112	14
Civil Engineering	144	144	2,961	896	55
Classics	60	60	1,815	688	23
Communication	333	333	8,973	1,615	19
Comparative Literature	65	65	996	455	28
Computer Engineering	36	36	1,762	871	22
Computer Science	260	260	9,875	1,760	57

TABLE 1
A Rating of 140 Undergraduate Programs in the United States

FIELD OF STUDY	Selected Number of Institutions Granting Degree	Total Number of Programs (Curriculum) Evaluated	Total Number of Areas of Study Evaluated	Total Number of Faculty Areas Evaluated	Institutions Listed In Part I
Dairy Sciences	43	43	412	66	11
Dietetics	127	127	1,273	454	15
Drama/Theatre	401	401	6,222	1,117	46
Earth Science	49	49	1,941	652	12
East Asian Studies	44	44	933	150	11
Ecology/Environmental Studies	151	151	1,020	406	13
Economics	627	627	10,730	3,696	46
Electrical Engineering	170	170	4,422	1,366	62
Engineering/General	22	22	1,210	639	10
Engineering Mechanics	21	21	854	352	6
Engineering Physics	17	17	761	139	8
Engineering Science	52	52	1,316	160	10
English	826	826	12,775	3,951	41
Entomology	55	55	1,122	495	26
Environmental Design	46	46	997	217	14
Environmental Engineering	33	33	1,104	366	11
Environmental Sciences	78	78	1,266	512	12
Farm/Ranch Management	20	20	788	152	9
Film	94	94	1,004	261	10
Finance	666	666	10,281	3,302	44
Fish/Game Management	51	51	1,645	724	12
Food Sciences	100	100	851	196	18
Food Services Management	72	72	666	122	12
Forestry	50	50	1,244	832	30
French	430	430	8,746	1,866	30
Genetics	30	30	884	298	13
Geography	83	83	2,300	647	30
Geological Engineering	18	18	777	144	12
Geology/Geoscience	115	115	5,549	1,090	50
Geophysics/Geoscience	47	47	733	169	28
German	301	301	3,901	988	30
Greek	77	77	995	183	16
Hebrew	50	50	388	104	20
History	690	690	15,360	5,431	46
Home Economics	177	177	1,790	798	30
Horticulture	77	77	1,071	312	36
Hotel, Restaurant, Institutional Management	132	132	843	95	23
Industrial Engineering	86	86	2,269	712	34
Information Science	60	60	995	228	10

APPENDIX A (Continued)
A List of Tables

TABLE 1
A Rating of 140 Undergraduate Programs in the United States

FIELD OF STUDY	Selected Number of Institutions Granting Degree	Total Number of Programs (Curriculum) Evaluated	Total Number of Areas of Study Evaluated	Total Number of Faculty Areas Evaluated	Institutions Listed In Part I
International Relations	62	62	1,273	469	15
Italian	58	58	1,001	345	22
Japanese	43	43	394	96	14
Journalism and Mass Communications . .	73	73	3,141	954	31
Labor and Industrial Relations	82	82	792	255	10
Landscape Architecture	39	39	663	105	33
Latin	49	49	1,117	307	11
Latin American Studies	51	51	655	96	16
Linguistics	62	62	1,185	489	30
Management	280	280	4,490	1,128	47
Manufacturing Engineering	7	7	133	34	6
Marine Biology	76	76	1,461	488	7
Marine Sciences	37	37	846	130	6
Marketing	531	531	9,766	2,481	41
Materials Engineering/Materials Science Engineering	38	38	1,303	186	32
Mathematics	166	166	17,829	2,696	58
Mechanical Engineering	200	200	10,814	2,998	58
Medieval Studies	44	44	872	116	10
Metallurgical Engineering	40	40	1,799	465	18
Meteorology	41	41	917	272	10
Mining and Mineral Engineering	24	24	1,303	654	18
Molecular Biology	33	33	1,885	746	22
Music	760	760	10,145	4,672	30
Natural Resource Management	68	68	837	222	15
Naval Architecture & Marine Engineering .	11	11	449	111	8
Near/Middle Eastern Studies	24	24	583	100	17
Nuclear Engineering	30	30	1,377	435	22
Nursing	507	507	7,278	1,131	39
Nutrition	218	218	1,644	722	28
Occupational Therapy	72	72	1,666	705	32
Ocean Engineering	8	8	450	86	6
Operations Research	40	40	971	230	10
Ornamental Horticulture	24	24	722	210	7
Parks Management	69	69	1,123	401	17
Petroleum Engineering	25	25	1,207	438	22
Philosophy	112	112	2,691	488	21
Physical Therapy	106	106	2,666	1,001	24
Physics	160	160	9,788	3,078	35

TABLE 1
A Rating of 140 Undergraduate Programs in the United States

FIELD OF STUDY	Selected Number of Institutions Granting Degree	Total Number of Programs (Curriculum) Evaluated	Total Number of Areas of Study Evaluated	Total Number of Faculty Areas Evaluated	Institutions Listed In Part I
Political Science	427	427	9,595	3,130	50
Portuguese	33	33	414	88	12
Poultry Sciences	26	26	416	89	13
Psychology	365	365	17,121	6,219	30
Radio/Television Studies	85	85	1,129	620	10
Religious Studies	104	104	3,860	894	21
Russian	83	83	1,161	760	20
Russian/Slavic Studies	91	91	1,488	490	18
Scandinavian Languages	16	16	281	73	8
Slavic Languages	24	24	999	154	17
Social Work/Social Welfare	221	221	1,670	485	17
Sociology	505	505	15,200	8,141	30
South Asian Studies	10	10	240	56	9
Southeast Asian Studies	10	10	239	54	9
Spanish	479	479	11,714	6,212	36
Speech/Rhetoric	307	307	8,690	2,120	14
Speech Pathology/Audiology	106	106	2,601	954	28
Statistics	70	70	2,370	722	25
Systems Engineering	14	14	310	74	12
Urban and Regional Planning	41	41	864	114	13
Wildlife Biology	33	33	851	110	16
Zoology	129	129	2,822	923	19

APPENDIX A (Continued)
A List of Tables

TABLE 2
A Rating of Prelegal Education in the United States[1]

Selected Number of Institutions Evaluated	1,726
Quality Prelegal Education: Institutions Listed in the Gourman Report	50
Total Number of Curriculum Fields Evaluated	203,006

Explanatory Note: [1]*The rating is evaluated and derived from data for 1,726 undergraduate institutions with reference to curriculum, instruction and "pre-law" programs. The quality of the curriculum and instruction is fundamental to the attainment of legal competence.*

TABLE 3
A Rating of Premedical Education in the United States[2]

Selected Number of Institutions Evaluated	1,726
Quality Premedical Education: Institutions Listed in the Gourman Report	58
Total Number of Curriculum Fields Evaluated	202,035

Explanatory Note: [2]*The rating is evaluated and derived from data for 1,726 undergraduate institutions with reference to curriculum, instruction and premedical education programs. The quality of the curriculum and instruction is fundamental to the attainment of medical competence.*

TABLE 4
A Rating of Ten University Administrative Areas

ADMINISTRATIVE AREAS	Selected Number of Institutions Evaluated	Institutions Listed in the Gourman Report	Total Number of Areas Evaluated
Administration	1,726	35	119,888
Alumni Associations	1,726	50	10,001
* Athletic-Academic Balance			
Comparative Competition for Fellowship/Scholarships	931	43	6,255
Counseling Centers	722	50	30,033
Curriculum	1,726	52	211,646
**Intercollegiate Athletic Departments			
Libraries	1,726	33	80,533
Public Relations	1,726	39	8,444
Institutions	1,726	1,277	215,222
Trustees/Regents (Public and Federal)	860	0	6,131
Trustees/Regents (Private)	489	92	2,660

* See Table 5.
**See Table 6.

APPENDIX A (Continued)
A List of Tables

TABLE 5
A Rating of Athletic–Academic Balance

Selected Number of Institutions Evaluated	906
Institutions Listed in the Gourman Report	126
Total Number of Areas Evaluated	14,099

TABLE 6
A Rating of Selective Intercollegiate Athletic Departments

Selected Number of Institutions/Athletic Departments Evaluated	906
Institutions/Athletic Departments Listed in the Gourman Report	127
Total Number of Areas Evaluated	7,665

TABLE 7
A Rating of Undergraduate Schools in Business Administration on the Approved List of the Gourman Report

Selected Number of Institutions/Business Administration Departments Evaluated	849
Institutions/Business Administration Departments Listed in the Gourman Report	228
Total Number of Areas Evaluated	32,070

TABLE 8
A Rating of Undergraduate Schools in Engineering on the Approved List of the Gourman Report

Selected Number of Institutions/Engineering Departments Evaluated	272
Institutions/Engineering Departments Listed in the Gourman Report	245
Total Number of Areas Evaluated	37,007

TABLE 9
A Rating of International Universities

ACADEMIC AREAS	Selected Number of Institutions Evaluated	Institutions Listed in the Gourman Report	Total Number of Areas Evaluated
Curriculum	761	44	92,046
Faculty	761	48	16,799
Institutions	761	49	96,049

(Curriculum, Faculty and Quality Institutions)

Listed below are the institutions included in Part VIII of the Ninth Edition.

COUNTRY AND SCHOOL

AUSTRIA
University of Vienna

BELGIUM
Free University of Brussels
Catholic University of Louvain

CANADA
McGill University
University of Toronto

DENMARK
University of Copenhagen

FRANCE
University of Provence (Aix-Marseilles I)
University of Aix-Marseilles II
University of Aix-Marseilles III
University of Besancon
University of Bordeaux I
University of Bordeaux II
University of Bordeaux III
University of Caen
University of Clermont
University of Dijon
Scientific and Medical University
   (University of Grenoble I)
University of Social Sciences
   (Grenoble II)
University of Social Sciences
   (Grenoble II)
University of Languages and Literature
   (Grenoble III)
University of Sciences (Lille I)
University of Law and Health Sciences
   (Lille II)
University of Human Sciences, Literature
   and Arts (Lille III)
University Claude-Bernard (Lyons I)
University of Lyons II
University of Jean Moulin (Lyons III)
University of Montpellier I
Languedoc University of Sciences
   (Montpellier II)
Paul-Valery University (Montpellier III)
University of Nancy I
University of Nancy II

FRANCE (Continued)
University of Nantes
University of Nice
University of Orleans
University of Paris I (Pantheon-Sorbonne)
University of Law, Economics, and
   Social Sciences (Paris II)
University of Paris III
University of Paris IV
University Rene Descartes (Paris V)
University of Paris VI
University of Paris VII
University of Paris VIII
University Paris-Dauphine (Paris IX)
University of Paris-Nanterre (Paris X)
University of Paris XI
University of Paris XII
University of Paris-Nord (Paris XIII)
University of Poitiers
University of Rennes I
University of Haute-Bretagne (Rennes II)
University of Rouen
University of Social Sciences (Toulouse I)
University of Toulouse-le Mirail (Toulouse II)
University Paul-Sabatier (Toulouse III)

FEDERAL REPUBLIC OF GERMANY
Rhemish Friedrich-Wilhelm University of Bonn
University of Cologne
Friedrich Alexander University of
   Erlangen-Nüremberg
Johann Wolfgang Goethe University
   of Frankfurt
Georg August University of Göttingen
Rupert Charles University of Heidelberg
Johannes Gutenberg University of Mainz
Philipps University of Marburg
Ludwig Maximilian University of Munich
University of Munster
Eberhard Karl University of Tubingen
University of Würzburg

ISRAEL
The Hebrew University of Jerusalem

ITALY
University of Bologna

(Curriculum, Faculty and Quality Institutions)

Listed below are the institutions included in Part VIII of the Ninth Edition.

COUNTRY AND MEDICAL SCHOOL

JAPAN
The University of Tokyo

NETHERLANDS
University of Amsterdam

SPAIN
University of Madrid

SWEDEN
University of Stockholm

SWITZERLAND
University of Geneva
University of Zürich

UNITED KINGDOM
University of Cambridge
University of Edinburgh
University of London
University of Oxford